Behind
a Curtain of Silence

Recent Titles in
Contributions in Military Studies
Series Advisor: Colin Gray

Arms Control and Nuclear Weapons: U.S. Policies and the National Interest
W. Gary Nichols and Milton L Boykin, editors

New Weapons and NATO: Solutions or Irritants?
Robert Kromer

The American War in Vietnam: Lessons, Legacies, and Implications for Future Conflicts
Lawrence E. Grinter and Peter M. Dunn, editors

Nuclear War and Nuclear Strategy: Unfinished Business
Stephen Cimbala

The Anglo-American Winter War with Russia, 1918–1919: A Diplomatic and Military Tragicomedy
Benjamin D. Rhodes

The Last Gaiter Button: A Study of the Mobilization and Concentration of the French Army in the War of 1870
Thomas J. Adriance

NATO Strategy and Nuclear Defense
Carl H. Amme

A Nuclear-Weapon-Free Zone in the Middle East: Problems and Prospects
Mahmoud Karem

Gentlemen of the Blade: A Social and Literary History of the British Army Since 1660
G. W. Stephen Brodsky

China's Military Modernization: International Implications
Larry M. Wortzel

The Painful Field: The Psychiatric Dimension of Modern War
Richard A. Gabriel

The Spit-Shine Syndrome: Organizational Irrationality in the American Field Army
Christopher Bassford

Behind
A Curtain of Silence

JAPANESE
IN SOVIET CUSTODY, 1945–1956

William F. Nimmo

Contributions in Military Studies, Number 78

GREENWOOD PRESS
New York • Westport, Connecticut • London

Library of Congress Cataloging-in-Publication Data

Nimmo, William F.
  Behind a curtain of silence : Japanese in Soviet custody, 1945–1956 / William F. Nimmo.
  p. cm.—(Contributions in military studies, ISSN 0883–6884 no. 78)
  Bibliography: p.
  Includes index.
  ISBN 0–313–25762–0 (lib. bdg. : alk. paper)
  1. World War, 1939–1945—Prisoners and prisoners, Japanese.
2. Prisoners of war, Japanese—Soviet Union. 3. Forced labor—Soviet Union—History—20th century. 4. World War, 1939–1945—Conscript labor—Soviet Union. I. Title. II. Series.
D805.S65N555 1988
940.54′72′47—dc19   88–5623

British Library Cataloguing in Publication Data is available.

Copyright © 1988 by William F. Nimmo

All rights reserved. No portion of this book may be reproduced, by any process or technique, without the express written consent of the publisher.

Library of Congress Catalog Card Number: 88–5623
ISBN: 0–313–25762–0
ISSN: 0883–6884

First published in 1988

Greenwood Press, Inc.
88 Post Road West, Westport, Connecticut 06881

Printed in the United States of America

The paper used in this book complies with the Permanent Paper Standard issued by the National Information Standards Organization (Z39.48–1984).

10 9 8 7 6 5 4 3 2 1

Copyright Acknowledgment

The author and publisher gratefully acknowledge permission to use the following:

Two *haiku* poems by Emperor Hirohito, courtesy of the Imperial Household Bureau, Tokyo.

To my Mother

Contents

Preface	ix
Acknowledgments	xi
Abbreviations	xiii
1. The August War	1
2. Japanese Settlers and the Red Army	17
3. Japanese in Stalin's Labor Camps	39
4. Marxist-Leninist Indoctrination	65
5. Attempts to Expedite Repatriation	83
6. Return to Japan	99
7. The Final Accounting	115
Notes	131
Selected Bibliography	141
Index	145

Preface

The Soviet Union attacked and defeated Japanese forces in Northeast Asia in the final days of World War II, and nearly three million Japanese fell into the hands of the Soviet Red Army. Repatriation from Manchuria, North Korea, southern Sakhalin, and the Kurile Islands was slow, and the Soviets took more than half a million soldiers and civilians to the USSR as prisoners for use on forced labor projects for several years. Large numbers of Japanese civilian residents and war prisoners died. The Soviets conducted an intensive Marxist-Leninist indoctrination program for war prisoners, and a professed acceptance of communism was a prerequisite for repatriation. This book examines the experiences of Japanese civilians and soldiers in Soviet-controlled areas after World War II; the efforts of American, British, Japanese, and United Nations officials to expedite repatriation; and the eventual return of internees to Japan.

The Soviet detention of Japanese in Northeast Asia and the USSR is not widely known outside Japan. In fact, most Americans know nothing about it. I was no exception when I first arrived in Tokyo in 1952 as a second lieutenant on the way to the Korean War, but in later assignments in Japan, where I held both military and civilian positions for 12 years, I became acquainted with Japanese who had been in Manchuria in 1945. Their revelations, along with news reports and stories in the Japanese press, aroused my interest. Over the years, I searched for more information on the subject, but found very little—in English—other than a paragraph or two here, or perhaps a chapter there, to describe the fate of Japanese held by the Soviets.

This curiosity followed me upon reassignment to the Pentagon in Washington, where I was able to find some official reports on repatriation, but nothing of a conclusive nature. After completion of military and civilian service with the Department of the Army, I returned to my hometown of Norfolk, Virginia, and entered a graduate program in international studies at Old Dominion University. My interest in the repatriation issue led me to the General Douglas MacArthur Memorial Archives, also in Norfolk, where I found a wealth of data on the subject in the records of General Headquarters (GHQ), Supreme Commander for the Allied Powers (SCAP), the Allied Occupation headquarters in Tokyo. This endeavor resulted in a thesis that was followed by additional research using Japanese source data—over 200 books have been published in Japanese on the subject—and other materials, ultimately leading to the publication of this book.

I have used the Hepburn system of romanizing the Japanese language, except that long marks have been omitted from well-known place names in Japan. Japanese personal names in the text of this book are written in accordance with Japanese usage: that is, family name followed by given name. The abbreviation "SCAP," which in a strict sense identifies General MacArthur personally, is more often used in works related to the Allied Occupation of Japan to refer to the general's headquarters and staff, and is so used in this book. References to General MacArthur are by name rather than title.

Acknowledgments

I received valuable assistance from many sources in the preparation of this book. Professor Thomas W. Burkman of Old Dominion University read the entire manuscript and made most helpful comments and recommendations. Professors Philip S. Gillette and Patrick J. Rollins of Old Dominion University offered advice in sections related to Russian and Soviet history and government. Assistance in translating Japanese books and articles was provided by Ms. Koh Shimizu and Ms. Chiyoko Quasius. Maps were prepared by Ms. Nancy A. Nimmo, my daughter.

The General Douglas MacArthur Memorial Foundation provided a grant that made this study possible. Colonel Lyman H. Hammond, Jr., USA (Ret.), executive director of the foundation, provided assistance and encouragement in seeing this project through to its completion. The staff of the MacArthur Memorial Archives was particularly helpful in identifying the comprehensive documentation needed for research. Archivist Edward J. Boone, Jr.; Assistant Archivist John M. Leeds, Jr.; and Curator Joseph M. Judge gave extensive assistance in the location and use of archive material.

Professor Marlene J. Mayo, University of Maryland; Professor F. Hilary Conroy, University of Pennsylvania; and Mr. Key K. Kobayashi, formerly of the Library of Congress; commented on related papers presented at regional meetings of the Association for Asian Studies. Others who provided assistance in writing this book include Ms. Yoshiko Yoshimura and Mr. Thaddeus Yoneji Ohta, Asian Division, Library of Congress; Mr. Carl J. Whiting, International Affairs Advisor, U.S. Forces, Japan; and Mr. Richard B. Finn, a Foreign Service officer who served in the Diplomatic Section of SCAP.

I am most grateful for the many forms of help provided in preparing the manuscript for this book. Final responsibility for errors of fact and interpretation, however, rests with the author alone.

Abbreviations

AFDC	Anti-Fascist Democratic Committee
ATIS	Allied Translator and Interpreter Service
BAM	Baikal-Amur-Main Line
CCCP	Soyuz Sovetchikh Sotsialisticheckikh Respublik (Union of Soviet Socialist Republics)
CIS	Civil Intelligence Section
CPSU	Communist Party of the Soviet Union
GHQ	General Headquarters
GS	General Staff
Gulag	*Glavnoye Upravleniye Ispravitelno-Trudovykh Lagerey*, Chief Administration of Corrective Labor Camps, the Soviet penal system under Stalin
IMTFE	International Military Tribunal for the Far East
JCP	Japan Communist Party
KGB	*Komitet Gosudarstvennoi Bezopasnosti*, Committee for State Security
LDP	Liberal Democratic Party
MIS	Military Intelligence Section
MVD	*Ministerstvo Vnutrennikh Del*, Ministry of Internal Affairs, 1946–53. Became a part of KGB after 1953.
NCO	Noncommissioned Officer
NKVD	*Narodnii Kommissariat Vnutrennikh Del*, People's Commissariat of Internal Affairs, 1934–46. Became a part of MVD in 1946.
POW	Prisoner of War
PRC	People's Republic of China
ROK	Republic of Korea
SCAP	Supreme Commander for the Allied Powers
UN	United Nations
USSR	Union of Soviet Socialist Republics

Behind
a Curtain of Silence

1

The August War

The sun rises early during midsummer in Manchuria, and dawn came before 5 A.M. on 8 August 1945 as Harbin residents began another day of midweek routine. Workers headed for jobs in the city's bustling rail yards, while others set off for offices, factories, shops, and arsenals to perform a multitude of tasks, primarily in support of Japan's war effort in the Pacific and other parts of Asia. Unknown to Harbin's early-morning risers, however, it was to be the last day of any semblance of normal routine for a long time to come.

Manchuria (Manchukuo since 1932) had scarcely been touched by the war. Except for a few B–29 bombings, Japan's colonial territories in Korea, Manchuria, southern Sakhalin, and the Kurile Islands had been among the most tranquil locations in Asia during the previous five years. However, in the summer of 1945 there was ample evidence of the major conflict being fought in other parts of Asia and the Pacific. The region's extensive natural resources were being exploited to feed Japan's war machine, and rationing of food, clothing, and other necessities were daily reminders of the homeland's fight for survival.

As the early August day progressed, oppressive heat began to build up from the monsoon blowing in from the south. Harbin buzzed with its usual weekday activity. The city was a cosmopolitan mixture of various nationalities, each with its own residential and business districts. Indigenous Manchurians and laborers from other areas of China formed the largest element of the population. Korean workers, brought to Manchuria by the Japanese, formed a sizable group. White Russians—residents of Harbin since their flight from the Soviets in the 1920s—gave the city a European appearance. Finally, there were the prestigious and powerful representatives of the Greater East Asia Co-Prosperity Sphere, the Japanese.

Later in the day, as twilight turned to darkness, lights in countless places of entertainment began to glow. Small groups of Japanese businessmen, bureaucrats, and military brass began to drift into their favorite drinking establishments for another evening's enjoyment. Yes, there was a war and defense efforts had top priority during the day—but nighttime was a different story. Harbin in prewar days had been called the "Shanghai of Manchuria," and there were still hundreds of bars, brothels, cabarets, cafes, saloons, and geisha houses to siphon off the yen of the many willing spenders.

However, there was anxiety among many of the more than one million Japanese civilians residing in Manchuria. This large element of overseas residents included government officials, executives and technicians of major Japanese companies, railway employees, professionals, farmers, and colonial settlers, together with their families. Some were in the provinces bordering on the Soviet Union or Outer Mongolia. Most residents of Manchuria knew that Japan was not faring well in the war—newspapers told of the B-29 raids on the home islands and the fierce battles that had been fought in the Pacific—and the mighty neighbor to the north was a source of much uneasiness. Nevertheless, Japan's army in Manchuria, the Kwantung Army, was invincible—or so the general public thought—and for years had been touted as Imperial Japan's most elite field army.[1] Fears of Soviet Army moves into Manchuria were allayed by the trust placed in the fighting capability of the Japanese defenders.

THE HISTORICAL SETTING

After its victory over Russia in 1905, Japan had projected an image of strength for many years. In September 1931, the Kwantung Army consisted of 10,400 men composed of one infantry division and several garrison battalions. Troop strength was increased to 164,000 by the mid-1930s, and to 270,000 by 1939, when it consisted of nine infantry divisions and numerous non-divisional units, equipped with 560 aircraft and 200 tanks.[2] A series of border clashes erupted between Japan and the Soviet Union in the 1930s; one of the major encounters occurred in 1938 at Changkufeng and Lake Khasan, adjoining the Soviet Maritime Province.[3] The most serious crisis took place in 1939 along the Khalkin Gol River, a remote western region on the border of Outer Mongolia and Manchuria. The border war, known as the Nomonhan Incident in Japan, began in May 1939 and became a major conflict by the end of June. Fighting reached a climax in August and ended the next month with the Soviets demonstrating military superiority heretofore unseen by the Japanese. The Soviet First Army Group in the Far East, under General Georgi K. Zhukov, decisively defeated its Kwantung Army opponents. However, the extent of this military setback was not made known to the public; the Imperial Japanese Army did not want losses publicized.[4]

The Nomonhan Incident led the army's high command to strengthen the Kwantung Army through the addition of more troops and equipment during the next three years. The border war caused the Japanese to be much more cautious in their dealings with Moscow and was one of the factors leading to a neutrality pact with the Soviet Union in 1941. In addition to the military weaknesses revealed at Nomonhan, Japan had other worries. The war against China was not going well; relations between Japan and the United States were not good and getting worse; Britain had declared war on Japan's Axis partner, Germany; and both the United States and the Soviet Union were providing increasing amounts of aid to Chiang Kai-shek. To counter these trends and to negate the prospects of a war with its northern neighbor, the Japanese ambassador to the Kremlin approached Soviet officials in 1940 concerning a neutrality pact. The Soviet Union, however, had signed a non-aggression pact with Germany in 1939 and, having recently demonstrated military superiority over the Kwantung Army, could see no benefit in the Japanese proposal. Nevertheless, several months of negotiations followed and, with a deterioration of relations between Berlin and Moscow in the spring of 1941, the Soviet Union finally agreed to a neutrality pact which was signed on 13 April 1941.[5] Only two months later, Nazi Germany launched a massive attack on the Soviet Union's western front, notwithstanding the Ribbentrop–Molotov pact of 1939.

After the Japanese attack on Pearl Harbor in December 1941, the United States and Britain began to pressure the Soviet Union to invade Japanese territories in the north. General Douglas MacArthur, then commander of American forces in the Philippines, sent a cable on 10 December 1941 to General George C. Marshall, chief of staff of the U.S. Army, requesting high-level efforts to persuade the Soviets to enter the war and attack Japan in Manchuria. Roosevelt and Churchill actively sought Soviet participation in the war against Japan, but Soviet Premier Joseph Stalin was preoccupied with the life-and-death struggle against the Germans in the European section of the USSR. In fact, Stalin pushed the Western Allies to open a second front against the Germans and showed little interest in ventures in Asia. However, at the Teheran Conference in late 1943, after the Red Army had turned the tide against Hitler's troops, Stalin finally consented to enter the war against Japan following the defeat of Germany.

At the Yalta Conference in February 1945, Allied leaders worked out terms that specified:

> In two or three months after Germany has surrendered and the war in Europe has been terminated the Soviet Union shall enter into the war against Japan on the side of the Allies on condition that:
>
> 1. The status quo in Outer Mongolia (The Mongolian People's Republic) shall be preserved;
> 2. The former rights of Russia violated by the treacherous attack of Japan in 1904 shall also be restored, viz:
>   (a) the southern part of Sakhalin as well as all the islands adjacent to it shall be returned to the Soviet Union;
>   (b) the commercial port of Dairen shall be internationalized, the preeminent interests of the Soviet Union in this port being safeguarded and the lease of Port Arthur as a naval base of the USSR restored;
>   (c) the Chinese-Eastern Railroad and the South Manchurian Railroad which provides an outlet to Dairen shall be jointly operated by the establishment

of a joint Soviet-Chinese Company it being understood that the preeminent interests of the Soviet Union shall be safeguarded and that China shall retain full sovereignty in Manchuria;

3. The Kuril Islands shall be handed over to the Soviet Union.[6]

The Soviet Union also expressed readiness to conclude a pact of friendship and alliance with Chiang's Nationalist Government in China, "in order to render assistance to China with its armed forces for the purpose of liberating China from the Japanese yoke."

When it became apparent in early 1945 that Germany would soon collapse, the Soviet Union began to make preparations for war against Japan. The terms of the Soviet–Japanese neutrality pact stipulated that it would remain valid for five years—until April 1946—with a provision for automatic renewal for another five years "in case neither of the contracting parties denounces the pact one year before the expiration of the term." On 5 April 1945, Soviet Foreign Minister Vyacheslav Molotov advised Satō Naotake, Japan's ambassador to Moscow, that the Soviet Union wished to denounce the pact. This action left Satō and officials of the Foreign Ministry in Tokyo with the impression that the pact would remain in effect for another year—in fact, Japanese *Gaimushō* (Foreign Ministry) representatives later insisted that Molotov had given assurances that the neutrality agreement was to remain in effect for another year—but subsequent events were to prove that the Kremlin had other intentions.[7]

By the time of the next summit meeting, held at Potsdam from 17 July to 2 August 1945, Truman had replaced Roosevelt as president of the United States upon the death of the latter in April. Germany had recently been defeated and the Western Allies were anxious to end the war in the Pacific. On 26 July 1945 the heads of government of the United States, China, and the United Kingdom issued a proclamation (the Potsdam Proclamation) calling for the "unconditional surrender of all the Japanese armed forces," with the promise that "the Japanese military forces, after being completely disarmed, shall be permitted to return to their homes with the opportunity to lead peaceful and productive lives."[8] However, Japan's cabinet ministers knew nothing of Soviet plans to enter the war and thought Moscow could be prevailed upon to mediate with the Western Allies to obtain some type of conditional surrender. In bluffing a position of strength, as if in a poker game, Prime Minister Suzuki responded to the Potsdam Proclamation by announcing on 28 July:

> I believe the Joint Proclamation by the three countries is nothing but a rehash of the Cairo Declaration. As for the Government, it does not find any important value in it, and there is no other course but to ignore it entirely and resolutely fight for the successful conclusion of this war.[9]

Even before Suzuki's reply, many American officials thought it would take another year to defeat Japan. Truman sought confirmation of the Soviet pledge made at Yalta to attack Japan and told Stalin that the United States planned to use a new bomb far more destructive than any other known bomb. Stalin announced that the Soviet Union would enter the war soon, and this news elated Truman. He said in a letter to his wife dated 18 July 1945, "I've gotten what I came for. Stalin goes to war August 15th with no strings on it. I'll say that we'll end the war a year sooner now."[10]

Most Japanese leaders knew by July 1945 that their nation was defeated but were divided over what course to follow. Militant hawks in the cabinet wanted to fight to the bitter end, even to the point of arming civilians with bamboo spears in a desperate last stand against the expected invasion. Admiral Ōnishi Takijiro, father of the Kamikaze corps, generously announced that he was "prepared to sacrifice twenty million Japanese rather than surrender."[11] Cooler heads were looking for a way to achieve a negotiated peace. These officials saw the Soviet Union as their last chance to salvage some type of arrangement with the British and Americans to allow Japan to retain its sovereignty and to forestall an Allied occupation. Attempts to obtain Soviet mediation continued in early August even though Ambassador Satō had advised the foreign minister in late July that there was no chance of persuading the Kremlin to aid Japan.

By the time the Soviets had denounced the neutrality pact with Japan, the Kwantung Army had been seriously depleted; its best troops and much of its equipment had been shipped off to the Pacific to fight the advancing Allied armies. For decades—since the 1905 victory over the Russians—Japanese strategy had relied on strong offensive operations; defensive operations were to be used only as a last resort. Furthermore, the Kwantung Army had, since the late 1930s, maintained contingency plans for an attack against Soviet territory. The overall plan was to secure Soviet territory north of the Amur River for about a hundred miles (more in some areas) in order to take over the Trans-Siberian Railroad east of Lake Baikal. These plans to invade Siberia were a closely guarded secret; only five Japanese officers knew of the complete concept.[12]

However, in September 1944, Imperial General headquarters in Tokyo had taken the highly unusual action of directing the Kwantung Army to abandon all offensive plans and, instead, to take up a defensive mission on all fronts. Under this plan the primary defenses were to be concentrated in the northern and northwestern portions of Manchuria. The mission of the Kwantung Army was to "frustrate enemy penetration of this zone by causing him to spread his forces thinly over the vast expanse of Manchuria, then defeating him in detail."[13]

Troop withdrawals from Manchuria reached a peak in March 1945. By the end of that month, the Kwantung Army had 11 divisions with a fighting efficiency of about 4. However, after the Soviet denouncement of the neutrality pact, Imperial General headquarters issued directives giving the Kwantung Army an order of battle signifying that it was on a war footing. Tokyo directed the commander-in-chief of the China Expeditionary Army to transfer 4 divisions and some smaller units to the Kwantung Army. Tokyo also instructed the 17th Army commander in Korea to transfer an infantry division and several smaller units to Manchuria. Eight new divisions were created by Imperial General headquarters in July 1945, staffed through a draft of all Japanese civilian men in Manchuria, most of whom were overage reservists or teenage students with little training. A few essential civilian men, such as employees of the South Manchuria Railway, were exempt from the draft. By 9 August 1945 the Kwantung Army strength had been increased to 24 divisions and 11 separate brigades, but combat effectiveness of these units ranged from as little as 15 percent to a high of 80 percent. Troop strength had been increased to approximately 780,000 men.[14]

Japanese Army intelligence planning, which had been lacking in modernization and systematic application, was strengthened after the Nomonhan Incident, but the Kwantung Army was not able to obtain a complete picture of Soviet intentions or strength. A postwar study prepared by former Japanese officers concluded:

> Japanese intelligence operations against the USSR were immensely difficult to carry out because of the so-called "iron-curtain" drawn across the border, and because of the peculiar internal situation of the country which is constantly in a state of alert. The category of intelligence most difficult to conduct was espionage by infiltrated agents.... The best information came from a large collection of fragmentary data.[15]

In spite of the 1941 neutrality pact, the Soviet Union and Japan had continued to keep a wary eye on each other. More than half a century of animosity between Japan and its northern neighbor had left the two nations deeply suspicious of each other. Japan could point to tsarist Russia's territorial aggrandizement in the late nineteenth century while some Soviet officials, especially Stalin, retained bitter memories of Japan's undeclared attack on Port Arthur in 1904. The Soviets, in turn, viewed Japan's participation in the Allied intervention in Siberia from 1918 to 1922 with 72,000 troops (more than the American and British forces combined) as an opportunist venture to thwart the Bolshevik victory.

Soviet intelligence had the upper hand, especially in the critical spring and summer of 1941, when it came to determining the intentions of its Far Eastern neighbor to the south. Richard Sorge, a Soviet agent posing as a German journalist in Tokyo, was able to inform Moscow that Japan's secret plan to attack the USSR would not be implemented in 1941, thereby enabling the Red Army to shift large elements of its forces from the Soviet Far East to the battered European front. Sorge's spy ring also had been able to provide detailed information on the Kwantung Army to the Soviet high command's Fourth Department (Intelligence) concerning matters such as order of battle, readiness condition, border fortifications, and location of units. Even after Japanese police arrested Sorge in October 1941, Soviet intelligence agents were able to discern that Japan could not maintain Kwantung Army units in a high state of readiness and fight a major war to the south at the same time.

By the end of 1941, the Red Army had transferred half of its Soviet Far Eastern troops and units to the European front. In all, 30 divisions were moved to the west. Japanese intelligence estimated the number of Red Army troops in the Soviet Far East in 1943 and 1944 at approximately 700,000. After the Yalta Conference, the Soviets began transferring troops and equipment back to the Far East, greatly accelerating the movements in April 1945. Eastbound trains transporting Soviet divisions increased to ten per day, and more were added in May and June. Japanese intelligence sources estimated that 25 Red Army divisions had been redeployed to the Far East by early August, and Imperial General headquarters calculated that the Soviets would attack in the autumn after transferring 10 or 15 more divisions. The Japanese estimates were wrong. Forty Soviet divisions had already been moved, bringing the total strength of the Soviet Far Eastern Army to 80 divisions consisting of 1.5 million troops with 26,000 field guns and mortars, 3,300 tanks, and nearly 3,900 combat aircraft.[16]

By early August, Japan's situation was desperate. Allied forces had captured Okinawa in June after 80 days of fierce fighting, the home islands' defenses were badly battered, an American B–29 had dropped the first "atom bomb" on Hiroshima, and foreign invasion troops were knocking at Japan's front door. The bomb that had destroyed Hiroshima was identified by Japanese scientists as a nuclear device, and it was amply clear that the weapon had a devastating effect far greater than anything seen before. No one in Japan knew if the United States would use more, or how many. Foreign Minister Tōgō Shigenori cabled urgent instructions to Japan's ambassador in Moscow to accelerate efforts to obtain Soviet mediation with the United States and the United Kingdom for a conditional surrender.

An urgent message was waiting for Soviet Foreign Minister Molotov when he returned to the Kremlin from the Potsdam Conference on the night of 6 August 1945: Japanese Ambassador Satō wanted to see him as soon as possible. Molotov also wanted to see Satō, who later recalled:

> On the 7th Molotov sent me a telephone message that he was available at 8 P.M. on 8 August. But in a later phone call, Molotov wanted to change this to 5 P.M. instead of 8 P.M. Accordingly I went to the Kremlin at the specified hour. When I went through the entrance and went into the palace everything seemed the same as usual. I proceeded to Molotov's study and, speaking in Russian, congratulated the Foreign Commissar on his safe return from Potsdam. But Molotov interrupted me saying, "I have today a communication to make in the name of the Soviet Government to the Japanese Government." He asked me to take a seat, then sat down himself, and read a notification to me. It was none other than a declaration of war by Soviet Russia.[17]

The Soviet Foreign Minister, his expressionless face framed by a bristle-like mustache and rimmed glasses, informed the Japanese ambassador that:

> After the defeat of Hitlerite Germany, Japan remained the only great power which still held out for continuing the war.... The demand of the three powers—the United States of America, Great Britain, and China—of July 26, 1945 concerning

the unconditional surrender of Japanese armed forces was refused by Japan. The proposal of the Japanese Government to the Soviet Union concerning mediation in the war in the Far East thereby loses all basis. . . . Faithful to its obligations to its Allies, the Soviet Government accepted the proposal of the Allies and adheres to the statement of the Allied powers of July 26, 1945. . . . In view of the foregoing, the Soviet Government declares that as of tomorrow, that is, as of 9 August, the Soviet Union will consider it is in a state of war with Japan.[18]

These formalities took no more than 10 or 15 minutes and Ambassador Satō left the Kremlin shortly after 5 P.M., but Red Army forces actually were entering Manchuria while the ambassador was in Molotov's office. The Khabarovsk and Maritime Province districts of the Soviet Far East are 4,000 miles to the east, and seven hours ahead of Moscow. In those areas bordering on Manchuria it was just after midnight, and the first moments of 9 August were beginning with advance elements of a huge army crossing the borders of the Soviet Union and Outer Mongolia to attack Japanese forces.

Even though recent months had witnessed a major effort to strengthen the Kwantung Army or at least give it an appearance of strength, there was no special alert order in effect on the night of 8 August 1945; in fact, the usual nightly reveling and carousing continued. Perhaps some vague premonition of the coming disaster led the wealthy and elite representatives of Japan's Greater East Asia Co-Prosperity Sphere to orgies of extravagance and debauchery at night, motivated by the desire to take advantage of these pleasures while there was still time. A first-hand account, provided by an army lieutenant who had arrived only a few months earlier, reveals the lack of foreknowledge concerning a Soviet invasion on that fateful night:

> the streets of Harbin were populated late into the night by drunken members of the privileged class. Each night had been the same since my arrival. Money flowed like water, thanks to the munificent subsidies of the Government to every enterprise that could claim a part in the general war effort. . . . Late into the night, the newly rich roamed from one cabaret to another, scarcely knowing how to spend their war-boom yen. Government officials, too, were flush with money. They had been given almost unlimited expense accounts for "entertainment" and social negotiations. . . . But, even these late night carousers slowly found, one after another, places of sleep; in bawdy houses, in brothels or geisha quarters. Silence and slumber eventually came to Harbin.[19]

If the former lieutenant's account can be trusted, an urgent warning was missed because of the nightly merrymaking. One of the revelers was an official of the Japanese Special Military Mission in Harbin. The mission was staffed by Russian-speaking experts whose primary function was to provide information on the Soviet Far Eastern Army to Kwantung Army headquarters in Changchun (Shinkyō). A vital radio message from an agent in Outer Mongolia warning of the impending Soviet attack had gone unheeded due to the official's absence.

The entire Kwantung Army was caught sleeping as a result of this intelligence failure.

THE SOVIETS ATTACK

Red Army divisions, under Marshal A. M. Vasilevsky, Commander of Soviet Forces in the Far East, began a three-pronged attack against the Kwantung Army in the early morning hours of 9 August 1945. The Transbaikal Front (Field Army), in a joint offensive with Outer Mongolian forces, moved eastward from Outer Mongolia along a broad front in a lightning attack against Kwantung Army units in northwestern and western Manchuria. About half of all Soviet troops in the Far East were involved in this action. By contrast, the largest elements of the Kwantung Army were based in eastern Manchuria, where about half of its units and troops were positioned. Soviet plans called for the Transbaikal Front to make a major drive from the west in two parallel thrusts through barren flatlands and mountainous regions to Mukden and Changchun. A second main assault was launched from the Soviet Maritime Region by the First Far Eastern Front, with the objective of penetrating Japanese border fortifications and advancing on Kirin and Changchun. Successful completion of these two main attacks would seal off escape routes for Kwantung Army units in northern Manchuria, thereby preventing them from reaching secondary defensive positions in the south. At the same time, Red Army units of the Second Far Eastern Front, positioned to the north, began crossing the Amur River for a southward move on Harbin.[20]

The Transbaikal Front of the Soviet Far Eastern Army mounted a relentless armored assault in western Manchuria, through 500 miles of desert and mountains, and carried out forced marches in extreme heat. Operations were made all the more difficult by an absence of road markers, place names, and reference points; and there was no drinking water, almost no vegetation, and virtually no indigenous source of supplies. For the most part, the Soviet attack met little or no resistance, but there were exceptions. In the Arshan area (about 150 miles east of the junction of the Soviet, Mongolian, and Manchurian borders), some Japanese units put up a fierce fight for four days. In another case, nearly 18,000 troops of the 107th Japanese Division, cut off from communication with higher headquarters, continued fighting for two weeks. Some scattered units kept up the fighting until 30 August. Nevertheless, the Transbaikal Front outnumbered the Japanese defenders so heavily that it was able to envelop positions of resistance and continue to advance toward the cities of central Manchuria.

Invading forces had a more difficult time in the east. Japanese troops occupied well-prepared, fortified positions, but the Soviet officers assigned to this front had been specially selected because of their experience in attacking through fortified areas of Finland. The Kwantung Army had begun construction of permanent border fortifications in 1935 and had concentrated its defenses in the eastern zone of Manchuria. Out of 13 defensive positions constructed from 1935 to 1940, 8 were located in the east, while 4 were built in the north and only 1 in the west. Japanese defenders put up strong resistance in the eastern fortified zones for two days but were gradually pushed back about 75 miles to the west to Mutanchiang (Botankō), where the defending garrisons fought a stubborn battle before finally surrendering on 16 August. Four days later, Soviet advance forces reached Kirin and Harbin. As in other areas of Manchuria, some Japanese units continued fighting but were bypassed and cut off by the invading forces.

Simultaneously, the Soviet First Far Eastern Front launched a secondary attack against northern Korea on 9 August. Soviet naval aviation attacked the port cities of Najin (about 20 miles from the short Soviet-Korea border) and Chongjin (60 miles below Najin) followed by Soviet landings on 11 and 12 August with almost no opposition. The Soviets captured other port cities on the coast of the Sea of Japan (north of the 38th parallel) in the next 10 days, meeting almost no resistance.

Yet another Soviet attack was initiated by the Second Far Eastern Front. Soviet divisions crossed the wide, fast-flowing Amur River (Heilungkiang in Chinese) from the north at several points and began rapid advances southward. The main crossing was at the border town of Tungchiang, in northeastern Manchuria (about 125 miles southwest of the Soviet Far Eastern city of Khabarovsk), followed by an advance to Harbin along the natural invasion corridor of the Sungari River. Although defending forces were weak, Soviet troops encountered strong fighting on 12 August about halfway to Harbin and were forced to fall back to Chiamussu two days later. It was not until 17 August that Soviet forces were able to clear the area.[21]

Kwantung Army defensive strategy called for a "last redoubt" (a secondary defense zone) in southeastern Manchuria around the town of Tunghua, an area adjacent to the Korean border. However, this plan was not fully implemented because of the rapidly unfolding series of events.[22] As it turned out, efforts to develop the defense zone would have been to no avail anyway; by making major thrusts across Manchuria from the west and east, the Soviet Far Eastern Army had sealed off retreat routes to the "last redoubt." In any case, another development was to make all defensive plans null and void.

Throughout the morning of 15 August 1945, frequent radio announcements advised listeners in Japan and its overseas colonial territories that the emperor would broadcast a special message at twelve o'clock. This was to be the first radio broadcast ever made by a Japanese emperor, a startling fact in itself. Most citizens, including many officers of the armed forces, expected an imperial command to exhort the army and navy to make a final and ultimate attempt to vanquish the enemy. At the stroke of twelve, an announcer from the government radio network in Tokyo, NHK, enjoined: "A broadcast of the highest importance is about to be made. All listeners will please rise. His Majesty the Emperor will now read his Imperial Rescript to the people of Japan. We respectfully transmit his voice." The Japanese national anthem, "Kimigayo," was played, and then the emperor began speaking (actually a recording had been made the previous day). The speech was heard throughout Manchuria where top officials of the Kwantung Army and many officers and soldiers, along with Japanese civilians, listened with undivided attention as the emperor began:

> To Our good and loyal Subjects:
> After pondering deeply the general trends of the world and the actual conditions obtaining in Our Empire today, We have decided to effect a settlement of the present situation by resorting to an extraordinary measure.
> We have ordered Our Government to communicate to the Governments of the United States, Great Britain, China and the Soviet Union that Our Empire accepts the provisions of their Joint Declaration....

Stunned beyond belief, listeners in Manchuria stood in amazement, not only at the surrender news, but at the sound of the emperor's voice. The speech continued with an explanation of the decision and an acknowledgment of the anguish and suffering that most citizens would experience over the capitulation:

> We are keenly aware of the inmost feelings of all ye, Our subjects. However, it is according to the dictates of time and fate that we have resolved to pave the way for a grand peace for all the generations to come by enduring the unendurable and suffering what is insufferable.[23]

Little did the dazed army troops in Manchuria realize at the time how prophetic that imperial injunction would prove to be in the months and years to come.

While it was clear from the emperor's broadcast that the war was to be terminated, the speech contained no specific details, and no official notification had been issued by Imperial General headquarters in Tokyo. The Kwantung Army had long existed as a semi-autonomous element of the Japanese Army, often ignoring instructions from Tokyo when they countered its goals and objectives, but this situation was different; the Imperial Rescript could not be ignored. Consequently, the Kwantung Army brass resorted to the bureaucratic solution of calling a staff conference the next day.

While Soviet forces were continuing their multi-directional attacks against continuing resistance from many Japanese units, top officers of the Kwantung Army began what was to be their last conference. Predictably, there were many hot heads among the staff who wanted to continue fighting to the last man. Years of indoctrination had conditioned Japanese warriors, especially the professional soldiery, to embrace the concept that surrender was disgraceful, constituting an act of utmost disloyalty to the emperor. Others argued that it was the emperor himself who had directed the capitulation and that the circumstances in this case, though highly unusual, were different. So it went into the night—with heated discussions and arguments over the fate of the Kwantung Army—until General Yamada Otozō, commander of Japanese forces in Manchuria, advised all that he accepted the emperor's dictate and would do his part to end the war.[24]

Winding down the war was no easy matter. Soviet forces were continuing their sweep not only across Manchuria and northern Korea, but also in Karafuto (southern Sakhalin) and Chishima Rettō (the Kuriles). A news release from the Soviet high command, explaining why the Red Army continued to fight, said that the emperor's announcement was "merely a general declaration." The Soviet statement explained:

> No order on cessation of hostilities has yet been issued to the armed forces and Japanese armed forces are continuing to resist. . . . The armed forces of Japan may be considered to have surrendered only from the moment when the Emperor of Japan issues an order to his armed forces to cease hostilities and lay down their arms, and when that order is carried out in practice.[25]

The Kwantung Army received orders on 16 August from Imperial General headquarters in Tokyo to stop fighting and to arrange for a truce with the Soviets. The next day, Prince Takeda Tsuneyoshi, personally representing the emperor, flew to Changchun from Tokyo to provide assurance that the Imperial Rescript was authentic and that the order to cease hostilities was an imperial command. Yamada called in representatives of his subordinate commanders on 18 August to officially inform them of the cease-fire and surrender orders.

Meanwhile, the Soviet Far Eastern armies continued to advance throughout Manchuria. Small, company-sized units made airborne landings at Harbin, Mukden, Changchun, and Kirin on 18 August to establish a Soviet presence in those major cities "to precipitate a real surrender and prevent unnecessary bloodshed." Major General G. A. Shelakhov, representing the Soviet Military Council of the Front, accompanied the troops arriving at Changchun. That evening, Lieutenant General Hata Hikosaburō, Kwantung Army chief of staff, arrived at the airdome to confer with Shelakhov. The next day, Hata and Soviet representatives flew to the First Far Eastern Front command post where Marshal Vasilevsky, commander of all Soviet forces in the Far East, dictated the terms of surrender. Vasilevsky specified that the capitulation was to be unconditional and that it must be completed not later than noon on 20 August. Yamada and his staff surrendered at Changchun on 19 August, and the once famous Kwantung Army officially came to an end. Even so, military action continued for two more weeks. Soviet troops made airborne landings at Port Arthur and Dairen on 22 August, and during the following days, Red Army divisions moved into the cities of Manchuria and northern Korea.

Japanese military forces in Sakhalin and the Kurile Islands were not a part of the Kwantung Army, and Yamada's surrender did not govern the actions of troops in those areas. Elements of the Soviet Second Far Eastern Front and the North Pacific Flotilla had attacked southern Sakhalin on 11 August 1945. The Japanese defenses consisted of one infantry division plus an artillery regiment, a naval base, and 13 landing fields, but no military aircraft. The defenders, about 20,000 troops, put up stiff initial resistance, and the Soviets were unable to make any significant advances until 14 August when Red Army battalions gained the upper hand and began moving southward. In the next three days, several cities and towns fell to the Soviet Army, and the Japanese commander announced cessation of all hostilities on 19 August. Nevertheless, fighting continued past that date, with many Japanese civilians and soldiers committing suicide when defeat became inevitable.[26]

The initial Soviet attack in the Kuriles came on 18 August, three days after the emperor's announcement. After a delay in positioning amphibious forces, Soviet troops invaded the northernmost islands of Shumshu and Paramushir, subsequently working their way down the chain toward Hokkaido. The attacking forces even captured four islands that had long been considered a part of Japan. These islands—still held by the USSR and known as the "northern territories" in Japan—remain contentious in Soviet-Japanese relations more than four decades after the war's end.

Stalin, recalling the Russian defeat in 1905, the Japanese intervention in Siberia, and the border incidents, hailed the Far Eastern victory:

> For 40 years, we the men of the older generation, have waited for this day. And now this day has come. From now on, Southern Sakhalin and the Kurile Islands will serve as a means of direct communications with the ocean and as a base for the defense of our country against Japanese aggression.
>
> We have won. From now on we can consider our country saved from the threat of German invasion in the West and of Japanese invasion in the East. The long-awaited peace for the nations of the world has come.[27]

The August War was over. In less than a month, Soviet forces had gained control of approximately 570,000 square miles of territory in Northeast Asia, an area nearly four times the size of Japan. Soviet-occupied territories held approximately 2.7 million Japanese, of whom 850,000 were military personnel. There had been no attempt to evacuate Japanese civilians since no one, in Tokyo or elsewhere, knew until the last frenzied days that Japan was going to surrender. *Pravda* reported on 12 September 1945 that Soviet forces had captured 594,000 Japanese officers and men. The Soviet Information Bureau said that 83,737 Japanese troops had been killed in action, but Japan's Foreign Ministry later estimated battlefield deaths to be about 27,000.[28] Soviet losses in the Manchurian campaign were stated as 8,219 killed in action and 22,264 wounded, while troops of the Mongolian People's Republic suffered only 674 casualties. Map 1 shows Northeast Asia at the conclusion of World War II.

THE LONG TRIP HOME

Not only was the short August War finished; the conflagration that had engulfed much of the world came to a final close with the Allied victory in Asia and the Pacific. Japan was defeated; it was the end of an era. Decades of expansionist

Map 1
Northeast Asia, August 1945

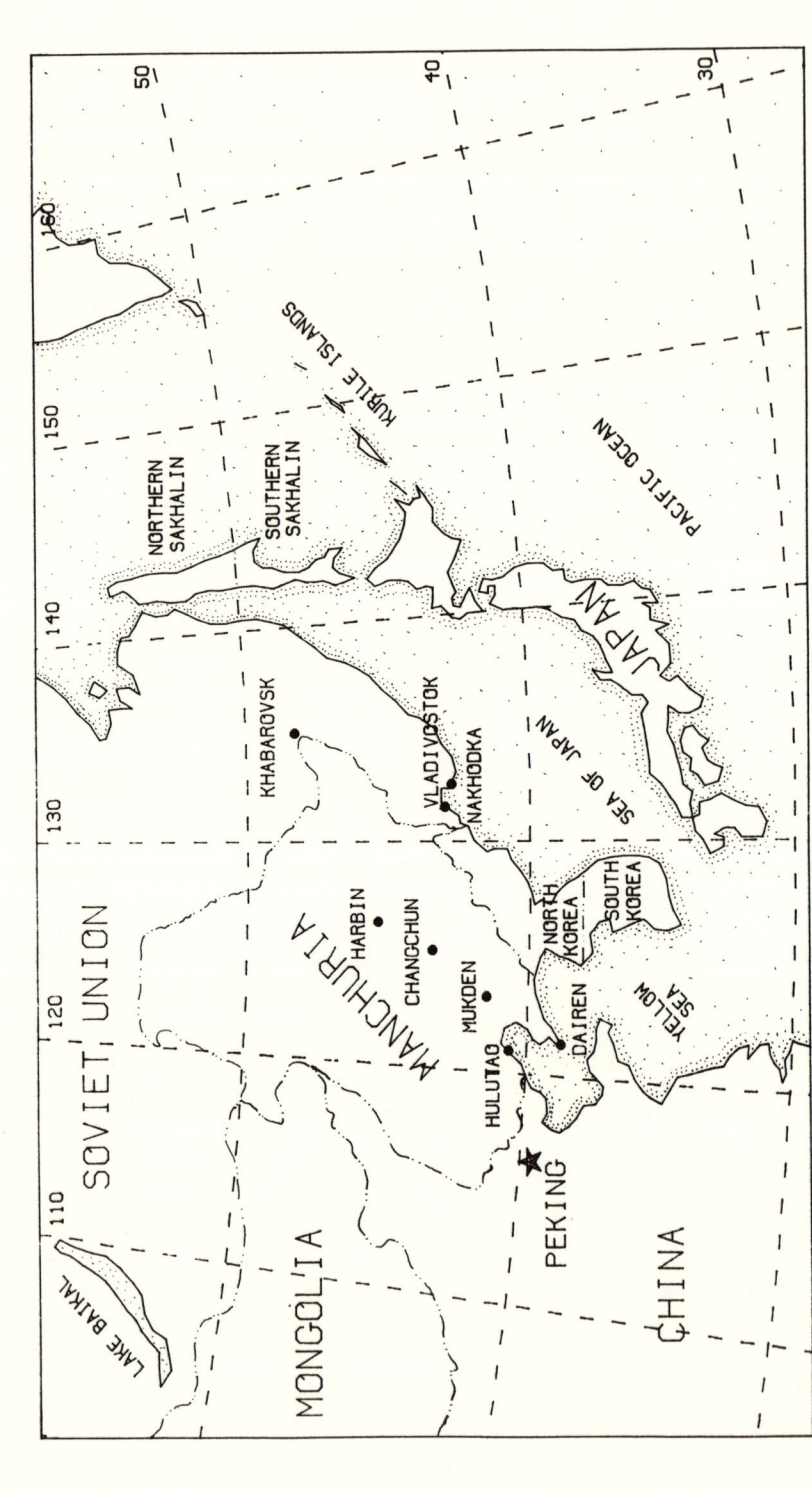

ventures had come to an end. Surrender found Japan's expeditionary forces and overseas colonial settlers dispersed throughout East Asia and the Pacific. Altogether, nearly seven million Japanese—evenly divided between military personnel and civilians—awaited what was to become the greatest overseas repatriation effort ever undertaken. Repatriation was mandatory. Roosevelt, Churchill, and Chiang had vowed—at the 1943 Cairo Conference—that Japan would be "stripped" of all colonial conquests and that the Japanese would be expelled from all territories "taken by violence and greed."[29] Stalin, a few days later at the Teheran Conference, added his agreement.[30]

When Allied forces entered Japan in late August 1945, one of the first tasks awaiting Occupation officials was the initiation of a program to return to the home islands those millions of soldiers and civilians in oversea areas. General MacArthur, newly appointed Supreme Commander for the Allied Powers (SCAP), set up a Repatriation Section in his headquarters to establish policy and monitor the return of soldiers and civilians, but actual operation of the program was to be carried out by the Japanese Ministry of Welfare using Japanese ships. It soon became apparent, however, that there were few seaworthy ships available in Japan, and that it would take several months of repair and renovation to put the disabled merchant fleet in a condition that would even meet bare minimum safety standards. To fill the gap, surplus American vessels (Liberty ships and large amphibious landing ships) were pressed into service. Japanese crews, composed of seamen formerly assigned to the navy and merchant marine, manned these American transports. Within six months, 167 Japanese ships had been repaired and modified to provide a total passenger carrying capacity of 87,600 spaces.[31]

Slightly more than one million Japanese had been repatriated by January 1946, but none were from Soviet-controlled areas. Repatriation from non-Soviet regions continued throughout 1946, and the number of returning Japanese reached four million by the first anniversary of the surrender. By March 1947, 97 percent of Japanese in non-Soviet zones had been repatriated, but only 53 percent of civilians and soldiers in areas occupied by the Soviets in August 1945 had returned to Japan.[32] Nearly all of those from the USSR-controlled territories, mostly civilians, had either trekked south on foot from North Korea or had been repatriated by China from Manchuria after the Soviets left in May 1946. About 1.3 million Japanese were still in Soviet hands. SCAP made many attempts to expedite repatriation and to obtain information on Japanese held by the USSR, but the Soviets rarely provided details on names, numbers, or deaths of internees under their control, leading one frustrated American official to refer to their posture as a *curtain of silence*.

Why were the Soviets so reluctant to release the Japanese who had so recently fallen into their hands? Was it due to animosity lingering since defeat in the Russo-Japanese War? Were the Soviets planning to use the defeated Japanese as hostages to insure Japan's peaceful behavior or, perhaps, as a bargaining lever to obtain a larger role in the occupation of Japan? Was there a plan to indoctrinate

Japanese in Marxist-Leninist logic and send them home to add to the strength of the Japan Communist Party, or did Soviet officials see Japanese manpower as part of the solution to their labor shortage in the industrialization of Siberia and the reconstruction of the war-damaged European region of the USSR?

Subsequent chapters will deal with these questions, but there are impediments to definitive answers. Personnel records were lost or destroyed in many cases. Casualty rates during the Red Army attack were never fully known, and Soviet announcements concerning deaths of prisoners of war and civilians were virtually nonexistent. A few Japanese refused repatriation, while others moved on foot from one country to another making it difficult to determine the precise number to be repatriated from any given area. Other problems arise in ascertaining the treatment of Japanese detained in areas under Soviet control. For one, half a century of enmity between Tokyo and the colossus of the north produced a negative bias in Japanese reports concerning Soviet treatment. The Russo-Japanese War had left a legacy of hostility that largely remained unchanged notwithstanding the 1917 demise of the tsarist government. There was bitterness over the Soviet abrogation of the 1941 neutrality pact. For Japanese pioneer settlers who had lived overseas for many years, the loss of nearly all their hard-earned possessions was a humiliating experience. Moreover, years of fervent rightist and nationalistic indoctrination in Japan had instilled fervid anti-Soviet and anti-Communist attitudes.

Cold War tensions between the Soviet Union and the United States began to mount soon after World War II. Perhaps this factor motivated some returning Japanese to unjustly malign their Soviet captors, but the evidence shows that most accounts of Soviet mistreatment were not exaggerated. SCAP reports show objectivity in the analysis of comments made by returning Japanese. Intelligence summaries often included straightforward pro-Soviet comments made by some returnees as well as remarks made by Japan Communist Party members, but the accounts of returning civilians and prisoners of war weave a basic thread of consistency in allegations of Soviet abuses. The reports, taken as a whole, are overwhelming evidence of the grim conditions faced by nearly three million Japanese in Northeast Asia at the close of World War II.

2
Japanese Settlers and the Red Army

Almost two million Japanese civilians were in areas overrun by the Soviet Army in August 1945. Most civilians were able to return to Japan by the end of 1947, but there were significant exceptions. More than 100,000 civilians were interned by the Soviets in Siberia and other parts of the USSR under worse conditions than those experienced by military prisoners of war, and Soviet officials detained some Japanese civilian technicians in Dairen for as long as four years after the war. The posture of the Soviets toward repatriation depended upon where the civilians were located. Japanese in southern Sakhalin and the Kuriles constituted the bulk of the population in those zones. These areas were to be incorporated into the Soviet Union under the provisions of the Yalta agreement, and Soviet officials made many attempts to persuade Japanese residents to become citizens of the USSR. Conversely, Japanese settlers in Manchuria and North Korea made up only a small portion of the total civilian population, and there were no serious efforts by the Soviets to convince them to stay there permanently. The Chinese Nationalist Government detained several thousand Japanese engineers and technicians in Manchuria for about two years because their services were necessary to operate essential industries. Some technicians stayed behind in both North and South Korea for similar purposes.

A separate section is provided in this chapter for Dairen and Port Arthur (the Kwantung Leased Territory) since the Yalta terms specified that the Soviet Union would resume the leasehold rights held by Russia prior to the Russo-Japanese War. This circumstance complicated repatriation of Japanese civilians from that area.

SOUTHERN SAKHALIN AND THE KURILES

When Soviet forces entered southern Sakhalin (Karafuto) and the Kurile Islands (Chishima Rettō) in August 1945, several hundred thousand Japanese suddenly became hostages of the Red Army. News of the Soviet attack across the 50th parallel had brought on a mad scramble to escape to Japan. Anything that would float across the La Perouse Straits (Sōya Kaikyō) for the 30-mile journey to Hokkaido was in great demand. Some 75,000 Japanese were able to flee just after the invasion, but Soviet military authorities prohibited all movement after 22 August. About 300,000 Japanese civilians still remained in southern Sakhalin and the Kuriles.

The southern half of Sakhalin had been transferred to Japan after the Russo-Japanese War. In subsequent years, the Tokyo government had promoted colonization and commerce in the 13,000-square-mile area and established a colonial government to manage the territory. Paper mills and seafood canneries were the primary industries. By contrast, the Kurile Islands, which Russia had ceded to Japan in 1875, had been administered by Hokkaido Prefecture as an integral part of Japan.

One of the first Soviet actions was to replace Japanese administrative officials and police. The Red Army commander ordered the entire police force of Karafuto's capital city, Toyohara (in Russian, Yuzhno-Sakhalinsk), to assemble at a public schoolhouse where they were arrested and led off to prison. Soviet officials viewed the Japanese officials and police as war criminals simply by virtue of the positions they had held, and most were sentenced to five-year prison sentences in Siberia.

Despite the ban on leaving Sakhalin, about 25,000 civilians escaped to Japan in the last three months of 1945. One escapee reported that the Soviets had taken over all schools and that some Russian language was being taught. Soviet officials, the escapee claimed, had sent about 50 recent graduates of Toyohara High School to other parts of the USSR for further study. In the latter part of 1945, there was no attempt to spread Marxist-Leninist doctrine, but some Japanese working for the Soviets attempted to interest local residents of Toyohara in Communism.[1]

According to other sources, there was some propaganda in the form of a Japanese-language newspaper published by the Soviets. An October 1945 edition of *Shinseimei* (New Life) was filled with articles praising the Soviet Union and urging Japanese to become Soviet citizens. One article explained:

> The most important matter for Japanese living in Southern Karafuto is to discard their ideas of repatriation and make ready, instead, for the immediate winter. Japanese should now consider the USSR their homeland; any place across the water is a foreign country.[2]

The Soviets followed similar policies in the Kurile Islands; there were no organized attempts to teach Communist principles, but efforts were made to induce civilians to remain in the islands. The supply of food, fuel, and winter clothing was sufficient for the residents, and Soviet officials claimed that conditions were better than in Japan. A resident of Kunashiri Island gave a glowing account of the Soviet occupation in the Kuriles. Talking to an *Asahi* reporter on a surreptitious visit to nearby Nemuro in Hokkaido, he claimed, "Life is better than under the Japanese."[3] Notwithstanding that enthusiastic report, Red Army officers implemented a compulsory work program for Japanese civilians on a "no work—no eat" basis. The harshest Soviet action was a warning against harmful acts toward Soviet military personnel; 10 Japanese would be executed for the injury of a Soviet soldier, and 20 would be shot for the death of a Red Army member. There is no record, however, of any incident requiring implementation of this policy.[4]

By the spring of 1946, Soviet soldiers in Sakhalin were telling Japanese civilians that armed conflict between the Soviet Union and the United States was inevitable. The possibility of war was a factor in the decision to prohibit repatriation, Red Army officers said, on the grounds that the Soviets and Japanese must fight side by side against the Americans. In addition, an abrupt departure of the Karafuto residents would have caused a serious labor shortage since few Soviet settlers had yet arrived. Japanese laborers worked on many of the defensive preparations built around harbor and military facilities in 1946. The Soviets also were making plans for extensive industrial development in Sakhalin, and the Japanese were the primary source of labor for commercial activities.

Soviet authorities initiated some espionage activity through use of Japanese and Koreans. (The Japanese government transported over 40,000 Korean laborers to southern Sakhalin prior to 1945.) One group reported on the activities of Japanese in Sakhalin, especially those suspected of escape attempts, while others infiltrated Hokkaido by boat to report on conditions in Japan. These ventures into Japan were financed by yen seized by the Soviets at the end of the war. Since many Japanese were attempting to leave, the Soviets established a network of armed coastal patrol boats to monitor escape routes. Korean informers—and some Japanese—provided information on escape attempts. The Soviets rewarded informers with 500 yen ($33) and a bale of rice for information on Japanese attempts to leave Sakhalin.

A year after the war there still had been no official repatriation and more Japanese were attempting to escape. To counter these attempts, a Soviet Army colonel told a group of Japanese that they were now Soviets and that they should abide by Soviet laws and "put forth an effort to further the Soviet cause." When questioned concerning repatriation, the colonel answered: "Because of involvement of various countries, it will be some time before Japanese can return to Japan."[5] On another occasion, a Soviet official in Sakhalin explained that living conditions were bad in Japan. He told civilian residents:

> Your return will only make the food situation in Japan worse. Moreover, Soviet Russia cannot afford to lose you for our industrial as well as our cultural development. We shall be very happy to add to our large family the Japanese race which the Russians in Sakhalin have always respected as highly civilized people.[6]

Nevertheless, escape attempts continued. Some were successful, but most attempts ended in capture and trial for illegal departure from the Soviet Union.

The penalty for unlawful exit from Sakhalin was a prison term of three to seven years at hard labor in a Siberian labor camp. Repatriated Japanese soldiers told American intelligence authorities in 1950 of civilians from southern Sakhalin who were working in Siberian coal mines. The civilians had completed three-year sentences but had no funds for transportation to a repatriation port. In many cases, upon release from prison after completion of a sentence, Soviet officials simply escorted the former inmates to the gate and left them on their own.

A real touch of irony was provided by the case of 20 pre–1945 Sakhalin residents who had been drafted during the war to work in factories on the Japanese mainland. After the war, they left Hokkaido illegally and clandestinely returned to Sakhalin to rejoin their families, but they were apprehended by Soviet officials there and held for illegal entry into the USSR. When they finally returned to Japan in March 1954, the hapless fugitives were questioned by Japanese police for their earlier illegal departure from Japan. In the end, police decided to take no action and repatriation officials announced that the unfortunate wanderers would be treated as "ordinary repatriates."[7] Soviet attempts to transfer some Japanese family members from the home islands to Sakhalin in 1946 are discussed in chapter 5.

The Soviet government initially interpreted the arrangements made at Yalta—for the transfer of southern Sakhalin and the Kuriles to the USSR—to mean that the residents were part of the deal. Escapees reported that "Soviet authorities regard Japanese living in Sakhalin as Soviet nationals." In addition, there were many cases where Japanese were identified as CCCP (the Russian abbreviation for USSR) on identification cards. "*Yaponsky* (Japanese) was entered on physical examination cards for soldiers, but cards for Japanese residents in Karafuto always indicated CCCP in the nationality column," according to a Sakhalin repatriate.[8]

Despite the Soviet attempts to induce civilians to stay in Sakhalin as citizens of the USSR, most Japanese wanted to return to the home islands. After several thousand Soviet settlers had arrived in Sakhalin by late 1946, the Red Army Kommandatura agreed to begin repatriation on a limited basis. The first group to return to Japan, about 2,000 men, women, and children, left Karafuto in December 1946. Repatriation accelerated during the next year, and about half of the Japanese civilians in Sakhalin and the Kuriles had been evacuated by the end of 1947. The heaviest repatriation activity occurred in the warm summer months of 1947 when up to 3,000 civilians left the port of Maoka (Kholmsk) almost every day. Repatriation continued for the next two years, but the return of civilians from Sakhalin and the Kuriles was much slower than from other areas under Soviet control.[9]

Most Japanese had been evacuated from Sakhalin by early 1950, but a Soviet announcement in April of that year that repatriation had been completed drew protests from many sources in Japan. SCAP and Japanese government records showed there were still several thousand more Japanese to be repatriated, but the Soviets stood by their statement.

Several years passed without any repatriation, but Moscow informed Tokyo in 1957 that approximately 1,000 Sakhalin residents wanted to return to Japan. Japanese ships made three voyages from 1957 to 1959 to transport repatriates, mostly Korean men with Japanese wives. One news account indicated that Korean men in Sakhalin were offering Japanese women "huge sums for 'formality' marriages." The report continued:

> There are more than 40,000 Koreans on the formerly Japanese peninsula off the Siberian coast . . . inducted by the Japanese Army as laborers and taken to Sakhalin against their will. Most of them want to come to Japan.
>
> The quickest way to realize their wish is to marry Japanese women and be repatriated. Hence Korean detainees are asking Japanese women for "formality" marriages. They are even asking married women to "divorce" their husbands for a duration to enter into make-believe marriages with them. As much as 1,000 rubles are being offered.[10]

More than a decade after the war, those who lost their lives in escape attempts were remembered. On a July 1957 voyage to Sakhalin, the crew of the Kōan Maru cast flower bouquets into the sea off Hokkaido "to pay homage to the spirits of 1,600 Japanese repatriates from Sakhalin who perished in the area soon after the war's end."[11] The final chapter on repatriation from Sakhalin was completed in February 1959 when 172 residents, mostly Korean men with Japanese wives and children, sailed for Japan. The Soviet census of 1967 showed no Japanese in Sakhalin, but a 1976 Japanese Foreign Ministry announcement indicated that 100 Japanese and 7,000 Koreans were still there.[12]

MANCHURIA

Even though more than 1 million Japanese civilians were in Manchuria when the Soviets arrived in August 1945, they constituted less than 3 percent of the total population. The largest element, about 40 million indigenous residents, was about to revert to Chinese citizenship. In addition, more than 1 million Korean laborers and their families plus some 70,000 White Russians were in Manchuria. Arrival of the Soviet Army would soon generate major changes in the life of these residents.

Manchuria had the greatest natural resources of any of the Northeast Asian territories recently occupied by the Soviets and was the scene of extensive Japanese industrial projects. The region is rich in mineral resources (especially coal, iron ore, magnesite, and oil shale), a circumstance which stimulated exploitation and led to Japanese development of large steel mills and manufacturing facilities. Arsenals located in major cities such as Mukden (Shenyang), Fushun, and Harbin produced weapons and ammunition for Japan's armed forces. Though extremely cold in winter, Manchuria nevertheless was blessed with fertile soil and a growing season sufficiently long to produce ample food for its residents and for export. Soybeans were the main cash crop. In the eastern highlands, vast forests provided timber resources to feed Japan's appetite for wood and paper products. Most of these operations were managed by Japanese while local residents (and transplanted Koreans) served as laborers. In addition, the Japanese developed extensive business and transportation interests throughout the region. Under Japanese dominance, Manchukuo expanded during the 1930s to encompass not only the provinces of Heilungkiang, Kirin, and Liaoning, but also the northeastern portions of present-day Hopeh Province (including Jehol) and Inner Mongolia. The three northeast provinces are now referred to as Northeast China; the designation "Manchuria," long associated with Manchu separatism and Japanese expansionist ventures, was discontinued after 1945.

Twentieth-century Japanese involvement in Manchuria began with the Russo-Japanese War of 1904–1905, when Russia's defeat led to the establishment of a Japanese foothold in the Liaotung Peninsula (the Kwantung Leased Territory). During the 1920s, Japanese influence expanded northward along the South Manchuria Railway, a development made possible by the Portsmouth Peace Treaty and the Sino-Japanese Treaty of 1915 which stated: "Japanese subjects shall be free to reside and travel in South Manchuria and to engage in business and manufacture of any kind whatsoever." Japanese interests initially were managed by the military under the Kwantung Army commander. Even though this system was changed in 1919 with the installation of a civilian as governor of the leased territory, high-ranking officers of the Kwantung Army continued to expand Japanese control aggressively, often without authority from Tokyo. The Mukden Incident of September 1931 served as a pretext for extending military control over a large part of Manchuria. In February 1932, at a meeting of governors of Northeastern China provinces and major cities, the All-Manchurian Assembly declared independence from China. The governors, with Kwantung Army backing, proclaimed the new state of Manchukuo (*Manchu land*) on 1 March 1932, making the entire 503,000-square-mile area of Manchuria a Japanese puppet state.

Although Manchukuo had an emperor, Henry Pu Yi, and its own prime minister, Chang Ching-hui, real power was in the hands of Japanese officials. The commander of the Kwantung Army and other top officers wielded extensive influence, and the top civilian leader was a Japanese, Takebe Rokuzō, who held the title of "Director of the General Affairs Bureau of the Manchurian State Council." From 1932 until the 1945 Soviet invasion, the Japanese were an elite group, firmly in control, and at the top of the pecking order among the various nationalities residing in Manchuria. This condition was reversed quite suddenly after the Soviet attack when Chinese and Korean residents exploded in revenge against their former colonial masters.

Aikō Hiroyuki, a Kumamoto Prefecture schoolteacher, was a 15-year-old student in Mukden in 1945. Years later he recalled:

> When the Japanese first came into Manchuria in the 1930s, some Japanese people became powerful and took advantage of the local people. In 1945, these Japanese

were attacked by Chinese in their offices and other places later on. . . . Some Japanese were severely wounded. Extensive outbreaks of violence against Japanese began to occur. A lot of Japanese were targets for the Chinese. Some Japanese were attacked and wounded by the Chinese, while others had their houses taken over by Chinese which made the Japanese homeless.[13]

The situation was further aggravated by abusive behavior on the part of Soviet soldiers, especially those in the initial contingents who viewed the Japanese and their possessions as war booty. Many of the Soviet troops were "crude and vulgar"—recently released convicts, according to most Japanese sources—and "they ruthlessly raped and made off with pretty and attractive Japanese women."[14] In northern Manchuria, where the brunt of the attack was first felt, Japanese settlers began evacuation on foot and soon were besieged by mobs. According to statements of repatriates, some evacuees were "robbed, murdered or otherwise outraged" by Soviet soldiers and Manchurian and Korean civilians.

The Japanese government had promoted emigration of Japanese from the home islands to Manchukuo since the early 1930s in an effort to resolve Japan's population problem. In 1933, the Agriculture Ministry, with a goal of settling five million Japanese in Manchuria by 1958, began providing financial incentives to pioneers to establish farms in northern and western Manchuria. These settlers, attempting to create farms out of barren lands that had never before been cultivated, were the first to feel the impact of the Soviet attack.

Pioneer settlers at the village of Halahei, about 250 miles west of Harbin and 80 miles east of the Mongolian border, were right in the path of the main onslaught of the Soviet Transbaikal Front's 39th Army. The last train came through at noon on 10 August, but villagers were unable to get aboard as it was already filled with other refugees who were bulging out of doorways, sitting on railway car roofs, and even hanging on to the locomotive. The settlers—including women, children, and old men—then began evacuation on foot through a vast, inhospitable territory. The group wandered on for more than two weeks, facing perils from the barren land and roaming bands of Mongol bandits. Many women and children dropped by the wayside, unable to keep up with the pace of refugee leaders. Cut off from all communication, they were unaware of the surrender and fired on a troop of Soviet cavalry, killing one soldier. Red Army reinforcements soon arrived on the scene, inflicting retribution with a vengeance. Soviet soldiers indiscriminately fired at the entire group and killed most of them. Later, a Soviet Army truck returned and carried away the few children still alive. Two surviving adults, hidden among the corpses, heard the children cry out, "*Otōsan, Okāsan, sayonara, sayonara!*" (Father, Mother, goodbye, goodbye!) as the truck pulled away.[15]

More than four decades later, 51-year-old Li Gui-qin arrived at Tokyo's Narita Airport from China searching for relatives. She was born to Japanese parents in Manchuria, but her mother and father were killed in the 1945 Soviet invasion.

Li, eight years old when the Red Army attacked, was part of a group of refugees ambushed by Soviet tanks. She recalled:

> Many people died, and I pretended to be dead, too. After two days, I crawled from the bushes and walked for about two miles. I came across a coal furnace and a Chinese man working there took me in as his adopted daughter.[16]

Anti-Japanese behavior soon erupted in all parts of Manchuria, resulting in the looting of private property and "violation of women." According to one repatriate, "Many of the Japanese moving south had to walk as they were not allowed to board trains and were subjected to all kinds of mistreatment. There were about 100 deaths per day, many from unnatural causes. A considerable number of Japanese women and children [were] being sold at prices of 70–80 yen."[17] Refugees in tattered clothing began pouring into Harbin, Changchun, Mukden, and Antung, bringing reports of brutal treatment—children abandoned by the wayside; homes sacked and burned by Chinese; women raped by mobs; children snatched from mothers' arms—breeding fear and apprehension in the large Japanese communities of major cities. A witness to the Soviet Army's entry into Harbin later recalled:

> As soon as darkness fell on the city, the Soviet soldiers launched into a headlong orgy of raping and looting. Like a pack of hungry wolves they roamed through the darkened streets into the wee small hours of the morning breaking into homes and shops and carrying off food, drink and women. Invariably, they chose the stores and houses of Japanese, especially those living in beautiful houses in the residential districts.[18]

Mukden, Manchuria's largest city, suffered similar consequences according to a former resident:

> There were many accidents caused by drunk Soviet soldiers who shot blindly in the streets. As a result of this, many civilians were wounded or killed. Almost all soldiers, including 16-year-old boys who were members of the Soviet Youth Troops, drank Chinese alcoholic liquor (*changchu* and *paichu*, to name a few) and diluted ethyl alcohol which they stole from warehouses. All of these liquors were very strong. Soviet soldiers stole merchandise from booths at open air markets. They did not even try to hide their actions. Japanese could not do anything but watch what was happening. However, Chinese people were different. When a Soviet soldier stole his merchandise, Chinese merchants would not turn loose of a Soviet soldier until he returned the stolen articles.[19]

Able-bodied Japanese soon were put to work stripping industrial equipment from factories for war reparations shipments to Siberia. In Changchun, the Soviets used a novel strategem to pick up Japanese civilians for work projects. Trucks were parked near an intersection, and a Japanese decoy would talk to people passing by; anyone who answered in Japanese was loaded on a truck. Even streetcars were searched, and Japanese were ordered off into waiting trucks. The civilians, varying in age from 14 to 55, were then transported off to work sites where the Soviets used them as laborers for periods of up to 15 days.[20]

South Manchuria Railway employees worked as laborers under Soviet and Chinese direction. In a few months, however, it became clear that Chinese and Soviet engineers and technicians did not possess sufficient skill to operate trains in a satisfactory manner. In October 1945, the Soviets reappointed Japanese employees to their former positions and paid them well. Some Japanese worked for up to a year under Soviet and Chinese transportation managers. Living conditions for these railway employees were exceptionally good in comparison to what others experienced in the first winter after the war.[21]

Most civilians in Manchuria, however, faced harsh conditions. It was severely cold, and inflation, poor transportation, and epidemics complicated the task of survival. These factors led to a high fatality rate in the winter of 1945–1946. The Japanese government estimated that 110,000 of its citizens died that winter and predicted the next winter would be worse. A former Manchuria resident explained:

> It was worse than you can ever imagine. . . . The worst thing was the number of people who died due to hunger and the extreme cold. A great number of refugees had come from northern Manchuria, on the border with the Soviet Union, to be sheltered in Mukden schools and other facilities. During the winter, we saw many people dying each day. There was no place to bury them in the city. Some people dug a large pit, about six meters square and four meters deep, in an uninhabited part of our neighborhood. The bodies were already frozen stiff because of the temperature. Then they were thrown into the hole and a thin layer of soil was spread over them.[22]

Comments from letters written in early 1946 pointed to abuses by the Soviets. SCAP officials intercepted postal communications during the occupation of Japan as an extension of wartime censorship; excerpts from letters quoted in GHQ Intelligence Section files illustrate the difficulties facing Japanese civilians:

> Generally speaking, the treatment of Japanese by the Soviet forces is cruel beyond description. Violence and pillage occurred frequently. They committed atrocities. . . . Above all, they violently demanded women, like brutes, and killed whomever opposed them. . . .
> When the Soviet troops first crossed the border into Manchuria they attacked the Japanese volunteers and other Japanese male civilians, taking them away together with the looted goods and money. Women also were taken, leaving children behind. The conduct of the Russians toward women is atrocious even at the present time.[23]

Aikō Hiroyuki explained that he first saw Soviet soldiers riding into Mukden on heavy tanks about 20 August 1945. "It was very frightening," he said, and he thought that "all Japanese people were going to be killed." Hashimoto Katsuyuki, a *Mantetsu* (South Manchuria Railway) employee in Harbin, explained:

> The Soviet soldiers in my work place had a low intelligence level. They lacked the power to reason and acted rudely. They behaved as if they were still at war. Although they were supposed to engage in a peaceful occupation, they were raping women in the street. In the Japanese residential areas, there were burglars day and night. According to rumors, the soldiers who had been sent to Manchuria were the bad ones.[24]

Japanese families were concerned for the safety of their teenage daughters. A merchant in Mutanchiang (Botankō) began preparations to leave for Japan soon after the attack. He set off on foot with his wife, two daughters, and one son, avoiding main roads. His two daughters, aged 15 and 17, wore boy's clothing and had their hair cut short to make them look like boys. This subterfuge worked, but wrist watches, fountain pens, jewelry, and other valuables were stolen by both Soviet and Chinese Nationalist soldiers. The family trekked more than 500 miles, and by the time they arrived in South Korea nearly all of their possessions had been plundered.[25]

While most reports deal with Soviet abuses, there were instances of misbehavior on the part of Chinese troops, both Communist and Nationalist. The *Kuomintang* (Nationalist) Government delayed repatriation of several thousand Japanese, including some women who were used as mistresses for officers or forced into prostitution. As Jack Belden writes in *China Shakes the World*, "Not only in towns did one see Japanese girls consorting with Kuomintang officers, but also riding on supply trains in the company of lieutenants and captains."[26] Chinese Communist authorities often forced Japanese civilians to work on labor projects without pay.

Reiko Schwab, now a faculty member at Old Dominion University in Norfolk, Virginia, was a teenage girl living in Manchuria with her family in 1945 and for much of 1946, in an area close to the Korean border. Chinese Communist forces, in control of that region much of the time, required her to work at various jobs such as kitchen helper, seamstress in a clothing factory, and nurse's aid. She received little or no pay for her work, but says she did not fear the Chinese Communist soldiers. On the other hand, Nationalist Chinese and Soviet soldiers often behaved badly. She explained:

> Chinese Red Army soldiers were very good. We were not afraid of them. We were really afraid of the Nationalist soldiers—they were the ones who raped many women and we feared them. We were also afraid of the Russians. Day and night we literally ran from house to house and hid from the Russians.
>
> We lived in continuous fear of the Russian soldiers. Two of them were former convicts, and they terrorized the community. They killed a Japanese man for his watch.[27]

Order was restored after a few months as Soviet military police began to function. Reports of misbehavior on the part of Red Army soldiers decreased after the Soviet high command issued instructions to curb the initial rampages of its soldiers. In some cases, Soviet military police shot their fellow soldiers in implementation of this policy. However, by early November the refugees faced new problems—starvation and extreme cold—with the onset of winter. Temperatures drop far below freezing in Manchuria, and the average mean January temperature for Harbin is four degrees below zero Fahrenheit. As the Japanese continued to flee from the countryside into the cities, food and clothing were available, but refugees lacked money to purchase goods. A relief fund of 40 million yen ($2.7 million) was raised by the Japanese Association of Mukden through the generosity of wealthier Japanese who still had money. The Iryumin Group, a residents association, distributed blankets, pillows, and food to refugees, but their efforts were not enough to save everyone. Japanese bankers and merchants made loans to some of their fellow countrymen, but financial resources still were insufficient to provide food and clothing for the 550,000 Japanese who had crowded into Mukden by December 1945.[28]

To add to the deplorable conditions facing Japanese civilians, the Chinese civil war was spreading throughout Manchuria. Until the end of World War II, Japan's Kwantung Army had protected Manchuria from both the Nationalist and Communist armies. The Soviets, in a treaty signed with Chiang Kai-shek on 14 August 1945, agreed to deal exclusively with the Nationalist Government in Chungking. Stalin even went so far as to bar Chinese Communist troops from entering Manchuria, but they infiltrated in large numbers through the countryside and managed to plunder and steal enough military equipment to establish an effective fighting force in large areas of Manchuria.

The Soviets initially agreed to withdraw from Manchuria by the end of 1945, but Chiang asked Soviet Army officials to delay their departure until the following February because of difficulties Nationalist troops were experiencing in entering Manchuria. The Soviets stayed beyond February, however, and blamed the delay on bad weather and lack of fuel. Control ostensibly was transferred to the Chinese Nationalists when the Soviets eventually left in May 1946, but the delayed departure provided ample time for Chinese Communist troops to become firmly entrenched in rural areas. General civil war between the Nationalists and Communists began in April 1946, and the Japanese were caught between opposing forces. Gradually, the Nationalists gained the upper hand in southern Manchuria, and ports were opened for repatriation.[29] Some Japanese were able to travel by train to ports, but many had to make the trip on foot.

Allied military officials worked out arrangements at the Potsdam Conference for Japanese troops in Manchuria to surrender to Soviet forces, but no specific agreement had been made concerning civilian repatriation. Since the Soviet presence in Manchuria was to be temporary and the region was to revert to Chinese control, the Nationalist Government assumed responsibility for civilian repatriation with assistance from the United States. The Soviets, however, rejected Nationalist requests to land at the major port of Dairen, and Chinese Communist forces occupied the smaller ports of southern Manchuria, thus delaying repatriation efforts. Evacuation of Japanese civilians finally was initiated in May 1946 when the Nationalists secured the port of Hulutao, about 80 miles northeast of the point where the Great Wall of China meets the sea. Meanwhile, about 30,000 Japanese found their way from Manchuria to North Korea, crossed the 38th parallel on foot, and were evacuated to Japan from South Korea.[30]

Former U.S. Navy ships manned by Japanese crews constituted the major element of the repatriation fleet. These ships evacuated about 7,500 Japanese daily in the summer of 1946, and repatriation continued until October. Then heavy rains caused the destruction of roads and bridges, preventing refugees from reaching Hulutao and causing some Japanese to spend a second winter in Manchuria. Repatriation resumed in the early spring of 1947, and more than one million Japanese civilians had been evacuated from Manchuria by the end of March. Nevertheless, death had claimed 162,000 Japanese residents in the preceding 19 months, and 86,000 surviving civilians were still there.[31]

Among those remaining in Manchuria were some 10,000 children, orphaned or abandoned in the confusing final days of the war. About half of them had been seized by "Manchurian brokers" and sold into slavery to farmers or shopkeepers, according to the report of one repatriate. More than 5,000 orphans were in the custody of the Eighth Route Army in areas of Manchuria controlled by the Chinese Communists. Orphan centers in Harbin and Mutanchiang provided care for the children, but many had forgotten Japanese and spoke only Chinese. Some did not remember their parents' names. A few orphans were inducted into the Chinese Communist Army upon reaching the age of 16. Also, Chinese families adopted many of the "left-behind" children.[32]

Some of the Japanese who stayed on in Manchuria were technicians who had been retained by the Nationalists because of a lack of skilled Chinese to operate industrial plants. In a May 1947 cable to the secretary of state, the American ambassador to China said that approximately 11,300 Japanese technical personnel (accompanied by about 30,000 family members) had been "commandeered" by the Nationalists for essential projects. SCAP intelligence summaries show that about 3,000 technicians voluntarily remained in Manchuria. They were induced to stay by high wages and good living quarters. Some even adopted Chinese names. The Chinese Nationalists offered many inducements to retain highly qualified technicians in Manchuria. To this end, Chiang's government established a Japanese War Prisoners and Civilians Administration in Mukden and made government-financed education programs available to Japanese residents.[33] Adverse factors, especially rapid inflation, soon set in and caused some Japanese to request repatriation. Many of the technicians and their families left in late 1947.

During the late 1940s, more repatriates came back to Japan from Manchuria. One group of about 2,000 returned in September 1949 and reported that they had experienced hardships first under the Soviets, subsequently under the Chinese

Communists, then at the hands of the Nationalists, and then again under the Chinese Communists. More than four years after the war, testimony before the Repatriation Committee of the Lower House of Japan's Diet (parliament) revealed that there were an estimated 45,000 Japanese still in Manchuria. Some had married Chinese citizens and refused repatriation, while others had elected to stay for a variety of reasons.

However, more Japanese came back in the fifties and even later. Four thousand Japanese returned from Manchuria in 1953, and nearly 3,000 more journeyed back to the home islands in the late 1950s. An April 1958 group of returnees was described as

> mostly technicians who had been employed in Communist China mines and railroads after the war, and farm youths who had been engaged in "pioneering work" in Manchuria and Mongolia before the war. . . . Many wore the blue "uniforms" typical of Communist China. None appears to be "fanatic," and they seem more mature than the 1949 repatriates.[34]

Four decades after the war's end, some of those who as children had been orphaned or abandoned in 1945—now middle-aged—were trying to make their way back to Japan. Beginning in 1972, after diplomatic relations were established between Japan and the People's Republic of China, Japan's Health and Welfare Ministry began an extensive search throughout northeastern China for Japanese who had been left behind in Manchuria. By 1987, more than 2,000 "left-behind orphans," *zanryū koji*, had been brought to Tokyo at Japanese government expense in an attempt to find relatives. Most of the "orphans" had been raised by Chinese families, spoke no Japanese, and found Japan to be "like a foreign country." Some returned to China, but others elected to stay in Japan. To facilitate their transition, the Health and Welfare Ministry established a Japanese language and culture training center at a former U.S. Army depot in Tokorozawa, Saitama Prefecture, about 25 miles west of Tokyo, where the *zanryū koji* received four months of intensive instruction. Health and Welfare Ministry officials planned to continue the search for Japanese left in China, and estimated in August 1987 that about 5,000 additional people wanted to come to Japan. The Japanese government announced plans in 1987 to build 5 new transition centers similar to the Tokorozawa site. In addition, the Health and Welfare Ministry also decided to extend the orientation period to one year, with 20 orientation centers to be constructed throughout Japan to provide additional help to the repatriates for eight months after completion of the initial four-month program.[35]

DAIREN AND PORT ARTHUR

Dairen and Port Arthur, though geographically a part of Manchuria, are classified separately because of their political uniqueness. Japan had initially obtained rights to this strategic area in the Liaotung Peninsula through the Treaty of

Shimonoseki in 1895 after defeating China, but tsarist Russia joined with Germany and France to force a revision of the treaty. A weak Chinese government, under obligation to Russia for financial assistance, was persuaded to grant leasehold rights for the peninsula to the Russians in 1898. The warmer climate of the Liaotung Peninsula, which juts out into the Yellow Sea, was an improvement over Vladivostok's harsh weather, and the port of Dairen (in Russian, Dalny) provided an outlet for goods shipped by the Russian railroad line from Changchun and Mukden, later known as the South Manchuria Railway. At the southern tip of the peninsula, the Russians began development of a naval base at Port Arthur. Resentment over Russian actions led Japan to a surprise attack on Port Arthur in 1904, and after Russia's defeat in 1905 the leasehold rights were transferred to Japan by the Treaty of Portsmouth.[36] Japanese development of Dairen made it second only to Shanghai as the major port on the East Asian mainland. The Japanese Navy converted the former Russian base at Port Arthur (in Japanese, Ryōjun) into a major facility for its own fleet.

After 40 years under Japanese rule, the peninsula changed hands again in 1945 when former Russian rights were transferred to the Soviet Union in accordance with the Yalta arrangements. The Soviets acknowledged in the 1945 treaty with the Chinese Nationalists that Dairen was to be a free port for commercial shipping, while the Port Arthur naval base was to be used jointly by the Soviet and Nationalist forces. The treaty, however, stipulated that Dairen would be placed under Soviet military control in the event of war with Japan. In short order, the Soviet Union declared that a state of war existed with Japan because a peace treaty had not been signed. Soviet troops remained on that basis, and Dairen became a closed port. Chinese Communist party members were placed in administrative positions in the city government, but they were subordinate to the Dairen Kommandatura, the Soviet commandant. The Nationalists never held any position of power in the city.

About 250,000 Japanese were in Dairen at the end of the war. In addition to its role as a major port, Dairen had become an important industrial center and headquarters for the South Manchuria Railway. Chinese in Dairen had received virtually no technical training and were not capable of operating the city's extensive industrial plants. This factor forced the Soviets to continue use of Japanese technicians, medical specialists, and railway employees, some for as long as four years after the war. As the Soviet occupation set in, living conditions deteriorated. The dismantling and subsequent shipment to Siberia of much of Dairen's power-generating and industrial equipment hit the civilian population hardest, leading to frequent disruption of power service, limited heating, and a shortage of basic consumer products. To make matters worse, individual movement was restricted, and police permits were required for spending the night away from home.

Dairen is a natural port and has a huge, well-protected, crescent-shaped harbor. Although the city bears traces of its Russian origins, the most extensive growth took place under Japanese rule. Soviet postwar stripping of Dairen's industrial base for reparations caused the port to languish. Commercial shipping in the late 1940s, limited to Soviet merchant vessels and an occasional Polish or Romanian freighter, was only a small fraction of what it had been in the 1930s.[37]

In early 1946, the Dairen Kommandatura ordered the formation of a Communist-oriented Japanese labor union to control daily activities of civilian workers. The union administered food distribution, employment, housing, and education for Japanese residents, and also recommended priorities for individual repatriation. One former official of the presurrender Japanese administration in Dairen later claimed that the union oppressed the majority of residents through people's courts, intimidation, fraud, and delays in repatriation. The official, testifying in 1949 before a committee of the Japanese Diet, said he had been tried in court on charges of being reactionary. He claimed the court did not permit him any defense, but forced him to stand before an audience of 1,000 spectators with a sign hanging from his neck reading "Reactionary Element." The court fined him 30,000 yen ($2,000 in 1946) and confiscated all his property. However, a former official of the Japanese labor union, in testimony before the same Diet committee, denied all charges and said the union worked for the interests of all Japanese in Dairen. He claimed that living conditions improved and that 25,000 Japanese were able to find employment "through the democratic practice of the union."[38]

Repatriation from Dairen and Port Arthur was much slower than that from Manchuria proper for several reasons. Foremost was the need for Japanese labor to do most of the work in removing production equipment for shipment to Siberia and to operate what was left to run the cities. Secondly, Dairen was closed to non-Soviet ships, and since the Soviets would not use their own shipping to repatriate Japanese, there was no way to begin evacuation. Protests by the American member of the Allied Council for Japan finally led the Soviets to agree in December 1946 to begin repatriation with American ships manned by Japanese crews.

The first shipload of repatriates left Dairen in December 1946 and, for the next few months, frequent voyages were made to evacuate Japanese civilians from the Liaotung Peninsula. Repatriation reached a peak in March 1947 when 82,000 residents left for Japan, and by April the total reached 218,000 for the four-month period. However, the Soviets retained about 7,500 professional and technical specialists, mostly physicians, nurses, engineers, and their families, for two more years. The last Japanese left Dairen in October 1949.[39]

Four years after the end of World War II, the Chinese Nationalists fled to Taiwan, and the People's Republic of China (PRC) was proclaimed. In a February 1950 treaty between the Soviet Union and the PRC, the agreement of 14 August 1945 between Moscow and Chiang's government was repudiated. Arrangements were made to transfer Port Arthur and Dairen to Chinese control. Even so, it was not until May 1955 that the Soviets finally turned over the Liaotung Peninsula to the Chinese. Dairen (in Chinese, Dalian), once again one of the busiest ports in Asia, and Port Arthur, known today as Lushun, together form the sub-provincial municipality of Luda.

NORTH KOREA

About 700,000 Japanese civilians were in Korea when the war ended. The Japanese had become firmly entrenched after 35 years of colonial administration in Korea and occupied all important professional and technical positions. Korean nationalism had been suppressed for decades, but leaders of a wartime provisional government in the United States had petitioned the major powers to establish an independent Korean government upon Japan's surrender. Allied leaders agreed in principle, but considered a transitional period a necessity before an independent government could be installed. In a private meeting at the Yalta Conference, Roosevelt and Stalin decided to place Korea in a trusteeship to be administered by Soviet, British, American, and Chinese representatives after Japan's defeat.[40] These arrangements were confirmed at the United Nations Conference in San Francisco in the spring of 1945 and at the Potsdam Conference, but Japan's surrender came about so suddenly that detailed plans for implementation were never developed. Soviet and American military representatives hurriedly worked out a decision to facilitate surrender of Japanese soldiers in Korea; troops to the north of the 38th parallel would surrender to the Soviet Army, while those south of the line would capitulate to the Americans. A trusteeship for all of Korea was to be established following the surrender, but the Soviets shortly made all territory to the north into their zone of occupation when they sealed and fortified the demarcation line. About 350,000 Japanese civilians were in North Korea in September 1945. American and Soviet officials conferred many times on the question of repatriating Japanese from the north. By the time negotiations were completed in December 1946, all but 15,000 of the Japanese civilians had trekked on foot from the north into South Korea.

Soviet troops entered North Korea in late August and early September 1945. As in other Soviet-occupied areas, the initial treatment of the Japanese was harsh. Leonard Barsdell, an Australian member of a team investigating the status of Japanese-held Allied POWs north of the 38th parallel, witnessed the behavior of Soviet troops during their first month in North Korea. He later wrote:

> the Russians, from the Manchurian border to areas below Kanko and Konan industrial districts, are indulging in widespread and indiscriminate looting of both Korean and Japanese property, and are indulging in rape and robbery of both Koreans and Japanese by armed force.
>
> On seven successive days I saw Russians looting in the Kanko and Konan districts, and areas to the south and north. On one occasion I asked, and was allowed to accompany a looting party. The procedure was this: the Russians, armed with tommy-guns, would drive up to a Korean or Japanese house, fire a few shots

in the air, then break into the house, drag out what women (mostly young girls) they could find, put them into the truck along with the furniture and any other articles that caught their eyes, and drive off to their barracks. After a day or two the girls are thrown on the street.

Barsdell went on to say that the attitude of the Soviets was bringing together Japanese and Koreans for the first time in 40 years. He explained:

> All along the line, from Kanko to the American lines, there is a stream of Korean and Japanese refugees trekking south. A few I interviewed said they were escaping from the Russians whom they feared. Their one desire was to get to American-occupied Korea. I saw this line just outside of Kanko, I saw it coming into Kanko from the Manchurian border, and I saw it entering the American zone, some 200 miles to the south.[41]

Returning Japanese had similar accounts to relate. Yamauchi Shinichi escaped from Manchuria and fled to Korea. He observed Peace and Red Guard units in Heijo (Pyongyang) composed mainly of Korean Communist students, some of whom had just come from the Soviet Union where their families had lived in exile during the Japanese occupation of Korea. They intimidated and stole from Japanese civilians. Yamauchi reported that in September the Red Army "began to round up male Japanese from the ages of 16 to 60 years, put them on trucks and take them away somewhere."[42] A former schoolteacher said the Soviets used Japanese POWs and civilians to construct and repair roads. Women and children were put to work as housemaids or as kitchen helpers in Red Army mess halls. Soviet guards shot Japanese if they tried to escape, according to the schoolteacher's report, but Japanese were not otherwise treated cruelly. The food supply, however, was extremely short.

Soviet officials initially attempted to prevent anyone from crossing the 38th parallel, but Japanese and Koreans were able to escape through remote mountain trails. Eventually these pathways became so well used that it would have been impossible for the Soviets not to have noticed. During a six-week period in April and May 1946, 34,000 refugees crossed from North Korea into the south.[43] By June, however, movement across the demarcation line had decreased significantly. The few Japanese who managed to escape during that month reported that the North Korean police were under orders to stop all refugees. By that time, however, more than half of the Japanese civilians in the north had crossed into South Korea on foot. American intelligence authorities soon discovered that the Soviets had indeed put a halt to all movements to the south, explaining their actions with these comments:

1. Do not think this is bad for the Japanese people. It is for the purpose of repatriating Japanese in a better manner.
2. We regret that we did not help the Japanese repatriate before. Also, we regret that repatriates had to walk without aid and protection of the Russian Army.

3. We made arrangements with Japan to use ships for repatriation of Japanese to Japan from North Korea directly.
4. Until the ships start coming in, the Japanese may, if they wish, sell their personal property.[44]

The ban on departure of the Japanese most likely was prompted by the Soviet decision to reopen Korean industries and the subsequent discovery that there was a shortage of professional and technical workers. The Soviets employed skilled and semi-skilled workers in metallurgical and chemical plants, with preferential treatment given to engineers. An article which appeared in a North Korean newspaper, appealing for an end to the friction between the indigenous population and their former masters, asked Koreans to show more respect to the Japanese:

> From the viewpoint of the laboring class, it is not good to hate, oppress or insult the Japanese laborers. Korean laborers in all workshops should give up their past attitude towards Japanese and strive to learn the skills possessed by the Japanese technical experts. In workshops and other places, leaders should be elected who will serve to solve the daily problems arising from the unrest, dissatisfaction and conflicts between the Japanese and Korean workers.[45]

However, the exodus of Japanese from North Korea soon resumed despite these appeals to stay. Since shipping from North Korean ports was limited, most of the remaining Japanese made the trek southward and and crossed into American-occupied Korea as those before them had done. Distances varied depending on the point of origin. It is about 75 miles from Pyongyang to the 38th parallel, but areas near the Manchurian and Soviet borders are 200 to 250 miles from the South Korean border. About 50,000 Japanese crossed into South Korea on foot in the summer and fall of 1946, but a Japanese relief official reported in November that over 70,000 still were in the north. Officials were concerned over the fate of the remaining civilians during the approaching winter in view of reports that many small children had died the previous year due to lack of food and winter clothing.

The Soviets forcibly detained a few Japanese civilians, but more frequently they employed subtle propaganda to persuade technicians to stay in North Korea. According to one refugee, the Soviets were spreading the word that American authorities in Japan felt that all Japanese in Soviet-occupied Korea were influenced by Communism and therefore deemed them undesirable. The Soviets claimed they desired the repatriation of all Japanese, but in cooperating with U.S. policies, it was considered best that the Soviet Government detain all Japanese nationals. The notice went on to state: "In order to make their stay as enjoyable as possible, the Soviet Army will aid Japanese desiring to make their homes in North Korea in any way possible."[46] Some Japanese elected to stay.

About 1,400 technicians in Hamhung refused repatriation and said they had comfortable homes and were receiving sufficient food.

The great majority of Japanese, however, wanted to be repatriated, but in the winter of 1946–1947 most were able to return only through the mountain route across the 38th parallel. Upon arrival in South Korea, Japanese refugees were given priority in obtaining train tickets for Pusan, much to the consternation of Korean citizens fleeing from North Korea. Nearly all Japanese had left North Korea by April 1947. SCAP records indicate that approximately 27,000 Japanese civilians returned by ship directly to Japan, but 296,000 Japanese refugees crossed the 38th parallel on foot and subsequently journeyed by ship from South Korean ports to Japan. Slightly more than a thousand elected to remain in the north, but most of these eventually returned to Japan. About 200 Japanese women, all married to Korean men, were repatriated from Pusan after the Korean War began.

As in Manchuria, some children were orphaned or separated from their parents in Korea. Many were lost in the long march to the south, several thousand died, and some were stranded when their parents returned to Japan without them. Even in the mid–1950s, photographs occasionally appeared in Japanese newspapers showing pictures of children searching for their parents. Some had made their way back to Japan on their own. Hirohata Kazutō, aged 13 in 1945, thought his parents died at the end of the war and was adopted by a South Korean family. He was inducted into the Republic of Korea (ROK) Army during the Korean War and fought alongside Americans against the North Koreans and Chinese Communists, but after four years in the ROK Army, Hirohata learned in November 1956 that his parents were alive and living in Hiroshima Prefecture. He rejoined his parents in Japan in 1957.[47]

SUMMARY

Nearly two million Japanese civilians found themselves in Soviet-controlled areas at the end of the war. Repatriation policy varied depending on location. Southern Sakhalin and the Kuriles were incorporated into the USSR, and Soviet officials appear to have embraced the doctrine that the residents went along with the territory. Repatriation from these areas was deliberately restricted for more than a year. In other regions, the Soviets recognized that sovereignty ultimately resided with other nations and did not show much resistance to repatriation, but did little to promote it. Large numbers of Japanese civilians had returned to Japan by March 1947 from two areas initially under control of the USSR, but the Soviets had little to do with these evacuations. Japanese civilians began leaving Manchuria after the Soviets had departed, and the great majority of refugees from North Korea were able to return to Japan only by first hiking to South Korea.

Soviet treatment of civilians in occupied territories was often abusive, especially in the first month after the war. However, to add some objectivity to the record of atrocities, it should be noted that Japanese in Soviet-occupied areas received treatment not unlike that which their own troops had meted out in China and other parts of Asia. Furthermore, Japanese treatment of Allied POWs and civilian internees was notoriously bad. To add another perspective of military behavior in newly occupied territories, there were many cases of misbehavior on the part of American and British Commonwealth troops in Japan. Although Allied Occupation personnel generally behaved well, there were ample instances of improper conduct such as public drunkenness, boorish manners, and crude and insulting behavior toward Japanese citizens. Misdemeanors were numerous

Table 1
Repatriation of Japanese from Oversea Areas September 1945 Through March 1947

Area	Estimated Number in Area August 1945[a]	Repatriated	Percent Repatriated
Soviet-controlled			
Manchuria	1,259,000	1,011,000[b]	80.3%
North Korea	359,000	320,000[c]	89.1
Dairen/Port Arthur	228,000	104,000	45.6
Sakhalin & Kuriles	305,000	12,000[d]	3.9
USSR	575,000	10,000	1.7
Soviet area total	2,726,000	1,457,000	53.4
All other areas	3,874,000	3,777,000	97.5
Total	6,600,000	5,234,000	79.3%

SOURCE: Derived from statistics shown in Daily Intelligence Summaries, Minutes of Allied Council for Japan meetings, and Japan Foreign Ministry Reports.

[a] After adjustment for 575,000 soldiers and civilians deported to the USSR for detention and forced labor. Initial SCAP estimate of 700,000 POWs was overstated.

[b] Repatriation initiated after Soviet withdrawal in May 1946.

[c] Includes escapees through South Korea.

[d] Does not include escapees.

and some Occupation troops committed felonies, such as murder and rape, causing concern on the part of SCAP officials. The Eighth Army Provost Marshal maintained records of crimes committed by Allied Occupation personnel against Japanese citizens. Representative data for 1946 show a monthly average of 534 offenses (54 percent against persons and the remainder against property).[48] These statistics, however, show that only a small percentage of Allied troops were involved in offenses against local residents. The average number of Occupation troops on duty in Japan in 1946 was 243,000, indicating an annual crime rate of 2,667 per 100,000 soldiers, significantly lower than the rate for the population at large in the United States. Even so, SCAP never condoned the acts of offenders, even in the early stages of the Occupation. Allied headquarters imposed court martial proceedings and prison sentences on the more serious violators. Statistics on crimes committed by Soviet Army troops in Manchuria and other former Japanese territories are not available.

Table 1 shows repatriation statistics as of March 1947.

3

Japanese in Stalin's Labor Camps

Although most Japanese civilians in Soviet-occupied areas suffered their share of trials and tribulations, soldiers in these areas endured even worse ordeals at the hands of the Red Army. The Soviets deported 450,000 members of Japan's armed forces to the USSR for use as laborers and held them for two to four years, often under subhuman conditions. In addition, 125,000 Japanese civilians, about seven percent of the total in Soviet-controlled areas, were caught up in this dragnet along with the military. While the Soviets repatriated most Japanese internees by the end of 1949, a few were held until 1956.

Not only did August 1945 see the sudden termination of the Greater East Asia Co-Prosperity Sphere, it also marked the first capitulation to foreign powers in Japan's long history. Since the inception of the modern Japanese Army in the late nineteenth century, a deep sense of pride and respect for authority had been instilled in its soldiers. Death in service to the emperor was seen as the most sincere act of loyalty, yet here was an army that had been overwhelmed in a matter of a week or two, whose emperor had decreed that the nation must accept the Potsdam Proclamation terms, and whose troops were demoralized and uncertain of the future. Although some officers and enlisted men followed what they saw as the only honorable way by committing *seppuku*, or suicide, most soldiers wanted to return to Japan. Some were secretly happy that the war was over, and almost all expected the Soviets to return them to Japan soon.

In the late summer and early fall of 1945, an uneasy malaise prevailed over the Japanese troops of the Kwantung Army in Manchuria. Some of them had heard the emperor's radio address on 15 August but did not really understand what had been said because the speech had been delivered in the classic language of the Imperial Court. Company commanders had disseminated the terms of the Potsdam Proclamation, especially the section that promised the return of Japanese military forces to their homes "with the opportunity to lead peaceful and productive lives." Nevertheless, several thousand members of the Kwantung Army—perhaps with a prescient view of the dark days ahead—deserted their units and struck out on their own. Some of them made it back to Japan in less than a year, but for most, no matter how much they tried to look like civilians, it was impossible to escape the Red Army search for deserters. There were cases of Japanese Army units deserting en masse—fighting as bandits—to survive. Some even joined the Chinese Communist Eighth Route Army; and a few fought in the Korean War on the side of the Communists. Several soldiers from an observation section in northern Manchuria became separated from their unit when the Soviets attacked. They eluded the Soviet Army by changing into civilian clothing and survived by raiding Manchurian homes. The deserters continued for several months, unaware of Japan's surrender, but Soviet troops eventually captured them after winter began.[1]

Most Kwantung Army units soon were disarmed, although there were numerous locations where Japanese soldiers retained their weapons temporarily to maintain order in areas of unrest until Red Army troops could take over. Japanese troops continued to perform the usual garrison duties associated with military life in any army. The Imperial Rescript for military personnel, dictating loyalty to the emperor and charging soldiers to defend the empire, continued to be read each morning in most units. This routine continued into the autumn, and some groups continued to recite the rescript for a few months even after arrival at POW camps in the USSR. Kwantung Army troops had been highly respected and feared by the inhabitants of Manchuria, but now the tables were turned. It was dangerous for Japanese soldiers to walk alone outside their garrison compounds. Angry mobs attacked several soldiers near Mukden, leading most Kwantung Army members to stay with their units or to walk in groups when it was necessary to visit other areas. A former Mukden resident explained: "Japanese soldiers were victims of attacks by Chinese. The Chinese would wait until a large group of Japanese broke up into smaller groups. And they attacked Japanese soldiers walking alone."[2]

A COLD BLAST OF SIBERIAN AIR

In the autumn of 1945, Soviet officers began preparations for transportation of Japanese military personnel to unannounced locations. Most units were broken up into groups of 50 men and taken to the northern border of Manchuria. Soldiers were puzzled at being taken in that direction instead of the southern parts of Manchuria, and, as with any army, rumors were rampant. Most still thought they soon would return to Japan, and the most common explanation was that they were going to Vladivostok where ships would be waiting to take them home. In some cases, to facilitate the boarding of trains, Red Army officers assured hesitant soldiers that they indeed were on their way home. Thousands of Japanese prisoners of war were at locations near the Amur River, known as Kokuryūkō in Japanese (Black Dragon River). Some troops crossed the wide, fast-flowing body of water on barges while others marched or rode trains across bridges. Trains departed at regular intervals transporting POWs to the northeast—a spur line runs for about 50 miles from Blagoveshchensk, a major crossing point, to the main line of the Trans-Siberian Railway—and POWs assumed they were on their way to Vladivostok. However, hopes faded as the trains slowly traveled on for day after day, and in some cases, week after week. The Red Army shipped the majority of Japanese POWs to labor camps in eastern Siberia, but about 100,000 prisoners went to other regions of the Soviet Union or Outer Mongolia, some even to areas near Moscow and Leningrad. One consistency in the Soviet treatment of captives was the absolute lack of any announcement as to what was happening. The hapless prisoners were never told of their destination or their destiny, not even the fact that they were to be detained in the USSR. One Kwantung Army member later recalled his experiences:

> After we got on the train, we thought that we only had to suffer and be patient until we arrived in Vladivostok. The train was supposed to go to the east on the Trans-Siberian Railroad to Khabarovsk. After a short nap, I was awakened by loud exclamations. "What's wrong?" I asked. "The sun is up but something seems to be wrong," one of my fellow soldiers cried out. "The train should be running toward the bright side if we are going east. But the train is going west, to the dark side." . . . Everyone looked outside and wondered why. "Really!" I said. "Something is wrong. This train is going west." All of a sudden the stark reality of it all hit us, like a cold blast of Siberian air. This was even worse than the surrender news we had heard on August 15.[3]

The once proud Imperial Japanese Army troops now were treated like cattle being taken off to the slaughter house. Troops were herded into box cars indiscriminately—counted off by Red Army guards—and former associations mattered not at all. Hashimoto Katsuyuki, a former South Manchuria Railways employee, recalled the departure of former Kwantung Army soldiers from Harbin:

> I saw Japanese soldiers boarding freight cars every day. Soldiers and officers often said they felt sorry to leave for Japan ahead of me. They also told me to come back to Japan soon. Although they told me they were leaving for Japan via Korea, I did not have the heart to tell them that their train, unfortunately, was not on the right track for traveling to the southeast. They were headed somewhere else, in the opposite direction.[4]

When the soldiers boarded trains, they found that some freight cars had been modified to provide makeshift bunks and a coal stove in the center. Others had no such luxuries. It was cold—Siberian winters start in early October—and heat was insufficient even in the modified box cars. Guards usually occupied the center area and monopolized whatever warmth was available. Some cars had four compartments—upper and lower racks to the front and similar arrangements to the rear—with about 15 men in each section. Usually there were no latrine facilities, but POWs were ordered off the train at periodic rest stops to answer the call of nature—outside in the snow—and the stops were never frequent or long enough. To make matters worse, lice were beginning to multiply. After a few days of these trying conditions, with inadequate and impure food, an increasing number of prisoners developed diarrhea or became constipated. The trains just kept going on, and floors became covered with human excrement accompanied by foul odors. In some cases, guards permitted POWs to chop a slit in the bottom of the freight car for use as a latrine, and this created an aperture that sucked in furious blasts of cold, Siberian air. Nevertheless, the Japanese captives were learning to adapt—makeshift expedients were to play an important part in their lives for the next four years—and soon made covers of wood and bits of clothing to put over the holes when not in use.

Shortly after boarding prison trains, POWs were introduced to a new diet. It was far different from the rations they had grown accustomed to in the Japanese Army, and most certainly did not typify the best in Russian cuisine. It provided calories—but often not enough. This was the unchanging circumstance they found during their stay in the USSR. Input versus output: the calories that went in were to be converted to energy for heavy labor projects. Vitamins, balanced diet, and taste did not matter. Energy was all that counted. The first food encountered by POWs was *kasha*, a porridge made with cereal grass, served as a mushy paste sometimes containing pieces of fish or meat. Black bread and *suhar*, dried bread, were the primary source of calories. During the train trip, which for some prisoners was as long as a month, food portions usually were inadequate and the supply of drinking water was insufficient. As the trains plodded on and the days grew into weeks, the primitive conditions began to take their toll. Many of the reluctant travelers became sick, and a few began to take on traits of animals—fighting over food and water—as the struggle for survival began.

Khabarovsk is 400 miles north of Vladivostok and Chita is about 1,000 miles to the west of Khabarovsk. In some countries—Japan, for example—these would be considered long distances, but not in the Soviet Union where all three cities are in the same corner of the country—eastern Siberia—a region which would become thoroughly familiar to Japanese POWs. Khabarovsk and Chita were major rail centers, as well as district headquarters for POW camps. For many of the former soldiers, one or the other of these cities provided the first opportunity to escape the cramped conditions of the prison train for something other than a periodic rest stop. Some captives were herded into barracks and told to get ready for a bath. Morale improved, but disillusionment was in store for any internee who thought he was going to experience anything similar to the *ofuro* (hot bath) he knew at home. The first task was counting. Convoys of prisoners always were counted whenever they made a move, whether across the country or across the street. The men always had to be in rows five abreast—to facilitate counting—but guards often came up with the wrong number, and the whole process had to be repeated. This task frequently took an hour—even in freezing cold—and was an event that would take place several times a day, for every day of the prisoner's stay in the Soviet Union.

Then there was the wait for the *banya*, the bathhouse, in freezing cold conditions. Usually one group would find that other POWs were ahead of them, resulting in more waiting. Once inside the *banya*, bathers found only cold water available—sometimes with only one bucket of water allotted for all functions—and bathing quickly ceased to be thought of as a pleasure. However, there was no need to hurry through the process in order to find warmth; clothing and shoes were being toasted in a *zhar kamera*, an oven-like device for killing lice. Prisoners had to sit naked on cold concrete slabs waiting for their clothes, which were scorching hot when the process was completed. More POWs were waiting outside, and guards forced the bathers to dress immediately, in spite of burns from the painfully hot clothing and shoes, to make way for others.

For some prisoners, these junction cities were the end of the line. They were assigned to nearby labor camps or somewhere within the same district. For others, however, it was back on the train again for distant journeys, and, as always, they were counted indiscriminately—five rows abreast—without regard to which group they were supposed to be with. When the soldiers climbed back aboard, the strong odor of carbolic acid, a disinfectant, permeated their environment. About 65,000 Japanese prisoners went on to the Central Asian region of the USSR to such places as Karaganda, Alma-Ata, Balkhash, Krasnovodsk (on the Caspian Sea near Iran), and Samarkand (near Afghanistan).[5] Some Japanese spent a month traveling without a stop for a bath, often being shunted off on sidings for hours at a time. Trains followed circuitous routes, sometimes doubling the straight-line distance. Central Asia, more than 3,500 miles from Japan, was a different world from the *taiga* (vast coniferous forests) of Siberia. It consisted of great plains with few or no trees. On some of the trains, POWs got a glimpse of the landscape and were fascinated by the immense size of the Soviet Union. Some rail cars had small windows at the corners, near the ceiling, and soldiers took turns climbing up to the top bunk to view the scenery, which one POW later described as "a vast land with extensive landscapes that made even Mount Fuji look like a minor work of art."[6]

Japanese prisoners destined for work projects in areas adjacent to Manchuria marched to their *lagers* (work camps). They did not have the "luxury" of a scenic train ride across half of the Soviet Union, but had to hike, as much as 400 miles in 10 days for some. Many perished along the way; in one unit, 30 out of 60 soldiers died of epidemics and fever. A survivor later recalled: "We could not resist the Russian soldiers as we would be knocked down and kicked to death." A few POWs were able to escape during these long marches before leaving Manchuria, but the Red Army simply drafted Japanese civilians to replace them. They had a quota to fill. Soviet Army officials took some prisoners to Outer Mongolia where nearly 40 percent died in the early stages of captivity. There were a few reports of good treatment at the hands of Soviet soldiers. These accounts stressed the absence of racial discrimination on the part of the Red Army. One former Japanese soldier reported: "They treat the Japanese without discrimination like the communists that they are, and the Japanese were deeply moved by their warm and impartial attitude."[7]

All told, about 575,000 Japanese were transported to some 700 work camps throughout the Soviet Union in a matter of a few months. Eighty percent were members of Japan's armed forces, while the remaining 20 percent included civilians from varying walks of life, for example, government officials, intelligence agents, police officers, railway employees, and private citizens. Several hundred women—some of them Army nurses, others civilians—also became Soviet prisoners. Forced into the same rail cars with men, they had no privacy during the long journey. Although the rapid movement of such a large number of Japanese may appear to be a remarkable feat, the Soviets had expanded the prison system of their tsarist predecessors and developed a highly efficient network for transportation of both political and criminal prisoners. Millions of Soviet civilians were relocated by this rail system during World War II. Furthermore, Red Army soldiers transferred from Europe to the Soviet Far East in the spring and summer of 1945 traveled on some of the same rail equipment.

Soviet officials retained several thousand Japanese soldiers in Manchuria and North Korea, some for as long as six months, to dismantle industrial equipment for shipment to Siberia. The concept of war reparations long has been a generally accepted practice; a defeated nation pays compensation to the victor for damages suffered during the war. Reparations payments normally are in the form of equipment and other goods, but the Soviets followed an even older concept—going back to the days of the Pharaohs—taking defeated enemy soldiers for use on labor projects. In other words, Japanese soldiers were viewed as part of war reparations. Although Premier Stalin had endorsed the Potsdam Proclamation concerning Japan's surrender, Soviet officials were not in agreement with the provisions for early repatriation. Kremlin officialdom was angered at British and American attempts to expedite repatriation. At the Conference of Foreign Ministers, held in London in late September 1945, Foreign Minister Molotov told U.S. Secretary of State James Byrnes that the practice of the Western Allies of merely disarming and repatriating Japanese soldiers was not sufficient. Instead, the Soviet official urged, the Allies should put them to work as the Soviets were doing.[8]

Although most Japanese prisoners were unaware of what the future held for them, they were on their way to participate in the development and rehabilitation of the Soviet Union, where a serious shortage of labor and technical personnel existed as a result of the war with Germany. To be sure, Japanese POWs were not alone in this task. Several million Germans, military personnel and civilians, spent three to five years in various parts of the USSR at hard labor. Some Germans, held on war criminal charges, stayed there for even longer periods of time. According to German documentation, about 3.5 million Germans were in the Soviet Union in March 1947, though the Soviets insisted the correct number was only 890,000.[9] About 800,000 German civilians had been carried off from Germany to the Soviet Union after the war, and there were persons of many other nationalities, including several million Soviet citizens, engaged in forced labor throughout the USSR.[10]

While the Kwantung Army was being transported to *lagers*, similar events were unfolding in southern Sakhalin and the Kurile Islands. Japanese soldiers in southern Sakhalin initially were interned in their own barracks, but during the fall of 1945 many were sent to various locations in Siberia. Twenty thousand troops in the Kurile Islands departed in October. Red Army officers told them their destination was Tokyo, but they too soon found themselves in Siberia. The promise of a journey to Tokyo was only a myth.[11] After completion of labor projects in northern Korea, about half of the Japanese soldiers in that region were sent to the Soviet Union, while nearly 10,000 went to Manchuria to assist in the stripping of machinery for Siberia. When the Soviets left Manchuria in the spring of 1946, the majority of this group fell into Chinese Communist hands. An additional 10,000 soldiers, disguised as civilians, escaped from northern Korea on foot to the south.[12] Just as in Manchuria, mortality rates were high in Korea. From December 1945 to February 1946, the death rate at the Puryong POW camp in the extreme northern part of Korea averaged 30 per day. Many of these deaths were attributed to typhus and malnutrition. At the Komusan POW camp, 4,000 out of a total of 20,000 soldiers died of dysentery in two months.[13] By June 1946, the Soviets had taken most of the surviving POWs to the USSR.

Most POWs were sent to established work camps in the Soviet Union, but Soviet officials later sent some internees to designated sites in remote locations where there were no facilities. Upon arrival, with only a few rudimentary tools, they had to build their own *lager*, even to the extent of setting up barbed-wire fences to keep themselves in. Prisoners received harsh treatment at the hands of guards, especially when they first arrived at camp. Soviet soldiers routinely took watches, fountain pens, personal belongings, and reading material; even clothing and blankets. There were other reports that treatment was generally fair, and it appears that POW care varied significantly depending on location and individual circumstances. Initially, mail privileges were nonexistent, but after the first year, some POWs occasionally received mail and were permitted to send letters to Japan once or twice a year. Some troops reported that the food given them was about half of what Soviet citizens received, but other Japanese POWs claimed they were provided with more food than Soviet civilians. By any standard, however, conditions were especially severe in the winter of 1945–1946. There were serious shortages of daily necessities, and Soviet citizens also led an austere life. The first winter was the worst for most Japanese, and the death rate was appallingly high in some camps. One POW put it this way: "Half our number, those who were physically weak, died one after another from the shortage of food and the cold."[14]

LIFE IN THE WORK CAMPS

There were two categories of Japanese prisoners in the USSR. The first and largest group consisted of rank-and-file POWs who lived in work camps and were assigned to labor battalions. The second category was composed of soldiers and civilians who had been convicted by Soviet courts on war crimes charges or other criminal offenses. Most Japanese prisoners were sent to work camps in the Soviet Far East and to locations along the Trans-Siberian Railroad, but about 20 percent went to other regions of the USSR or Outer Mongolia. An analysis of the regions where Japanese prisoners were located shows:

Region	Number
Siberia	472,000
Outer Mongolia	13,000
Central Asia	65,000
European	25,000
Total	575,000[15]

Map 2 shows a representative selection of Japanese prisoner work sites.

Lagers were under the administration of the MVD (Ministry of Internal Affairs), identified prior to 1946 as the NKVD, and later to become associated with the KGB. Japanese in the USSR quickly learned the meaning of *vlast*, which could be translated as "ruling bureaucracy." At the pinnacle of power for the whole nation was the Kremlin in Moscow, but each element of government and every bureaucratic organization had its own *vlast*, and so it was with the POW camps. At the top was the camp commander, often an MVD captain or senior lieutenant. Other members of the *vlast* included the deputy commander, the labor officer (who controlled the use of POWs on work projects), and a political officer responsible for the Marxist-Leninist indoctrination of the internees. In addition, there were the garrison commander who supervised the guards, a quartermaster officer, and the hospital staff (in larger camps). POWs were under the direction of a district headquarters—there were more than 100 such headquarters throughout the USSR to administer the camps for German, Japanese, and other prisoners—and the districts were under a regional headquarters which, in turn, reported to the MVD in Moscow. Throughout all these layers of administration were special police investigators who seemed to roam about at will—their appearance always caused apprehension among POWs—to detect the identity of reactionaries and prepare criminal cases against them.

However, even Japanese prisoners had a part in running the camps. The senior Japanese leader was responsible to the MVD camp commander for the condition of the barracks and operation of routine functions of the camp, and to the labor

Map 2
MVD Labor Camps for Japanese Prisoners

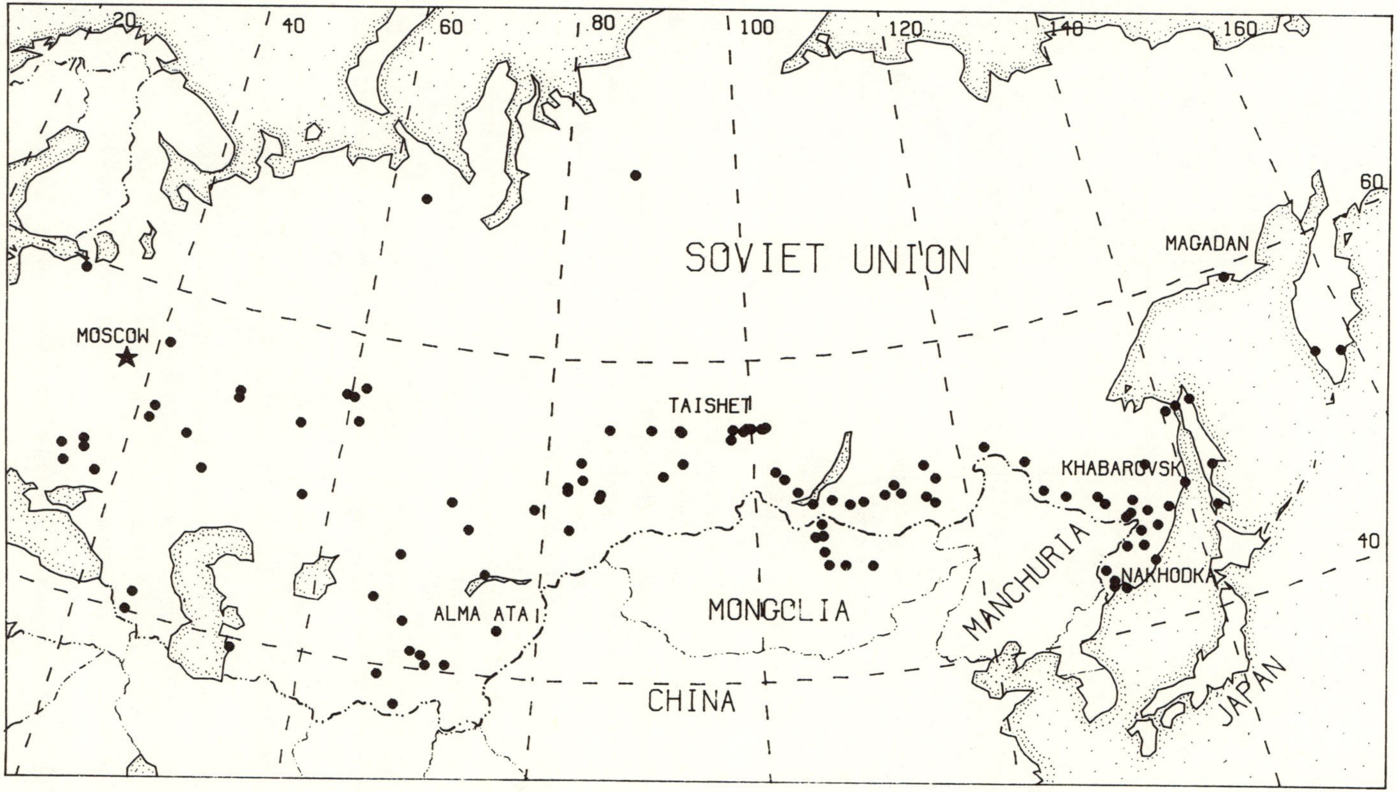

officer for assuring the maximum amount of work from the POWs. Labor camps composed of 600 to 1,000 men were subdivided into companies of from 100 to 200 prisoners. They were headed by a Japanese company commander, under the direction of the senior Japanese camp leader. Companies were organized into sections of about 30 men, again under Japanese leadership. These organizational units frequently were known by Russian names, such as *brigada*, and POWs often called their own leaders by Russian names, for example, *brigadir*, or sardonically, *kommendant*. Initially, leadership positions were filled by former Japanese officers or noncommissioned officers (NCOs), most often the same commanders that the men had known in presurrender days, but as time went by and the indoctrination process began to take effect, the positions began to be filled by activist POWs. Japanese leaders were in a precarious position; they were forced to carry out MVD staff directions, often at the expense of driving POWs beyond the limits of human endurance, but any shortcomings in the labor production of the *lager*, or in the political indoctrination programs, could lead to criminal charges against Japanese leaders. About the best the average prisoner could hope for was to have a *brigadir* who gave fervent lip service to the political slogans and indoctrination campaigns, but who, at the same time, would attempt to be fair in the treatment of POWs.

Some camps initially held prisoners of several nationalities. German POWs were predominant in the European districts of the Soviet Union, but some were in the Soviet Far East. Often there was no way for Soviet guards to communicate directly with their Japanese charges as neither spoke the other's language. German prisoners became a communication link since many Germans and some Japanese could speak English. The Soviets would first issue instructions to a Russian-speaking German. Directives were then translated into English and relayed to an English-speaking Japanese, who would interpret for his fellow countrymen. At most camps, however, White Russians, who were former residents of Manchuria, and fluent in Japanese and Russian, were interpreters.

POW camps varied considerably depending on location, but generally fit a pattern of several large barracks buildings, an administrative building, and utility structures, all surrounded by a fence. One camp in Siberia was about 1,300 feet by 800 feet with barbed wire strung along both sides of a wooden fence. Guard towers were located at the corners of the compound. Large tents provided housing with a capacity of 200 POWs in each tent. At Karaganda, in Central Asia, some barracks were of brick construction, and 140 prisoners lived in each building. POWs slept in bunks with straw mattresses on wooden boards, and there were several stoves to provide heat in winter. Other camps were overcrowded, with some barracks buildings housing as many as 600 occupants. In these buildings, which were about 200 feet in length and between 30 and 60 feet wide, bunks consisting of bare boards with no mattresses were stacked three and four layers high, occupying long rows throughout the main section of the structure. This arrangement provided each POW with about 10 or 12 square feet of space to call his own. It was impossible to provide adequate heat in the barracks during bitter cold periods, and men slept back to back in a single bunk to keep warm.[16]

In some camps where diets were totally lacking in salt, it was not unusual for a POW to develop a medical condition requiring an abnormal frequency of urination. Some men needed to urinate every 15 minutes, but with the exhaustion that followed a day of strenuous work, it simply was not possible to wake up during the night. If the man with this condition occupied a top bunk, his hapless comrades in lower bunks became victims of a nocturnal spray. Some rapid changes in bunk assignments came about in such cases. Latrines usually were outside of the barracks building and could accommodate only a small number of camp residents at any one time. The problem was that everyone wanted to go at the same time—in the morning before going off to work—resulting in long lines and lengthy waits. The outhouses were primitive affairs, with no privacy, but the former soldiers grew accustomed to it. What other choice did they have?

Daily routine varied from camp to camp, but one topic which was always of major importance to POWs was food. MVD regulations, often posted on kitchen walls, prescribed what would certainly have been an adequate diet. Major items on the daily food ration list were: 350 grams of black bread, 100 grams of polished rice, 350 grams of cereals, and 600 grams of vegetables, plus smaller amounts of fish or meat. In truth, however, POWs rarely saw any of these items in the prescribed quantities, and never saw the total ration list fulfilled. A survivor of four years in the Soviet Union later recalled:

> the *norm* was a farce that seemed to taunt us at mealtimes from the walls of the barracks and the kitchen. Japanese prisoners of war were never impressed so much by the difference between propaganda and fact, common in every phase of Soviet life, as in the case of food promised them but never provided in full.[17]

Another POW had a different story to relate about food in his *lager* at Morshansk, about 250 miles southeast of Moscow:

> The soup the Russians served us was beyond the knowledge of anything we had ever seen before. We could see a bit of grain and oil on top, but so much salt was in it we called it "the salty water." Sometimes we were late for dinner. . . . In this case, we had the last part of the soup bucket and we had more grain for ourselves because the grain sank to the bottom. We were really happy when this happened to us, and said to each other, "Tonight's soup has real calories!" The camp's best, the most tasteful food was the salty soup with peas. . . . We were given a very little amount of sugar. We licked and used all of it as soon as it was sent to us. The abundant salt which we had was quite useful for us to boil with wild flowers and plants whenever we found them outside.[18]

Prisoners in good physical condition who cooperated fully with Soviet officials usually received the best treatment. Work categories were assigned based on individual condition, and frequent physical examinations were conducted to determine category. The most routine examination required POWs to strip before a Soviet medical officer (often a female medical assistant) who would pinch the prisoners' buttocks, much in the same way a veterinarian would examine the rump of a farm animal to determine its condition. Those who were healthy and able-bodied, that is, with sufficient flesh on their buttocks, were categorized as Class 1 and worked at least eight hours daily (usually more), six days a week. Those in Class 2 (physically fit, but not strong) worked five hours daily, and Class 3 POWs (with chronic, but not serious disorders, for example, hernia or hemorrhoids) worked three hours a day. Prisoners who were chronically ill, convalescent, or debilitated (or physically handicapped) were placed in Classes 4 through 6. Hospital patients, the only prisoners exempt from work, were in Class 7. Class 1 POWs received the most food while those in Classes 2 and 3 were given proportionately smaller quantities of food. The logic behind this method was quite utilitarian; those who did the most work burned up the largest amount of calories and therefore needed the most food. Weak POWs who needed more nourishment to regain strength were able to obtain additional food only by doing extra work or through the charity of fellow prisoners.[19]

It was possible to escape from some POW camps, but very few attempts were made as there was almost no chance of survival after escape and nowhere to go. Guards were strict in convoying POWs from camp to work sites and back. Usually there were two guards in front, two in the rear, and two on either side, all armed, and there was the constant counting—in rows five abreast—as many as eight or nine times daily. Attempts to flee were especially dangerous in winter. One POW escaped, but later was found frozen to death in the snow. However, some POWs walked off from construction sites undetected and headed for the nearest train station. A stationmaster's suspicions were aroused on one occasion when an escapee asked for a ticket to Tokyo; the hapless POW was back in MVD hands in short order. In another case, a fleeing POW was detected on a train—he had no internal passport—and was apprehended. Treatment of captured escapees varied; some were executed, but most received criminal sentences from Soviet courts and were transferred to convict labor camps.

A few POWs, after return to Japan, spoke highly of their treatment in Soviet camps, but most were critical. Of 81 interviews reported in a SCAP study, 78 returnees made unfavorable comments concerning Soviet treatment. Much of the criticism was related to the first year of captivity. However, that year was a bad time for everyone in the Soviet Union, and Japanese prisoners had no way of knowing the general situation. Most POW complaints involved food, medical care, and working conditions. A 1948 repatriate revealed the grim conditions he experienced in Siberia:

> I led a wretched life for about 18 months in a detention camp at Kalanguy between Manchuli and Chita. Within about 50 kilometers from Kalanguy, there were three detention camps. Kalanguy was the 12th camp of the 24th Chita District. There

were about 1,500 Japanese soldiers and civilians there. While there, about 500 Japanese died of food shortage, overwork, or scarlet fever. Russian soldiers carried the dead bodies away in a truck and buried them in the snow. I fell ill of typhus, but still had to work eight hours per day. I fainted on 6 September 1946 and was carried into camp. I was sent to a hospital in a truck with 18 serious cases. Thirteen died in the truck.[20]

Japanese soldiers repatriated in 1948 were usually older or in worse physical condition than those who were to come home a year later. In addition, the 1948 repatriates had not experienced the intensive indoctrination campaign which befell those who were to follow them in 1949. Their comments concerning internment in the Soviet Union often were bitter. Asano Fukuichirō of Mie Prefecture spent three years at Krasnoyarsk in central Siberia, west of Lake Baikal. He was in a POW camp located about 1,200 miles northwest of the place where he had been captured, Hailar, in northwestern Manchuria. A letter from Asano dated 24 August 1948, just after his repatriation, reveals the harsh circumstances he faced in the USSR:

At first, there were about 1,500 Japanese POWs in our camp, but, after three years, the number had fallen to 643, as about 850 POWs died. Then, 150 of the survivors were returned home. We received 200 grams of black bread and a half-liter of potato soup at breakfast, a bowl of millet gruel at lunch, and 200 grams of black bread and a bowl of soup at supper. The above menu remained unchanged all through the years we were there. I think often of those prisoners still there, who are feeble and without nourishment, and are working in a mechanical way without any initiative, except the honest desire to return home.[21]

Food was one of the main topics of conversation among POWs, with much thought given to ways of obtaining more. By contrast, sexual desire was almost nonexistent—sheer exhaustion and poor physical condition relegated such matters to the lowest priority—and, with a few exceptions, POWs rarely had opportunity for intimate contact with women. Nevertheless, after the passage of many years, some former POWs were able to look back on their stay in the Soviet Union with a philosophical, sometimes humorous, frame of mind. Yabe Akira of Yokohama, in the September 1982 issue of *Bungei Shunjū*, a well-known Tokyo monthly, relates an anecdote involving a group of POWs walking back to camp on a dark and cold wintry night in temperatures well below zero degrees Fahrenheit:

On the way back to camp, we found potatoes here and there alongside the railway track.... Later we were cooking the potatoes in boiling water on the stove in the darkened barracks, and we talked about food in our home towns, as usual. When we took the lid off the pot when we thought they were done, we found something unusual. What we had picked up in the dark was not potatoes, but frozen horse manure. We felt stupid and miserable. But this unexpected result was so funny that it brought back the long forgotten laugh.[22]

Medical treatment was generally poor for most POWs, but not much different from what the average Soviet civilian received, especially in Siberia. Seriously ill prisoners frequently were forced to continue working until they collapsed. Some died due to a lack of medical personnel and proper medication. A 1950 repatriate said the only medicine available was aspirin for high-fever patients and creosote for stomach trouble, and that seriously ill patients usually died. In other cases, however, MVD officials sent prisoners who had labored strenuously to the point of exhaustion, and whose health was failing, to rehabilitation camps. They stayed there for several weeks and were provided with highly nutritious food, but after recovering their health, Soviet authorities sent them back to labor camps where more hard work and a poor, low-nutrition diet were waiting.

Over and again, Japanese and American authorities interviewing returning repatriates at Maizuru (the primary port in Japan for returnees from the USSR) heard favorable comments concerning the lack of racial discrimination on the part of the Soviets. Most Japanese were familiar with the racial prejudice faced by Japanese residents in the United States during the first half of the twentieth century. The whole matter of discriminatory treatment at the hands of British and Americans had been a sore point in Japan for years. A 1947 repatriate explained: "Except when working, Russian soldiers seem to regard Japanese as their equals or even superiors. Treated without racial discrimination, the Japanese sometimes forget they are POWs."[23]

In an odd twist of fate, Japanese POWs occasionally encountered "Oriental-looking" men in Siberia and, to their great surprise, found that some were Japanese. In fact, they were former Kwantung Army soldiers who had been captured in the Nomonhan Incident of 1939. Reported as "killed in action," they preferred to remain known in that category to their families and hometowns in Japan. Death was honorable; surrender was a disgrace. Most could not be persuaded that the emperor's rescript of August 1945 obviated the dishonor previously associated with surrender. One Nomonhan veteran, who had become a Soviet citizen after marrying a Russian woman, was known only by his adopted name, Ivanov. He refused to reveal his Japanese name or his home prefecture in Japan and said that

> he must have been considered killed in action and there must be a grave in his hometown. So why trouble his family needlessly now? It would be best if he endured matters alone. After all, his life in the Soviet Union was quite comfortable, and the Russians did not evince racial prejudice.[24]

As in any grouping of human beings, there were opportunists among Japanese POWs who were clever in taking advantage of situations where they could improve their own lot at the expense of others. Soon after arrival in the USSR, some POWs ingratiated themselves with camp authorities, quickly learned Russian, and obtained a large degree of power and control over other Japanese prisoners. MVD officials soon accorded special privileges to these sympathizers, and, as time went by, they were often free to come and go as they pleased. Some were able to enjoy the occasional companionship of Russian women. These opportunists soon earned the hatred of their fellow countrymen, but there was little that could be done about it at the time. POWs who had curried favor with Soviet officials often were influential in determining work assignments and improvements in living arrangements. They also advised authorities of reactionary POWs, a designation that could result in a criminal sentence, and recommended priorities for repatriation. Thus, the average POW stood up to the conspirator at his own peril. Revenge was to come later, on the eventual return voyage to Japan.

Prison camp life improved as the USSR began to recover economically and socially from the devastation suffered during World War II. Between October 1946 and March 1947, conditions gradually became better as the Soviets began to put more emphasis on the indoctrination program. Food improved and, by the end of 1947, ration quantities no longer were dependent upon the amount of work done. An intensive program was underway by 1948 to imbue the POWs with Marxist-Leninist principles, and the Soviets were anxious to impress POWs with the advantages of living in a Communist society. Life in the average *lager* still was very much below first-class living conditions, but internees could not help but notice improvement over the miserable, subhuman existence they had endured in the first year.

CONSTRUCTION AND WORK PROJECTS

Japanese POWs and civilian internees were put to work by the Soviets in almost every type of endeavor imaginable during their stay in the USSR in furtherance of the postwar Five-Year Plan for national reconstruction (1946–1950), continuing the Soviet goal of transforming the nation into an industrial society. Stalin, long obsessed with making the USSR into a great power, had admonished Soviet citizens in a 1931 speech: "We are fifty or a hundred years behind the advanced countries. We must make good this distance in ten years or they crush us."[25]

Millions of Soviet citizens were conscripted as laborers in the 1930s to fulfill industrial goals set by Stalin. Millions more were arrested on the flimsiest of pretexts and sentenced to five or ten years in corrective labor camps. The Soviet Union did indeed make significant advances in the decade prior to World War II, but at an agonizing cost of physical and mental suffering of its citizens. After the war, there was much to be done in recovering from the extensive damage and depletion of resources suffered as a result of the German attack. There were several million German and Japanese prisoners available, along with Soviet citizens and people from other countries, for the task at hand. The Supreme Soviet of the USSR established a Five-Year Plan for the Re-creation and Development of the National Economy of the USSR for 1946–1950, which called for large increases in the production of iron and steel, coal, machine-building, and food, and for extensive expansion and improvement in transportation and communication facilities.[26]

Japanese prisoners made significant contributions to fulfillment of the Soviet postwar Five-Year Plan and were used primarily in labor projects requiring heavy exertion, such as lumbering, loading and unloading of rail cars, mining of coal and iron ore, repairing roads and railroads, construction of new rail lines, and building factories. Japanese worked throughout the USSR, but the largest number were employed in the Soviet Far East, where conditions were severe and work the most demanding. Soviet officials also used Japanese internees in the construction of military fortifications, defensive positions, airfields, and naval installations. Not everyone performed hard labor, however. Some POWs with technical ability were assigned to projects where their skills could be used. MVD officers assigned weak and debilitated POWs to clerical or light labor jobs such as cleaning streets or working in hospitals. Every POW was required to perform some type of work unless seriously ill. The Soviets looked upon the resources provided for care of POWs, meager though they were, as a form of investment, and insisted on a profitable return. There was no such thing as languishing in a cell with nothing to do (except for those facing criminal charges, and then only until a confession was obtained).

Soviet officials measured the progress of work projects throughout the USSR by standards expressed in units of production for both individual workers and operating entities. These standards, known as *norms*, applied to POW labor and theoretically set a goal for doing a reasonable amount of work in a prescribed period of time. However, the *norms* were set so high that most POWs had to work longer than the scheduled eight-hour day, and even then few POWs had sufficient strength and stamina to fulfill the goals. Meeting the *norm* was extremely important, especially during the first two years when POWs received food based on fulfillment of quotas. Weak prisoners, unable to satisfy production goals, received less than the usual ration of food. This lack of adequate nourishment led to even more physical debilitation, thereby creating a vicious circle. After the first year, the MVD began paying small amounts to some POWs for their work, but pay was reduced when the *norm* was not met. Prisoners were not paid at all when output fell below 60 percent of the *norm*.

After several months of working at the same job, POWs became more skillful and could complete their tasks in less time. Unfortunately, improved productivity only brought forth calls for higher output. Ishii Takashi, a POW at a lumber camp in Siberia until 1948, explained:

> POWs fixed the tools so that they could use them more easily. They made simple tools that they needed for their convenience. They rearranged the machines and materials in the shops and plants in order to work better and more efficiently....
> As soon as all this was done, and it became easier for the Japanese prisoners to

produce the standard output, the Russians raised the *norm*.... The Russians were always setting the *norm* ahead before the Japanese got trained to do the work.[27]

So important, and so complicated, was the *norm* system that the Soviets created a specialized occupation solely for the purpose of monitoring work measurement standards. The *normarofshik*, as he was known, was consulted by construction supervisors, foremen, workers, and labor officers to resolve the many disputes that arose over what type of work was to be counted toward fulfilling the *norm* and who was to receive credit for it. The whole system evolved into a bureaucratic perplexity which was to overshadow the POWs' existence throughout their stay in the Soviet Union. As an example, there were more than 40 volumes of *norms* applicable to construction work alone, and each of these contained about 60 or 70 pages. These instructions, published by the Ministry of Construction in 1947, covered every conceivable aspect of construction work, such as: 1) architectual planning, 2) surveying, 3) site preparation, 4) excavation, 5) transportation, 6) materials handling, 7) laying of foundations, 8) concrete work, 9) bricklaying, 10) carpentry, 11) plastering, 12) plumbing, 13) welding, and 14) electrical work, to name a representative sampling.[28]

Pay rates were related to the complexity of tasks and the amount of work accomplished. The *norm* instructions dictated that workers be divided into seven classes (in addition to the seven classifications related to physical condition), extending from Class I (Unskilled) through progressively higher levels of skill to Class VII (Master Craftsman). As an example of how this system worked, the *norm* for a Class II worker (minimal skill, no training) transporting materials, in increments of less than 25 kilograms, using a *nosilki* (wooden litter) with another worker, for a distance of 10 meters, dictated that 1 metric ton be moved in 36 minutes. For this work, he would earn 96 kopecks (100 kopecks = 1 ruble). To fulfill this goal, it would be necessary for a POW to move 13,330 kilograms (29,326 pounds) of materials (such as bricks) over a 10 meter distance in an 8-hour period, for which he would earn 13 rubles.

These procedures, though cumbersome and unwieldy, would appear to provide a yardstick by which work progress could be determined and pay for the POW could be calculated—except for two major problems. First, it was physically impossible for most POWs to do the work established by the *norm*. (Twenty-nine thousand pounds in eight hours works out to more than 14 tons, or assuming an average weight of 4 pounds per brick, it would amount to more than 7,000 bricks.) A few POWs—those in the very best physical condition with a strong physique—could meet the *norm*, but only by working like a machine, without any wasted motion, for every second of an eight-hour period, and without one moment's rest. Even a gulp of water would have to be taken on the run. Secondly, the workers' "earnings" were earned not for their own account but for the POW camp. Each one of the MVD *lagers* was on a complex cost accounting system. The cost of operating the camp had to be paid for by the labor of its residents. *Lager* authorities said it cost an average of 456 rubles a month, per prisoner, for operation and maintenance of the camp and for upkeep of each internee. When POWs worked on a construction project, for example, the Ministry of Construction would pay the Ministry of Internal Affairs (MVD) for labor per the *norm* standard. Similar arrangements were in effect for work performed under the auspices of other ministries such as Transportation, Agriculture, and Armed Forces. POWs received pay only for "earnings" in excess of 456 rubles—minus what some camp labor officers claimed was a 30 percent "income tax"—and even then, no more than a maximum of 150 rubles per month would actually be paid out in cash.[29] Some MVD officers promised that amounts earned over the maximum were being held in a bank and that a lump-sum payment would be made just prior to repatriation, but POWs who expected to receive these deferred payments were to be disappointed. The promised savings were never paid. As a matter of fact, POWs were not permitted to keep any Soviet currency when they eventually left the USSR, not even as a souvenir.

Even for the few POWs who received some payment for their work, opportunities to buy commodities were infrequent. A ruble in 1947 officially was worth 19 cents in American money, but this was an arbitrary rate established by the Soviet Government. The ruble's actual value was about 3 cents. Furthermore, POWs had to pay exorbitant prices for getting a guard or Soviet worker to purchase items for them on the outside. A one-kilogram loaf of black bread, priced at 1 ruble at government retail stores, cost POWs between 40 and 100 rubles.[30]

The *norm* system and its "earnings" arrangements led to an intricate bookkeeping operation which in itself employed many people. First of all, the project manager had a *norm* to achieve for his operating entity, for example, coal mine, construction project, factory, or farm. Any shortcoming would cast him in a bad light with the next higher level of bureaucracy. Subordinate to the manager, each foreman had a *norm* to fulfill for his particular area of responsibility. Thus, managers at these levels of supervision had to look in two directions—upward and downward—first to satisfy those over them and, secondly, to ensure that the collective performance of laborers under their direction was adequate to fulfill the *norm* of the work unit. For the POW-laborers, it was vital to their well-being that they be properly credited for their work. To keep track of their daily performance, foremen maintained work sheets (in Russian, *nariad-zadanii*) which ultimately decided not only whether the POW would receive any pay, but also (during the first two years) how much food he would receive.[31]

Disputes often broke out among POWs over credit for work performed. On large construction projects there were workers of varying nationalities. In addition to Japanese, German, and other POWs, there were several categories of Soviet workers: political prisoners, criminal prisoners, labor conscripts, exiles who had completed prison sentences but had not received internal passports, military laborers, and "free workers," a term the MVD applied to ordinary citizens who worked for wages. Japanese POW-leaders faced a constant struggle to assure the proper maintenance of records to reflect work performed. In the first months,

Soviet foremen often put Japanese laborers to work at tasks for their own personal profit, such as chopping wood into kindling which the foreman later could sell to supplement his own meager wages. Also, it was not unusual for a construction supervisor to credit a work unit of his own countrymen for labor actually performed by Japanese POWs. The POWs quickly learned to work only on projects assigned to their unit and to diligently review each day's *nariad-zadanii* to see that proper credit was received.

The next lesson POWs learned was that the *norm* regulations were rigidly followed. Soviet officials gave POWs credit only for work done in accordance with the *smeta*, cost estimates based on construction plans, or "blueprints." Specifications for site preparation, for example, might require that a trench, 30 centimeters in width, be dug, but if the supervisor wanted the trench to be 40 centimeters wide, work credit could not be applied to the extra 10 centimeters of earth removed. In this example, one-fourth of the POW labor would go unacknowledged. As might be expected, this situation led to the creation of a specialty among Japanese POWs, a *norm* interpreter. The specialist frequently spent many hours in the evening pouring over *norm* specifications so as to be prepared to defend his work unit's position against unwarranted demands of construction supervisors, foremen, and labor officers.

The Japanese penchant for hard work proved to be a boon for those who were physically fit and was also of great benefit to Soviet officials in meeting production goals. Japanese POWs earned a reputation for being hard workers. An account of the operation of a brick factory at Tambov, about 300 miles southeast of Moscow, illustrates how some Japanese benefited from their industrious efforts. There were 110 Japanese POW-workers at Brick Factory No. 1 along with 60 Soviet workers, mostly women. The daily factory *norm* was 18,000 bricks, but production in June 1947 amounted to only 14,000 bricks per day. The factory manager demanded that the *norm* be met and warned that freedom, such as it was, might be restricted otherwise. Daily working records for each individual were reported to the prison camp head, and each POW's compensation and food allotment was increased if he met his *norm*. Production soon increased to 18,000 bricks daily, and Japanese workers received extra food and tobacco rations as a bonus. They were also allowed to go to town after work, see movies, and drink beer. The Japanese ended up working harder than anyone else, and eventually Soviet workers were taking orders from Japanese. The *norm* applied equally to both Japanese and Soviet workers, and no distinction was made concerning age or sex.[32]

Most work situations faced by Japanese POWs, however, were not as humane as the Tambov brick factory. There were frequent accidents in coal mines, resulting in permanent injury or death. POWs unloading coal and iron at a wagon factory in the Lake Baikal region were forced to labor in temperatures of 50 to 60 degrees below zero Fahrenheit. As one survivor later recalled: "Threatened by the bayonets of Soviet soldiers and beaten by them, we went on working half unconsciously."[33] Even recovering hospital patients had to work. POWs in the convalescent ward at the 888th Hospital in the Amur District unloaded lumber and coal at the train station or worked in a soap factory. Some, assigned to burial sections, frequently dug graves for deceased Japanese prisoners.

MVD officials often forced POWs to work to the point of exhaustion, especially in the hazardous coal and ore mines. At Karaganda in Kazakhstan, prisoners of many nationalities labored at coal mines in shifts 24 hours a day. The same was true at Vorkuta, north of the Arctic Circle, which had about 30 pits. Only a few Japanese were at Vorkuta, but large numbers of Soviet and German prisoners worked there. The total prison population at Vorkuta was estimated at 235,000.[34] Japanese POWs worked the mines at Magadan, in the far north of eastern Siberia near the Sea of Okhotsk. Thousands of Japanese POWs labored at coal mines in eastern Siberia; implements were crude and machinery was almost nonexistent. It was all pick and shovel work. Great numbers of other Japanese prisoners worked at lumbering camps—all with axes and hand saws—especially along the Sikhote Alin Mountain Range paralleling the Sea of Japan, in the Soviet Maritime Province. The German, Joseph Scholmer, writing in *Vorkuta* of his lengthy imprisonment in the USSR, estimated that half of the entire coal production of the Soviet Union and 80 percent of the wood supply in the late 1940s and early 1950s were produced by forced labor.

Another major endeavor involving Japanese POW labor was the construction of new railroad lines. Former Kwantung Army soldiers worked in the bitter cold of frozen central Siberia between Taishet and Bratsk, to the west of Lake Baikal. Mid-winter temperatures often dropped to 40 or 50 degrees below zero Fahrenheit, and POWs quickly learned to put snow in their mouths (and to keep their mouths closed) whenever they entered a heated building. The rapid change in temperature could cause tooth enamel to crack without these precautions. In July, temperatures rose to 100 degrees Fahrenheit; and swarms of huge mosquitoes eagerly extracted blood from the hapless POWs. Several thousand Japanese labored on construction of the first stretch of tracks for what was to become, decades later, the new Baikal-Amur-Main Line, the BAM. POWs cleared land through virgin forests and laid about 200 miles of track from Taishet eastward from 1946 to 1949. The BAM, finally completed in 1984, provides a main east-west rail route running between 200 and 300 miles north of the Trans-Siberian Railway, with an eastern terminus at Komsomolsk on the Amur River, about 200 miles north of Khabarovsk. Completion of the BAM in September 1984 was widely publicized in the Soviet Union, but no mention was made of the forced labor used on the project.[35]

These illustrations show the variety of experiences encountered by POWs working in the Soviet Union. In most cases, Japanese traveled daily from the *lager* to the work site, usually on foot, and they became a familiar sight to local citizens who often spoke to them in Russian. Children frequently shouted: "Hallo, Japonsky. Kudavy idëte?" (Hello, Japanese. Where are you going?) to which some Japanese would reply, "Na rabotu" (to work). When the people in one village heard that the POWs were being repatriated, they called out to them:

"Japonsky, damoi, da?" (You Japanese are going home, aren't you?). The POWs responded, "Da, Da! Damoi, harasho!" (Yes, yes! Going home. Wonderful!) to which the villagers echoed, "Harasho!" and "Japonsky, Dasbedania!" (Goodbye, Japanese!).[36]

Just as the Japanese were highly regarded in one village, officials of the Soviet Union must have had a great appreciation for their labor. A conservative calculation reveals that POWs worked nearly five billion manhours in the rebuilding and enhancement of industry in the USSR. Even at the low wages prevailing in Japan in the late 1940s, Japanese prisoners performed work valued at a minimum of 250 billion yen, or nearly 700 million U.S. dollars at the 1949 exchange rate. Expressed in 1987 values, this labor would be worth approximately 8 trillion yen (64 billion U.S. dollars).[37]

CRIMINAL SENTENCES

Life for the average Japanese POW in the Soviet Union was harsh, but there was a second category of soldiers and civilians, those under criminal sentence, who suffered even more hardships. MVD officials held generals, high-ranking staff officers, and some civilians responsible for "aggression against the Soviet Union." Soviet military courts convicted prisoners in this group on the grounds that the leadership positions they had held were *prima facie* evidence of their intent to launch and wage a war of aggression against the USSR. In addition, MVD officers charged an even larger number of prisoners with "anti-Soviet behavior" for impeding the Marxist-Leninist indoctrination program and for trivial misdemeanors, such as stealing small quantities of food. Some junior officers and NCOs were classified as war criminals for having performed duties expected of any leader in combat. In one case, a Soviet court convicted a former lieutenant on the charge that he was "responsible for anti-Soviet movements of a platoon." The MVD charged others for refusal to cooperate with *lager* authorities, an accusation often based on information from POW-informers.

Kremlin leaders went to extensive lengths to portray Japan as an aggressor in Northeast Asia. In an unusual move, MVD officers flew three Kwantung Army officers to Tokyo in September 1946 in a Catalina amphibian airplane (lend-lease equipment from the United States) to testify as witnesses in the war crimes trials of the International Military Tribunal for the Far East (IMTFE). Moscow had a twofold objective: first, to prove "anti-Soviet aggression" on the part of Japan; and, secondly, to substantiate Soviet charges that Emperor Hirohito was personally responsible for war-making policy. Three days after their arrival in Tokyo, one of the witnesses, Lieutenant General Kusaba Tatsumi, committed suicide by taking poison, most likely cyanide. Soviet officials intensified their surveillance of the other two officers, Major General Matsumura Tomokatsu and Lieutenant Colonel Seijima Ryuzō, who were compelled to testify at the Tokyo IMTFE hearings, held at the site of the former Imperial Japanese Army headquarters in Ichigaya, not far from the Imperial Palace. These two officers gave only grudging assistance to their Soviet captors, but the IMTFE upheld charges of Japanese aggression against the Soviet Union. The attempt to show that the emperor had taken an active part in directing the war was not successful. Soviet officials returned the two former Kwantung Army officers to Siberia—again by the Catalina amphibian—on 11 November 1946.[38] A Soviet military court at Khabarovsk later tried Matsumura and Seijima on charges of plotting aggression against the USSR. Both officers received lengthy prison terms.[39]

The Soviets conducted trials at Khabarovsk in December 1949 against General Yamada Otozō, the former Kwantung Army Commander-in-Chief, and 11 of his subordinates, not only on charges of planning war against the USSR, but also for "manufacturing and employing bacteriological weapons." The trial resulted in conviction of all defendants with sentences ranging from 2 to 25 years, but Moscow later reduced most periods of imprisonment. Biological warfare charges stemmed from experiments conducted in Manchuria under the auspices of the Kwantung Army. The Soviets claimed that three experimentation centers, Army Units 100, 731, and 1644, "devised methods for mass breeding of fleas, for their subsequent infection with plague and utilization for war purposes."[40] Allegations of germ warfare preparations were substantiated by revelations made in later years, but there is no evidence that the Kwantung Army actively employed biological agents against the Red Army. Akiyama Hiroshi, a former army technician at Army Unit 731, explained in a 1955 *Bungei Shunjū* article that his facility was disguised as a large medical corps unit and that attempts were made to produce biological agents which could cause cholera, diptheria, typhus, and plague. Army Unit 731, located about 25 miles south of Harbin, was cloaked in secrecy and allegedly used Chinese, Korean, and Russian prisoners as "human guinea pigs." Akiyama's duties involved extraction of germs from wild rats and the cultivation of infected bacteria. Extensive testing continued in the early days of August 1945, and, according to Akiyama, between 1,500 and 2,000 victims died on 9 August 1945 alone. The Soviets, at the Khabarovsk trial, charged that 3,000 human beings were killed in germ experiments.[41]

A 1976 television documentary, produced by Yoshinaga Haruko and aired by Tokyo Broadcasting System, added further credibility to the Soviet charges of germ warfare preparation. Dr. Akimoto Sueo, also a former staff member of Army Unit 731, substantiated Akiyama's earlier allegations.[42] In addition, several books have been published in Japan, including Morimura Seiichi's 1982 best-seller, *Akuma no Hōshoku* (Gluttony of the Devil), which provide extensive details on the development of bacteriological agents by Japanese researchers in Manchuria and elsewhere.[43] John W. Powell's comprehensive analysis of this hidden chapter in Japan's history cites evidence that Army Unit 731 also used American POWs in germ warfare experimentation.[44] When the Soviet Army attacked on 9 August 1945, medical technicians poisoned the remaining "human guinea pigs" at Army Unit 731, leading to their deaths before sunset. Staff members burned the bodies, ground up the bones, destroyed all evidence, and began the demolition of facilities. Germ warfare center personnel were given top priority in returning to Japan. Akiyama returned by way of Pusan and arrived in Japan on 23 August 1945, an amazing feat when compared to the ordeals experienced by other Japanese in Manchuria. All of the commentaries on this topic confirm that medical and technical personnel of Army Unit 731 were hastily evacuated to Japan along with their research data. These sources also charge that the former biological warfare experimenters escaped prosecution as war criminals in exchange for handing over detailed information on their tests to U.S. Army officials. However, Army Unit 731 personnel in support functions, such as maintenance staff and office assistants, remained in Manchuria, and the Soviets later prosecuted them as war criminals notwithstanding their rather tenuous connection to the actual conduct of experiments.

Soviet charges against their Japanese captives often were arbitrary and capricious; in some cases, a lack of enthusiasm for the Marxist-Leninist indoctrination program could lead to hastily concocted charges without any substantive basis. Japanese prisoners naturally were reluctant to admit their "crimes" in such cases, but MVD authorities extorted confessions by means of intimidation, starvation, beatings, and other forms of torture. Trials often were "mockeries of justice," and Soviet military court officials viewed the defense counsel function for Japanese prisoners as merely a *pro forma* requirement which could be performed in a perfunctory manner. Trials were conducted in Russian, often with no translation into Japanese. There were "frequent heavy and arbitrary sentences for unsubstantiated or trifling misdeeds," according to a 1950 repatriate. Prisoners serving criminal sentences lived under worse conditions than those of the usual POW camp, often sharing accommodations with Soviet criminals, or *blatnye* (thieves), who were "pretty bad characters." MVD guards treated released prisoners as discharged convicts—in the same manner as they did for Soviet citizens who had completed criminal sentences—and provided no transportation beyond the prison camp gates.

Thousands of Japanese civilians in Manchuria and southern Sakhalin were arrested by Red Army and NKVD (later MVD) authorities in late 1945 in a dragnet cast to ensnare government officials, intelligence agents, policemen, and anyone else who aroused the slightest suspicion of enmity toward the Soviet Union. As the months after the surrender slowly passed, residents of Manchurian cities began to note the disappearance of Japanese acquaintances, one by one. Nothing ever was said or announced, and hardly anyone ever saw the missing residents leave. By late November, however, it had become obvious that sinister developments were taking place. The explanation for the mysterious disappearances, often not revealed until years later when the internees finally returned to Japan, was that NKVD officials operated in a furtive manner, usually making their arrests in the dead of night. In fact, everything was done at night—arrest, questioning, transfer between prisons, and boarding of trains for Siberia—and by daylight hours nothing was overtly discernable. The most trivial pretext could serve as a basis for arrest—listening to a Soviet radio station, possession of maps showing Soviet territory, official duties involving research on Soviet economic matters, a careless anti-Soviet remark, membership in the Concordia Association (an organization aimed at assimilating various ethnic groups in presurrender Manchukuo)—and lengthy criminal sentences to prison and corrective labor camps.

Ordinary POWs in the USSR constantly faced the threat of arrest on criminal charges for some infraction of the rules or for "anti-Soviet" behavior. Again, the arrests usually were made at night. A POW, gently awakened by someone tapping him on the shoulder, would depart in stealth accompanied by guards to be taken to a local MVD headquarters for interrogation. When the remaining POWs awoke in the morning, they were completely clueless as to their comrade's departure. Intimidation and uncertainty were key weapons in the initial stages of arrest. Suspects frequently were abused physically and put in a solitary confinement cell, an "isolator," or they were put with other prisoners in cells barely large enough to contain inmates in a sitting position, with little opportunity to stretch out for sleep. Food was meager, and human beings frequently descended to the level of animals in fighting over scraps of bread. Sanitary facilities were filthy. The toilet consisted of a foul-smelling *parasha*—nothing more than an infrequently emptied barrel—and the newest cell occupant would always find himself seated next to this primitive form of humiliation. Prisoners were not allowed to talk, except when questioned by interrogators. Guards carefully controlled the movement of suspects from cell to interrogation room so that messages could not be exchanged with other prisoners. This process went on for days, weeks, or even months; for whatever period of time it took to extort a confession from a hapless "enemy of the people." Worse yet, prisoners were forced—under duress—to implicate fellow Japanese as reactionaries.[45]

Why were Soviet authorities so determined to obtain confessions? Why not use other evidence—even if it was contrived—to convict suspects? Stalin's "enemy of the people" concept, originated in the purges of the 1930s, stressed "confession," and it was on the basis of such "admissions of guilt" that Stalin ridded himself of what he perceived to be ideological enemies. The "show trials" of 1937 served not only to eliminate "enemies of the people" but also to warn others and to justify the need for discipline and vigilance. These purges widened in scope in the latter part of the decade and penetrated all levels of Soviet society. An estimated eight million people, 5 percent of the population, were arrested. Furthermore, conviction always was based on the confession. About 800,000 purgees were executed, and the remainder were sentenced to labor camps in the Soviet penal system, which was termed the *Gulag* (Chief Administration of Corrective Labor Camps). The concept of forced confession continued until Stalin's death in March 1953. The words of a later Secretary-General of the Communist Party of the Soviet Union (CPSU), Nikita Khrushchev, sum up the methods used against the millions of unfortunate souls (including Japanese prisoners) caught up in the NKVD and MVD network:

Stalin originated the concept "enemy of the people." This term automatically rendered it unnecessary that the ideological errors of a man or men engaged in controversy be proven; this term made possible the usage of the most cruel repression.... The only proof of guilt used, against all norms of current legal science, was the "confession" of the accused himself; and, as subsequent probing proved, "confessions" were acquired through physical pressures against the accused.[46]

Most Imperial Japanese Army soldiers were accustomed to discipline more severe than that experienced by British and American soldiers. Japanese troops were known for their atrocities against enemy personnel, but they did not have the experience or long history of harsh treatment of prisoners which was so well practiced in Stalin's *Gulag*. Unfortunate Soviet citizens who found themselves in a corrective labor camp quickly learned that cooperation with authorities, though not a guarantee of survival, was essential to even a chance of survival, as exemplified by this account of conditions:

> The men were compelled to work by force. Those who resisted were put in jail (in unheated cells, without clothes, and with a food ration of 300 grams of bread and a bowl of soup once a day). Flat refusal to work entailed a death sentence. Such sentences were often read to us. But before recording a refusal, the camp authorities would force the prisoners to work by beating, kicking, dragging them by their feet through mud and snow, setting dogs on them, hitting them with rifle butts, and by threatening them with revolvers and bayonets.[47]

In light of the intense nationalistic indoctrination earlier received by Japanese Army officers and soldiers, it is understandable that some POWs would attempt to stand up to their Soviet captors by refusing to cooperate. Those who did so paid a severe penalty. These examples from a Japanese Foreign Ministry report show the treatment given recalcitrant POWs:

1. Sergeant Major Nagao Yoichi was confined in the guard room of the Branch Camp for several months. He was struck and kicked by officers of the Soviet Army and lost consciousness many times. Rations were suspended four times, for 21 days in total. Blankets and overcoat were taken away at midnight in hard winter.
2. At the Third Branch Camp, Angren, about October 1948, Second Lieutenant Nishihara Yasuhiro became almost unable to walk because of ill treatment, including non-supply of bedding, interruption of sleep, and suspension of rations (for three days at a stretch). Water was not supplied either.
3. At the 20th Branch Camp, Karaganda, during October and November 1949, about 75 persons were forced to sign false records, and undergo a 25-year sentence, by a Japanese group who had received instructions from Senior Lieutenant Anoshkin of the Soviet Army.
4. POWs were compelled to sign a record prepared unilaterally and arbitrarily by Soviet authorities when mental condition was abnormal as a result of a series of examinations over a long period, suspension of rations, beatings, intimidations, and so on.[48]

The Foreign Ministry report also included an analysis of 305 POWs repatriated in April 1950. Sixty-two of the returnees had drawn 25-year sentences for violations such as: "served with the Special Intelligence Division," "intercepting radiograms to Soviet Russia," "served with Special Services Agency," and "stealing of 'social property' of Soviet Russia." Actual terms served ranged from two months to two and a half years. Some Japanese held under lengthy criminal sentences were involved in rebellions and strikes at the Kengir camps in Karaganda where Soviet troops shot and killed about 700 prisoners on 25 June 1954. The uprising involved 150,000 prisoners (Japanese made up only a small number), but repatriates returning to Japan in April 1955 said that prison life improved markedly after that incident. Even so, a Japanese Red Cross report stated that 760 Japanese prisoners at a camp in Khabarovsk defied guards for four months in early 1956 before being subdued by 2,000 Soviet troops.[49]

More than 1,000 Japanese, many of them generals and staff officers of the Kwantung Army, returned to Japan on 26 December 1956. Some civilian officials also were in this group. Concurrently, the Soviet government said there were no more Japanese prisoners from World War II in the USSR, but the government of Japan contended that more than 10,000 POWs and civilians were missing.[50]

Life in Stalin's detention camps was indeed an agonizing ordeal for most Japanese POWs. Substandard sanitary facilities, inadequate nourishment, hard labor in extreme temperatures, the mystery and secrecy shrouding every Soviet move, crowded barracks, and poor medical treatment all contributed to a miserable existence for *lager* residents. However, one facet of Japan's "Siberian experience" was to overshadow all other phases of detention: the Marxist-Leninist indoctrination program. It was to effect a radical transformation among some POWs and create a treacherous atmosphere that turned Japanese against Japanese.

4

Marxist-Leninist Indoctrination

The initial experiences of Japanese prisoners in the Soviet Union could hardly be considered as evidence that any type of indoctrination program was about to begin. Conversely, an account of the degrading and grim conditions faced by Japanese during their first months of captivity would lead to a conclusion that the Soviets wanted only to punish the vanquished foe of the East and install hatred for the land of Marx and Lenin. As time passed, however, a scheme for one of the most thorough indoctrination programs in history began to unfold. The first step, as indeed in any intensive indoctrination effort, was the complete degradation and dehumanizing of formerly proud soldiers so that they would be receptive to any new idea so long as it led to an improvement in living conditions and held out hope for a return to the homeland. It was this first stage that POWs experienced as they traveled to labor camps throughout the USSR and struggled to maintain life itself. POW leaders during this phase, for the most part, were the same officers soldiers had known in presurrender days. Through an evolutionary process, however, rank-and-file POWs began to understand that living and working conditions would improve only when internal leadership became more "activist" oriented, thus paving the way for elimination of conservative, or "reactionary," influence.

Four well-defined stages marked the course of Marxist-Leninist indoctrination from 1945 to 1949. In addition to the degradation and dehumanizing of POWs, the Soviets inaugurated a program during the first phase to eliminate devotion to the emperor and banish class distinctions between officers and enlisted soldiers. In addition, Soviet political officers made the first attempts to diminish hatred of the Soviet Union. Progress was slow during the first year because of the poor living and working conditions, but POW camp life began to improve by January 1947, and a second phase of indoctrination began. POWs received instruction in Communist theory for the next several months, with the intent of giving the internees new ideas to replace old ones. The Soviets initiated a third phase in the late spring of 1947 by changing the emphasis of instruction to discredit Allied occupation policies in Japan. The objective was to show that the United States was practicing imperialist principles by converting Japan into an American colony. POWs learned that the only way to achieve a truly democratic reconstruction of Japan was through a close alliance with the USSR.

Gradually, more and more Japanese POWs were converted to "scientific socialism" (Marxist-Leninist principles), and those who were active proponents of the Soviet line came to be known by other POWs as *akuchibu*, a Japanese phonetic variation of the Russian *aktiv*, or "activist." In Soviet terminology, *aktiv* refers collectively to the most active and politically minded members of an organization, as in Party *aktiv*, trade union *aktiv*, or youth group *aktiv*.

By the summer of 1947, the indoctrination program and the work of young Japanese *aktivs* resulted in a purge of influential conservative leaders. They were replaced by advocates of "democratic action," ushering in the fourth phase in August 1947 with a more direct and intensive approach. Previously camouflaged terms, such as "Democratic Group," were changed to more specific descriptions such as "Communist Group," and the stage was set for a two-year period of thorough indoctrination.

Conversion to Soviet ideology took place in most POWs after they realized that a professed acceptance of Communism was a prerequisite to repatriation. Moreover, approximately 20 to 25 percent of the Japanese prisoners became "left-wingers" and eagerly assisted the Soviets in the indoctrination program. Most of the POWs in this group were young, uneducated, and from poor families.[1] The leadership of this left-wing element frequently participated in development and presentation of various facets of the program, and internees who showed themselves to be serious adherents of Communism were sent to political schools for training. Additionally, a few Japan Communist Party (JCP) members, exiled from Japan in the 1930s, turned up at POW camps in the USSR. Dan Tokusaburō, an early JCP member, had left Japan for France in 1935 to escape arrest and prosecution. German troops captured Dan in Paris in 1940 and held him in Berlin for the next five years. Soviet officials freed the JCP veteran in 1945 and sent him across Siberia to Manchuria where he was to await further transportation to Japan, but Dan, instead of returning to Japan, accompanied Japanese POWs to Karaganda, in Central Asia, where he was instrumental in developing Marxist-Leninist indoctrination programs.[2] The Soviet Mission in Japan also served as a focal point for coordination with JCP leaders. Several of the Mission officials had contacts with Japanese Communists and were able to relay information to the USSR for use in political indoctrination of Japanese prisoners.

As word of the "brainwashing" program began to filter back to Japan, MacArthur's headquarters in Tokyo became increasingly concerned. Documentation compiled by the Civil Censorship Section of SCAP in March 1948, based on an analysis of about 1.5 million letters and postcards sent by Japanese POW's and repatriates, revealed a radical transformation of beliefs and attitudes on the part of the Soviet-held prisoners. Comments concerning the first year were predominantly negative, but a new trend appeared in January 1947 when letter writers reported improved living conditions and enthusiastically acclaimed the instruction they were receiving. Letters written in early 1948 indicated that a high-pressure indoctrination program had been initiated. This revelation led a SCAP staff officer to comment:

> It is impossible to depreciate the Communist propaganda technique. It is dangerously effective. The Soviet Union, apparently, realized that it has in its hands a group, which if sold on the idea of Communism, is large enough to disrupt the economy and perhaps even the governmental structure in Japan. Certainly close watch should be maintained over the situation and perhaps thought should be given to countering the well-known Communist dogma in the minds of war prisoners immediately after repatriation.[3]

NIPPON SHINBUN

Once the initial move of Japanese POWs to labor camps had been completed, the former soldiers began to notice that one of the objects confiscated by MVD guards during periodic searches was printed matter of any kind. The Soviets took away books, letters, old newspapers—any object that contained writing—regardless of language. Coming from a nation with one of the highest literacy rates in the world, Japanese POWs craved reading material second only to food. This longing soon was satisfied by the appearance of a Japanese-language newspaper, the *Nippon Shinbun*, which was distributed throughout the camps. The *Nippon Shinbun* began as a crude, two-page publication, with articles about poor conditions in Japan and criticism of the emperor system. Soviet political officials used former Kwantung Army printing presses, taken from Manchuria shortly after the surrender, to print the newspaper. Some sources put the initial date of publication as early as 15 September 1945.[4] A SCAP study shows that the first issue was published in the autumn of 1945. In any event, the Soviets began publication of the *Nippon Shinbun* shortly after Japanese POWs arrived at labor camps. The newspaper, printed at Khabarovsk, was published twice weekly for a few months, but production was increased to three issues per week beginning in June 1946 when the staff was enlarged and the number of pages was expanded from two to four. A significant improvement in quality resulted from these enhancements.

MVD political officers, assisted by Japanese POWs with previous journalistic experience, staffed the *Nippon Shinbun*. *Tass* dispatches and radio broadcasts from Japan provided a major source of news items for the newspaper. Japanese staff members wrote new articles based on the monitored radio broadcasts from Japan, playing up negative aspects of American occupation policies. Soviet staff members, most of them fluent in Japanese, rewrote POW-prepared articles but were careful to preserve the Japanese "flavor" of the news material. The chief editor of the *Nippon Shinbun* was Lieutenant Colonel Vladimir Khobarenkopf, a Moscow University graduate, who wrote under the pen name of Ōba Sanpei.

About 60 Soviet officers were on the newspaper staff, and 70 Japanese POWs, including editors, reporters, typesetters, and printers, worked in the Khabarovsk office.

Some POWs, especially those who had no qualms about participating in the Soviet political indoctrination program, eagerly sought assignment to the *Nippon Shinbun* headquarters. Staffers were excused from hard labor, received a small salary, and enjoyed a much greater degree of personal freedom than the rank-and-file POWs in the USSR. Yanami Hisao (alias Aikawa Haruki) served almost four years on the newspaper's editorial staff. MVD officers provided Yanami with an internal passport, and he traveled alone to many of the POW camps. Yanami wrote extensively about poor economic conditions in Japan—certainly a true state of affairs in the late 1940s—but his articles were slanted to attribute the difficulties to malevolent American occupation policies. Yanami (Aikawa) contended that the solution to Japan's economic problems could be found through implementation of Marxist-Leninist principles. After his return to Japan in November 1949, Yanami became an editor of *Akahata* (Red Flag), the JCP newspaper, and specialized in repatriation issues until he was purged by SCAP order on 7 June 1950.[5]

Format of the *Nippon Shinbun* generally followed the lines noted in a SCAP report:

Page 1. Soviet and world affairs, usually direct translations of *Tass* dispatches.

Page 2. News of Japan, dealing particularly with economic and labor problems and Japanese relations with the United States.

Page 3. Editorials and essays dealing with life in the Soviet Union, for example, collective and state farming, the Soviet constitution and system of government, biographical sketches of important Soviet leaders, and articles depicting the Soviet Union as a workers' paradise.

Page 4. Items of special interest to POWs, such as: short stories, cartoons, announcements, and news concerning camp activities (often contributed by POWs).[6]

Articles in the *Nippon Shinbun* usually reflected the four chronological phases of POW indoctrination. Throughout most of 1946, the paper advocated elimination of officer-enlisted class distinctions, thus setting the stage for removal of conservative officer influence; and establishment of the Friendship Society, an informal organization in POW camps for the advancement of Marxist-Leninist ideas. The next phase of the indoctrination program, stressing the ideological aspects of Communism labeled as the "New Democracy," began in early 1947. Soviet editors, sensing that it was too early to promote Communism openly, directed the theme of articles to the proposal that POWs, after repatriation, should "democratize" Japan along Soviet lines since "that is the only way of true democracy." The third phase was introduced in May 1947 with a series of articles critical of the United States and the Japanese government. POWs read reports in the *Nippon Shinbun* alleging abuses in Japan, such as:

GHQ has made warning to the Japanese people concerning public meetings and demonstrations in order to hold in check the labor class and to persecute democratic organs.

... US Occupation Forces have employed former Japanese officers in government posts and positions. These men, at present wearing civilian clothes, are to fight in the coming war in US uniform.

... The Americans are murdering Japanese. The Japanese who even slightly oppose the looters have to expect great sacrifice. Even the American newspapers were forced to report that the number of Japanese killings has reached an extreme point and has increased considerably. The drunken American soldier looks upon Japan as a conquered nation and regards the Japanese people as his slaves. The laborers and farmers of Japan are gasping for breath under the colonial slave system created by American reactionaries.[7]

The *Nippon Shinbun* editorial staff reoriented its policies in the summer of 1947 to coincide with the fourth phase of the indoctrination program. Previous euphemisms, such as "democracy," were replaced by more specific terms, like "Communism." However, this change generated friction among the Japanese staff members and led to the formation of two factions. Radical *aktivs* on the staff favored a direct approach of sharply criticizing and denouncing all actions of the American and Japanese governments. This group also proposed that the *Nippon Shinbun* strongly advocate elimination of the emperor system. The second faction argued that most POWs would see through the tactics proposed by the radical group and grow skeptical of the Soviets and their intentions. They preferred the use of more subtle techniques, such as the theoretical approach to Communism, but the radicals had more power and succeeded in winning their case by persuading the Soviet staff to transfer the dissident faction to another camp. The chief Japanese editor, Asahara Masaki, a member of the radical faction, was instrumental in developing an anti-American and anti-emperor theme that continued until the newspaper discontinued publication in late 1949. Asahara traveled to POW camps throughout Siberia to implement pro-Soviet programs and was a key figure in the organization of an elaborate network for the propagation of Marxist-Leninist ideology.[8]

From mid–1947 until its discontinuance in late 1949, the *Nippon Shinbun* made an intensive effort to discredit the United States and the emperor system in Japan, as revealed in one article:

American Occupation authorities are supporting former military police (*kempeitai*) and the financial oligarchy (*zaibatsu*) in Japan and have aided the Emperor, the number one war criminal, in re-establishing the former militaristic and fanatic constitution. They have extorted and repressed workers as in the past and have given political power to the former imperialists and the landlords.[9]

At the same time, articles praising the Soviet system were printed in almost every edition of the newspaper. One of the constant themes was the Soviet claim that repatriation delays were caused by refusal of the American and Japanese governments to send ships. Imai Genji, in his account of internment in the Soviet Union, explained:

> We saw unfamiliar words, such as the "Emperor system," "reactionary," and "class war strife" in the newspaper. Another foreign word, "American imperialism," was also seen in the paper and it seemed as if the United States and the Soviet Union already were at war against each other. Articles often had headlines such as: "The Great Leader, Stalin," and "The Soviet Union, A Rapidly Progressing Country." . . . Our main concern, repatriation, was discussed in a manner with which we simply could not agree. "Several unavoidable incidents have happened in Japan. It is rather impossible for the Japanese Government to send ships to the Soviet Union because they have been suffering from food shortages and other events." They made it sound as if the Soviets were keeping us as adopted children while our parents (Japan) could not support a family.[10]

Other articles in the *Nippon Shinbun* portrayed the United States as being near a total collapse as a result of inflation and labor disputes. The Marshall Plan was represented as a capitalistic trick to gain control of the European countries, and the United States was accused of attempting to enslave and colonize Japan. Other Stories claimed that the tentacles of American imperialism were stretching across the world. One such article, under the heading of "Expansion of American Power Until It Controls the World Is Aim of Trumanism," explained:

> Since the conclusion of World War II, American "expandists" have been trying to form a front line of security by bringing Greece, Turkey, Iran and the Arabian countries under United States control. The U.S. is moving to become a threat in the Mediterranean Sea. This reaction in Truman's policy has engendered the bitter opposition of not only world-wide Democratic countries, but of progressive elements in the United States itself.[11]

Japanese staff members of the *Nippon Shinbun* wrote favorable reports about the Japan Communist Party and its leaders, Tokuda Kyūichi and Nosaka Sanzō, explaining that the only way to achieve a free society in Japan was through application of Marxist-Leninist ideals. The newspaper also published frequent reports criticizing the Japanese government for "oppressing labor unions and government workers." One such article in the 29 December 1945 issue was headlined: "Labor Union Broken Up. No Progress toward Democracy—Breakup Order Given by MacArthur."[12] In 1948 and 1949, the *Nippon Shinbun* persistently advocated membership in the JCP upon repatriation as the only solution to counter the "anti-democratic practices of the United States." At a 1950 hearing conducted by a committee of the Japanese House of Representatives in Tokyo, former POW Yoshida Kōhei testified:

> about the time of May Day 1949, the *Nippon Shinbun* sponsored an "Oath of Allegiance to Comrade Stalin" which prisoners were required to take. This oath

consisted of joining the Japan Communist Party *en masse* upon returning to Japan, becoming "Repatriates Loved by the Millions," and telling the truth about the Soviet Union.[13]

Although Soviet political officers and Japanese *aktivs* had indoctrination purposes in mind, rank-and-file POWs soon found other uses for the *Nippon Shinbun*. Even though Japanese prisoners avidly sought reading material, the scarcity of paper in *lagers* led them to place a high value on old newspapers. POWs initially cut the newspapers into small pieces for use as toilet paper, but soon found more important purposes—rolling cigarettes with their *makhorka* (an inferior tobacco) ration—and developed a plan for maximum use of the *Nippon Shinbun*. In order to prevent soiling of the paper through excessive handling, one or two copies of each issue were posted on the barracks wall for reading while remaining copies were cut into small pieces for immediate distribution in equal shares.

Soviet officials repatriated most POWs by the end of 1949, and Japanese staff members of the *Nippon Shinbun* were among the last to return. They were interrogated at Maizuru and Tokyo for several days, but Japanese government agencies took no legal action against the "Siberian journalists." The *Nippon Shinbun*, with its monopoly on news dissemination, was highly effective in influencing POW attitudes. Although most prisoners viewed the newspaper as a propaganda device at first, the frequent repeating of anti-emperor and anti-American themes caused younger and less-educated *lager* residents to fully believe the articles and even led conservative and mature Japanese to become skeptical of American occupation policies. After returning to Japan, however, repatriates expressed amazement that conditions were far better than they had been led to believe.

POLITICAL SCHOOLS

MVD political officers began a systematic indoctrination program in the spring of 1946 to convince POWs of the advantages of Communism over capitalism. The Soviets established political schools as a foundation for this program and sent promising Japanese POWs to the schools for periods varying from one week to three months. Graduates returned to POW camps where they served as instructors and group leaders. The one-week school, widely known among POWs as the "short course," provided basic education in Marxist-Leninist principles. At least two POWs from each camp attended these sessions, which were conducted at several regional locations. The longer-term political schools, known quite appropriately as the "long course," provided more detailed instruction on Communism and scientific socialism to those POWs considered sympathetic to the Soviet Union and capable of strengthening the JCP after return to Japan.

The "short course" was an intensive training program designed to prepare internees as instructors and group leaders in POW camps. Each day was crammed with about ten hours of instruction followed by discussions and group meetings in the evenings. A typical "short course" schedule of instruction included:

1. Current Events of the Soviet Union.
   a. History of the Red Army.
   b. The Advancement of the USSR since World War II.
   c. Stalin's Five-Year Plan.
   d. History of the Communist Party of the Soviet Union.
2. Current World Situation.
   a. President Truman, Seeking World War III.
   b. Failure of the Marshall Plan.
   c. Henry A. Wallace, Champion of the U.S. Communist Party.
   d. Democratic Nations in Eastern Europe.
   e. The Laborers Fighting for Freedom in China and India.
   f. The Korean Problem.
3. Current Events in Japan.
   a. Violation of the Potsdam Declaration by the United States.
   b. American Colonization of Japan and Preparations to Launch an Aggressive War Against the USSR Using Japan as a Base.
   c. Oppressing Labor by the Importation of U.S. Dollars.
   d. Oppression of the Labor Class.
4. History of the Japan Communist Party.
   a. The Struggles and Steady Climb of the JCP.
5. People's Control of the Japanese Government.
   a. The Solid Front of Labor Unions to Overthrow the Present Government with the Aid of the JCP.[14]

Long-term political schools were from one to three months in duration, and instructional sessions were held six days a week, eight hours a day. Students at the "long courses" were thrust into the milieu of complete immersion in Marxist-Leninist thought; every moment of the day involved some aspect of intensive indoctrination, including discussion sessions held well into the night. Soviet political officers organized students into groups related to their prewar backgrounds along the following lines: 1) farmers and laborers, 2) small merchants, 3) middle school graduates, and 4) high school and university graduates. Most courses were held in Khabarovsk, but MVD officials and Japanese *aktivs* also conducted long-term schools in Vladivostok and Moscow. The staff consisted of Soviet and Japanese personnel, as typified by the Vladivostok school where the commandant and vice-commandant were Soviet officers and the principal was a former Japanese Noncommissioned Officer (NCO). Faculty members included a former lieutenant of the Kwantung Army and three NCOs. Political school students were excused from manual labor and received pay of 50 rubles a month. Japanese instructors received 100 rubles monthly and were given special privileges. The course of instruction at long-term political schools included:

1. History of the Japan Communist Party.
2. Structure of the Soviet State.
3. Dialectics and Materialism.
4. Imperialism.
5. Evils of the Emperor System.
6. Advantages of Socialism over Capitalism.
7. The Path which the Soviet Races have Taken.
8. Peaceful Revolution or Violent Revolution in Japan?
9. Operation of Cells in Cities and Villages.[15]

As word of the political schools spread throughout the POW camp network, thousands of willing applicants clamored to sign up. For most, the major appeal was exemption from all labor and the good living conditions enjoyed by students. POWs vied with one another to show political officers what "good democrats" they had become and enthusiastically attended evening political lectures in large numbers. Schools usually were composed of 60 to 100 students, but only a small percentage of POWs—probably about 1 percent—attended the "long courses." When students returned to their camps after a month or more of schooling, they were almost unrecognizable to their former comrades. The exhausted and sickly appearance of the rank-and-file POW had been replaced by robust and exuberant converts overflowing with self-confidence.

Soviet authorities modeled political indoctrination courses for Japanese POWs after similar programs for Red Army soldiers and POWs of other nationalities, primarily German and Romanian. A former high-ranking Japanese officer interned near Moscow later reported: "Separate schools were established at Morshansk Camp No. 7064 for Japanese, German and Romanian officer internees. . . . Some of the German POWs were sent back to Germany, smuggled into the American and British zones, and used as Russian agents."[16]

Political school graduates became the keystone of the Soviet program to educate Japanese POWs in pro-Communist theories and were influential in leading discussions at *lager* Friendship Society meetings. These *aktivs* also were instrumental in monitoring the indoctrination progress of each POW and determining eligibility for repatriation, based on an appraisal of the internee's knowledge and acceptance of Marxist-Leninist principles. By late 1948, an elite class of Japanese POWs, the *aktiv* leadership, had been formed from graduates of the political indoctrination courses. This special group, estimated at between 1 and 2 percent of the total POW population, controlled the destiny of other Japanese POWs during their final year in the USSR.

THE FRIENDSHIP SOCIETY

Soviet political officers encouraged the formation of informal camp groups to stimulate discussion of political and social thought along Marxist-Leninist lines.

POWs organized clubs, societies and youth groups at various *lagers*, but the principal body for propagation of Soviet doctrine was the Friendship Society, the *Tomo no kai*. The society had its beginnings as a spontaneous, natural product of group living and served as an agency to regulate and facilitate interaction between POWs and Soviet authorities, and among internees. This "human desire to organize" ideally suited political objectives for the propagation of ideas favorable to the Soviet Union and for the spread of unfavorable criticism of American occupation and Japanese government policies. The *Nippon Shinbun* made frequent appeals for POWs to join the Friendship Society.

Although organizational efforts varied, MVD political officers often called upon POW leaders to form social clubs at the camps and used informal networks to give the appearance of spontaneous action on the part of the POWs. The Soviet staff made special efforts to convert natural leaders to their side and sent cooperative POWs to the "short course." Leaders who refused to attend were eased out of their positions and replaced by others. Soviet political officers maintained a close liaison with Japanese leaders of the Friendship Society but were careful to conceal the relationship. MVD authorities gave guidance and direction in the form of suggestions rather than orders, but POW-leaders soon learned that failure to adopt "suggestions" could lead to disciplinary action. MVD officials actively participated, on occasion, when POWs were slow or ineffective in accomplishing desired goals, but only as a last resort. Political officers continually stressed "class conflict" with frequent allegations that officers had exploited enlisted soldiers under the emperor system.[17]

Imai Genji, in *Shiberiya no Uta* (Song of Siberia), recounts his experiences with the Friendship Society:

> One day, several unfamiliar Soviet officers appeared in camp and a few members of *Tomo no kai* were called to meet them. . . . We were asked about the current condition of the Friendship Society in our camp. We had not gotten organized very well yet, so we answered that we were studying socialism. When the political officers told us we should be doing more, I responded: "All of us are exhausted after working every day, and it's impossible for us to do much work with the *Tomo no kai* on top of everything else." Then a Soviet lieutenant said: "Why don't you choose three representatives among yourselves. And those who are chosen will be excused from work beginning tomorrow. Just concentrate on *Tomo no kai*. We'll speak to the camp commandant about setting up an office for you."[18]

Membership in the Friendship Society was voluntary, and only about a fourth of the internees belonged to the society in its first year of existence. Most POWs were resentful of their harsh treatment at the hands of the Red Army and MVD. Even Soviet officials often were more interested in completing work projects in the first year after the war. As time passed, however, camp authorities placed more emphasis on the indoctrination program and offered inducements for membership in the Friendship Society. Distribution of the *Nippon Shinbun*, for example, was made at the rate of one copy for every 3 to 4 members of the

Friendship Society. For non-members, however, the rate was one copy for every 40 POWs. In some camps, *Tomo no kai* members were given such advantages as choice of job assignments, more food, and favorable bunk assignments.[19]

The indoctrination program was in high gear by the summer of 1947, and the Friendship Society served as a basic forum for political discussions, lectures, songfests, amateur plays, film showings, and other activities oriented to Marxist-Leninist principles. *Aktivs* used the *Nippon Shinbun* as a principal source of material for Friendship Society discussions. Soviet political officers made additional resources available—books on socialist economics, history, and political philosophy—enabling interested POWs to acquire an extensive knowledge of Communism and the Soviet Union. The predominant discussion theme was criticism of U.S. policies, especially those concerning the occupation of Japan. Some of the topics were: "Ruthless Exploitation of the Defeated Japanese People," "Evils of American Imperialism and Capitalism," and "Blessings of the Soviet Way of Life." Discussions often centered on conditions in Japan—*aktivs* accused the Americans of attempting to restore imperialism, emperor worship, and class structure—and the severe economic and social problems in the home islands were attributed to the "anti-democratic" stance of the United States. A SCAP analysis, based on comments of repatriated POWs, concluded: "Discussions usually contained subtle propaganda that Japanese POWs had a solemn and truly patriotic duty to strive for establishment of a 'democratic' Japan."[20]

The Friendship Society was so important to Soviet indoctrination goals that *aktivs* applied increasing pressure on recalcitrant POWs in attempts to achieve solidarity and further isolate "reactionary" internees. A former POW explained:

> there was an uneasy feeling between the *Tomo no kai* members and those who did not join. The Soviets wanted to re-educate all Japanese POWs to communism. Soviet officials used the leaders and members of the *Tomo no kai* to reach the rest of the POWs. To achieve this goal, several POWs were educated to be new *aktivs*. ... These new *aktivs* talked to their friends and acquaintances, encouraging them to join. This procedure was repeated several times, and most POWs eventually joined the Friendship Society when they saw how much better life would be for them as members.[21]

The Friendship Society did indeed grow to large numbers. In some camps, only a handful of strong-willed POWs held out, often resulting in criminal sentences for their "reactionary" attitudes. Many in this category were not repatriated until 1950 or later.

As the Friendship Society became well entrenched, posters extolling the virtues of Soviet socialism proliferated. Pamphlets promoting the advantages of Communism over capitalism were in abundance. These pamphlets, often used as discussion starters, bore such titles as: "The Life of Soviet Youth," "The Constitution of the Soviet Union," and "Speeches of Nosaka Sanzō." Soviet films were shows occasionally, and a former POW gave a summary of a movie on racial discrimination and the ensuing discussion:

> An American woman, a caucasian, gave birth to an illegitimate Negro baby, and for this reason was driven out of the U.S. with sticks and stones. She sought sanctuary in the Soviet Union, where she joined a circus in Moscow. She attracted the attention of two circus men, one a Soviet citizen and the other a German. When the German learned she favored the Russian, he decided to ruin their act by showing her illegitimate child to the circus audience during one of her performances. The Russian snatched the child from the German who then tried to take it away. The German was arrested by the police for violent behavior, while the audience cheered. The Russian man and the American woman lived happily ever after.
>
> After the movie, a representative of the *Nippon Shinbun* gave a speech on the picture and stated that the story was true, and that the Negro child is now a cadet at the Moscow naval academy. At the end of every such program, each prisoner was ordered to cast a signed ballot either for communism or capitalism.[22]

The Friendship Society served as an important element in the Soviet program to inculcate Japanese POWs with pro-Soviet and pro-JCP attitudes. It was a natural organization in which men were drawn together as comrades with common interests. By subtle manipulation of Japanese attitudes, Soviet political officers were able to create conditions that compelled POWs to accept, or at least pretend to accept, pro-Soviet and anti-American ideas. Indoctrination efforts were accelerated prior to repatriation; POWs knew they needed to make a fervent show of how well they had learned their lessons. Once this hurdle was passed, internees were transferred to screening camps for intensive monitoring and more indoctrination prior to repatriation.

THE ANTI-FASCIST DEMOCRATIC COMMITTEE

An informal network of politically active Japanese POWs evolved from contacts made in the political schools and in the Friendship Society. This network grew into an elaborate bureaucracy known as the Anti-Fascist Democratic Committee (AFDC), and was organized along Communist Party lines. POW camps (cells) were under a district headquarters, and the entire organization was managed (by Japanese) from a central headquarters in Khabarovsk. A conference held in Komsomolsk in May 1948 articulated AFDC goals: 1)Acceleration and coordination of propaganda programs throughout the entire POW camp system; 2) greater stress on the functioning of youth organizations in the individual camps; 3) reproduction of Communist cells in the *lagers*; and, 4) increased effort to discover the identities and activities of known and potential "anti-democratic" elements among internees. AFDC programs were integrated with the JCP platform and "mass participation was to be the watchword of the future."[23]

The Anti-Fascist Democratic Committee, under the general direction of the Soviet Area Political Department, was entirely a Japanese organization. Chairmen and officers at each camp and at district and central headquarters were all Japanese *aktivs*. Soviet officials provided internal passports to some AFDC officials, thereby permitting them to travel throughout the USSR. AFDC *aktivs* also received a small salary and were exempt from hard labor. These privileges, as with those who served on the *Nippon Shinbun* staff and in the Friendship Society, constituted a strong motivation for Japanese POWs to further Soviet interests. At the policy-making level in Khabarovsk, *Nippon Shinbun* and AFDC Central Committee leaders worked in close coordination to expedite indoctrination program objectives. Each camp and district AFDC consisted of a chairman and three subordinate officers responsible for propaganda, culture, and a youth organization. Local newspapers, frequently referred to as *kabe shinbun* (wall newspaper), flourished under AFDC direction and were hand-printed and posted, as the name would suggest, on barracks walls.

AFDC officials held periodic regional and national meetings to coordinate indoctrination programs and to "standardize leadership in the democratic movement." The schedule for a five-day symposium held in July 1947 reveals the main points advocated for education of POWs. This meeting, with 113 participants, started off with the adoption of a slogan: "Overthrow Fascism and the Emperor." General objectives were announced as:

1. There can be no Democracy without Battles against Fascism.
2. Democratization of Japan along Soviet lines.
3. Implementation of the general tasks of the democratic movement.

Each session of the symposium opened with the singing of the "Song of the Red Flag." On the last day of the conference, unanimous agreement was achieved in developing a statement on the nature of fascism:

> What is fascism? Fascism in Japan is the Emperor System. It includes every kind of fascist element, and feudalism is used to hide the secret of it. Our mission is to reveal this secret, and it will give us energy to fight against fascism. Oh! Our brothers who were the victims of feudalism! It is time for you to be awakened! Now we have revealed the secret of fascism. All of us, including the ones who have just received our message, are prepared to rise against fascism.[24]

Then the AFDC delegates, as if they were salesmen who had just attended a company pep rally, trooped back to their districts and camps with great enthusiasm for the "anti-fascist" battle. Representatives of district headquarters regularly visited POW camps to give lectures and participate in discussions of the Friendship Society. Yabe Akira, a former navy man captured in the Kurile Islands, recalled an incident that occurred in the Soviet Far East in 1947:

The Anti-Fascist Democratic Committee sent its organizer to camps in the Sikhote-Alin area. . . . He described several examples concerning hatred against the officers who repeatedly committed crimes by using the Emperor's power. He asked us to agree with him. . . . If someone expressed an opinion that was not to the AFDC representative's liking, he shouted at him, "You are not conscious enough of class conflict yet. Criticize yourself!" Most of the older soldiers listened in silence. They appeared to say, "There he goes again." They also agreed quietly. When questioned, they simply replied, "That's exactly true."[25]

The Anti-Fascist Democratic Committee also acted as a quasi-judicial agency. AFDC members were on "hearing boards" established in POW camps to consider and recommend punishment in disciplinary cases, for example, violations of camp regulations, and evidence, or suspicion, of "anti-Communist utterances" and uncooperative attitudes. By 1948, rank-and-file POWs had far more to fear from Japanese *aktivs* than from MVD officials. "Hearing Board" recommendations often resulted in criminal sentences for POWs and extensive delays in repatriation.[26]

INDOCTRINATION AND DAILY LIFE AT THE *LAGER*

Daily routine in the POW camp milieu was ideally suited to an indoctrination program. Soviet political officers and Japanese *aktivs* were able to control all news, discussions, recreational activities, work—indeed, the total camp atmosphere—and *lager* residents never had an opportunity to hear opposing arguments. In fact, ordinary POWs were so busy attempting to fulfill their *norm* at work, maintaining the barracks, performing special jobs at the behest of MVD officers, maintaining their own clothing and meager personal belongings, and participating in the political indoctrination program, that there were only rare occasions when they had a moment to reflect on their situation. Imadate Tetsuo, a former POW, explained:

> Every POW was just trying to do his daily work, and did not have a second to think on his own. He did not have any chance to have his own ideas or thoughts. Also, he was not allowed to possess an individual identity. . . .
> The POWs' constant hunger also did not help them. If anyone could manage to think on his own, it was usually about food. The Soviet method of keeping Japanese prisoners under control consisted of providing miserable living conditions and making them work. Keeping the Japanese prisoners so busy that they were not able to think on their own was part of the Soviet plan. Group activities were the basis for the Japanese POWs' daily life.[27]

A day in the life of a POW followed this typical schedule: 6 A.M., wake up, prepare for the day, clean up around camp, breakfast, sing a song of praise for the Communist brotherhood, group reading of *Nippon Shinbun*, and study of Marxist-Leninist principles in groups; 7:30 A.M., line up for work, roll call, count-off by fives, march to work site; 8 A.M. to 12 noon, work; 12 noon to 1 P.M., lunch (often carried by POWs from camp), workshops, group reading of newspapers, political lecture; 1 P.M. to 5 P.M., work; 5 P.M. to 8 P.M., return to barracks, count-off by fives, roll call, supper, repair work around camp, clean latrine, song and dance practice, prepare for political lectures; 8 P.M. to 10 P.M., political lecture.[28]

POWs were never alone and never quite sure who would hear their remarks. This condition led to a reluctance to talk about anything that could possibly be interpreted as "anti-Soviet agitation." The constant hunger of the POWs was a weapon MVD officials used in a skillful manner. Some POWs were transferred to special camps for temporary periods—ten days, or so—and asked to report on their comrades. Extra food was an incentive for information on reactionary statements made by fellow POWs. This created an atmosphere of distrust throughout each *lager*, leading rank-and-file POWs to refrain from talking unless absolutely necessary. The standard response to *aktiv* statements at political lectures or elsewhere was, "That is exactly correct. Long live the Soviet!"

May Day was the biggest celebration during the year, and intended to commemorate the "brotherhood of the working class." POWs participated in demonstrations, plays, singing, and political lectures, and had three days off from work to celebrate the annual event. Watanabe Shigeru, a POW at Chita Camp No. 12, reported:

> On May Day we gathered under the red flag and shouted, "hurrah for the Universal Labor Union." Next we had a demonstration parade with portraits of Lenin and Stalin in front. After these activities, we had various kinds of games during the daytime, and we had a play in the evening....
>
> Group singing centered around Soviet marching songs, such as "The Internationale," "Red Flag," "Comrades, Be Firmly United," and "Song of Dedication to the Communist Party."[29]

These events provided diversity to the grim conditions faced in the daily POW routine and created an air of festivity throughout the *lager*. However, there was a problem—as POWs later discovered—that marred this short vacation from hard labor. The days off for the celebration had to be made up; and camp inmates had to work the next three Sundays to make up for lost production. For most of the POWs, it was 21 straight days of hard labor before they could catch their breath again.

Work and indoctrination programs were linked closely. POWs were reminded daily that their labor was instrumental in building the socialist world. In the all-pervasive pro-Soviet atmosphere, *aktivs* convinced most POWs to sign statements that their work was performed on a voluntary basis. When the highly indoctrinated 1949 repatriates returned to Japan, an American intelligence officer observed: "They maintained that manual labor was not obligatory in the camps, although they said they had been glad to work voluntarily."[30] Posters and "wall newspapers" prominently displayed in each *lager* enjoined POWs to fulfill the norm and join the camp "democracy movement." The 10 August 1946 issue of *Dai San Rageru Kabe Shinbun* (No. 3 *Lager* Wall Newspaper) urged: "Fill our labor *norm* by 100%. Let's join the Soviet's 5-year plan! Democracy is a rightful strife for workers to make better living conditions. Clean up the reminder of fascism!"[31]

At the beginning of 1949, the Soviets still held approximately 100,000 Japanese prisoners in the USSR. Political indoctrination proceeded at an intense pace up to the day repatriates sailed from Nakhodka. In the spring of 1949, only the most zealous converts to Communism could be considered for the initial repatriation voyage, and POWs vied with one another to show how well they had learned their lessons.

SELECTION FOR REPATRIATION

Soviet political officers and Japanese activists subjected candidates for repatriation to extensive testing to detect anti-Soviet or poorly indoctrinated POWs. The MVD established an "intermediate screening camp" in the Blagoveshchensk district for this purpose, and POWs were sent there prior to shipment to the port of Nakhodka. AFDC representatives conducted intensive "semi-final propaganda barrages in conjunction with a systematic attempt to weed out anti-Soviet personnel and former Japanese police and intelligence officers." An undercover Japanese POW-informer monitored suspected POWs and provided data to the AFDC, and information from Soviet officials was used to "cross-check" results. Prospective repatriates who failed the test were detained for more indoctrination or for trial as war criminals.[32]

Prisoners selected for repatriation happily boarded trains bound for port and thought they could relax, but Japanese *aktivs* had other plans for them. The most intensive and crucial period of their stay in the USSR was just now beginning. Indoctrination efforts continued on their train trip to the port and were intensified at Nakhodka. In all, a period of about one month elapsed from the time POWs left their "home *lager*" until they sailed for Japan. Some POWs spent even longer periods at Nakhodka—weeks, even months for some—for additional indoctrination. Not only did "screening" and testing continue, but *aktivs* drilled repatriates intensively to prepare them for a program of activity upon arrival in Japan "to counter the colonial slave system created by American reactionaries."[33]

Soviet authorities and Japanese *aktivs* conducted an extensive program to convert POWs to pro-Soviet and pro-JCP attitudes. Most of the indoctrination endeavors emanated from Japanese sources such as the *Nippon Shinbun* and the Anti-Fascist Democratic Committee, and POW were acutely aware of the need to show their enthusiasm for Marxist-Leninist thought. Some POWs later alleged that JCP General Secretary Tokuda had written a letter requesting that Soviet authorities retain reactionary POWs and return only those who had become

MARXIST-LENINIST INDOCTRINATION

"democratic." These charges were made by a group of 44 repatriates at hearings conducted by the Japanese Diet in 1950. Press comments in Japan reflected widespread anger over revelations that Tokuda had asked the Soviets to retain POWs who refused to become Communists.[34] Tokuda and the JCP denied these claims, but several repatriates gave testimony at the Diet hearings that Soviet MVD officers had told them of the request to delay repatriation of reactionary POWs.

The intense desire to return home made many Japanese POWs go along with whatever would convince authorities of their conversion to the Soviet program. There were some genuine converts, but most repatriates later disavowed their professed faith in Marxist and Leninism. During their three or four years in the Soviet Union, POWs were led to believe that no one in Japan was concerned about their repatriation. Nothing could have been further from the truth. By 1946, several associations of Japanese citizens, formed to expedite repatriation from Soviet-controlled areas, were in existence. Throughout the late 1940s, these organizations petitioned SCAP and Japanese government agencies to pressure the Soviet Mission in Japan for an early return of their missing sons and husbands. Demonstrations to publicize the plight of the Soviet-held Japanese were a regular occurrence in Tokyo and other cities. SCAP officials, Japanese government agencies, and later the United Nations, all undertook extensive efforts to expedite repatriation. Some of these endeavors were to go on for more than ten years.

5

Attempts to Expedite Repatriation

Two facts concerning repatriation had become obvious by the first anniversary of the war's end. First, most Japanese in areas controlled by American, British Commonwealth, and Chinese forces had been returned to Japan; and, secondly, the Soviets had not begun any type of repatriation program. As repatriation from non-Soviet zones neared completion by the end of 1946, attention focused on the large number of Japanese held by the USSR. The subject became a matter of heated and lengthy debates in meetings of the Allied Council for Japan, an advisory body in Tokyo consisting of four members: the Supreme Commander (represented by the Diplomatic Section chief), who was chairman and United States representative; a representative each from the Soviet Union and the Republic of China; and a member representing the British Commonwealth (United Kingdom, Australia, New Zealand, and India).[1] Foreign ministers of the United Kingdom, the Soviet Union, and the United States, meeting in Moscow in December 1945, established the council to provide representatives of the Allied Powers with a voice in the conduct of the American-dominated occupation of Japan. Biweekly meetings began in April 1946.

Even before creation of the Allied Council, SCAP officials requested in October 1945 that the Soviet government make Japanese ships in its occupied areas of Northeast Asia available for repatriation of Japanese soldiers and civilians. There was no response to this request until April 1946, when the Soviet member provided information on shipping at the first meeting of the council but stated that "none was suitable for repatriation purposes."[2] With repatriates flowing back to Japan from other areas in the spring of 1946, concern was beginning to grow over the fate of Japanese held in regions occupied by the USSR. The subject rapidly became a major issue at Allied Council meetings. George Atcheson, SCAP Diplomatic Section chief and council chairman, summarized repatriation problems at a June 1946 meeting in Tokyo and pointed out the Potsdam Declaration terms calling for a "return to their homes" of Japanese military personnel. However, the Soviet Council member, Lieutenant General Kuzma N. Derevyanko, protested that the subject of repatriation was not within the

Allied Council's jurisdiction. Instead, Derevyanko insisted, the council should have been discussing integration of repatriates into Japanese life and elimination of the Demobilization Bureau, an agency staffed primarily by former Japanese Army and Navy officers to facilitate return of military personnel to civilian life.[3] This tone set the pattern for council meetings for the remainder of the Occupation era. Derevyanko constantly badgered other members with questions and comments about procedural matters and refused to consider the repatriation issue. In fact, attempts to discuss the matter became so counterproductive that MacArthur instructed his Diplomatic Section chief, after the 29 October 1947 meeting, to drop the issue from the council agenda. The topic was not brought up again until December 1949. During most of the 26-month period, the Allied Council met only on a perfunctory basis.

Prior to MacArthur's edict, however, General Derevyanko frequently complained about the Demobilization Bureau, asserting that it was a subterfuge to continue the Japanese General Staff, and proposed that the bureau be restructured to eliminate all former military officer. In one heated exchange, council chairman George Atcheson explained the purpose of the Demobilization Bureau—to pick up ex-soldiers at ports of debarkation, deliver them to their hometowns, maintain personnel records, and aid family members—and then went on to discuss reasons for its continued existence:

> As a matter of fact, if the Soviet authorities had been willing to repatriate the 800,000 or a million Japanese soldiers in their hands as a part of our general repatriation program, the activities of the Demobilization Bureau would now be drawing to a close.[4]

REVERSE REPATRIATION

One month before the first Allied Council meeting, however, a bizarre series of events began to unfold. General Derevyanko, on 12 March 1946, requested SCAP to arrange for transportation of some 8,500 Japanese from Japan to Sakhalin. According to Soviet Mission officials, the requests were made by "Japanese fishermen on the southern part of Sakhalin to allow their families, who entered Japan during the period of hostilities, to return." General Derevyanko outlined plans to send a Soviet ship to the ports of Niigata, Aomori, Hakodate, and Wakkanai to transport family members to Sakhalin.[5] Two weeks later, SCAP agreed to the Soviet general's proposal, subject to several conditions:

1. The movement of any Japanese families concerned must be entirely voluntary on their part.
2. Prior to the commencement of travel, the Soviet Government will furnish to the Supreme Commander a list, in the form of an individually signed request for return of their respective families to Sakhalin, of the Japanese fishermen concerned. This

list should include, further, the full name of each member of each family in Japan, the address . . . and the relationship.
3. Complete supervision of the movement of these families will be effected by the Occupation Force authorities and not by representatives of the Soviet Government.
4. The Supreme Commander for the Allied Powers will specify the ports, the dates, and, within reasonable limits, the time of arrival in Japan of the Soviet vessels for transport of families.[6]

These stipulations set off a long series of correspondence between the Soviet member and SCAP, marked by unusually polite language, masking the growing hostility between Moscow's representative and the Western Allies. However, the "Reverse Repatriation" issue was never discussed at Allied Council for Japan meetings, no doubt due to Derevyanko's insistence that repatriation was not a proper topic for the council. Major General A. P. Kislenko, Deputy Chief of the Soviet Mission, advised SCAP in April that compilation of a list together with the specified information would be "technically very difficult" and suggested that "it would be very desirable that the Chief of Staff grant permission for the immediate arrival in Japan of the Soviet boat with representatives of the Japanese fishermen in Sakhalin." After an exchange of several letters, the USSR Mission chief, on 1 July 1946, submitted to SCAP a "list of 757 persons, which compose 210 families of Japanese fishermen who are petitioning to be sent from Japan to Southern Sakhalin."[7] Derevyanko signed his letter, "With complete deference." Three weeks later, in a response with the salutation, "My dear General Derevyanko," Atcheson added a new stipulation:

> Until there may be reasonable assurance of facilities and permission for Japanese nationals to travel freely from as well as to Sakhalin, it will not be possible to send Japanese nationals to Sakhalin in what, in fact, would amount to deportation with no assurances of their freedom to return should they so desire.[8]

One month later, Derevyanko expressed "extreme astonishment in regards to the new demands of Mr. Atcheson, concerning some special guarantee of freedom of movement to and from Sakhalin," and again, "with complete deference," announced "I have the honor to request a prompt answer to this question."[9] SCAP's answer was prompt. Six days later, the Diplomatic Section chief ended the matter, explaining:

> so long as any of the Japanese individuals concerned do not possess freedom of movement or choice of residence, the necessary conditions for acquiescence in your proposal have not been fulfilled. . . . I accordingly regret to inform you that this Headquarters is not in a position to give favorable consideration to your request.[10]

Thus the "Reverse Repatriation" case came to a close. Why were Soviet officials so eager to have families join the fishermen in Sakhalin? In that first year after the war, Moscow's plan was to colonize its recent territorial acquisition with residents already there, and the movement of families to rejoin the fishermen would enhance prospects of their staying on a permanent basis. However, by late 1946, with the arrival in Southern Sakhalin of Soviet settlers, this policy was relaxed and repatriation to Japan began on a limited basis. Even so, as described in chapter 2, a small number of family members clandestinely left Japan and journeyed to their former homes in Sakhalin.

General Derevyanko never brought up the matter again. The issue received no publicity, and the Soviets lost a propaganda opportunity to rebuke SCAP and American officials for delaying the reunification of families. Instead, it was to be an American and British diplomatic offensive over the next six years, with the Soviet representative cast, albeit often deservedly, as the villain.

INITIAL SOVIET AGREEMENT

Soviet and American staff officers met often in 1946 in an attempt to expedite repatriation from USSR-controlled areas. They held 13 working-level sessions in the last three months of the year, but talks bogged down over who was to pay for fuel and other supplies. Conferees finally resolved the issue on 19 December 1946 and agreed that 50,000 Japanese would be repatriated monthly. SCAP assumed responsibility for providing ships, fuel, food, and supplies; all the Soviets had to do was deliver internees to the ports.[11] In the first five months of 1947, Soviet repatriation of Japanese was at a level much in excess of the established quota. Soviet officials sent 90,000 Japanese home in March, straining the resources of Allied port teams. The large number of returnees was due primarily to heavy shipments of civilians from Dairen and Port Arthur from January to April 1947. Afterward, monthly repatriation dropped considerably below 50,000. Although the number of returnees dwindled after May, SCAP provided shipping to accommodate more than requested by the Soviets in hopes of accelerating the flow of repatriates. However, the ships consistently returned to Japan with more than ten percent of passenger space unused.[12]

Several SCAP offers to provide additional shipping in 1947 went unanswered until October, when the Soviet member replied that repatriation could not be increased due to "transportation and technical reasons." General Kislenko, acting for the Soviet representative while Derevyanko was on an official visit to Moscow, claimed the repatriation issue was outside the scope of the Allied Council's charter and that SCAP was using the subject to divert attention from the "deplorable state of the repatriates who, on their arrival in Japan, get no proper assistance with regard to getting employment and who are virtually left to the mercy of fate." This charge led to a spirited exchange between Kislenko and William J. Sebald, who had become council chairman after the death of George Atcheson in an airplane crash at sea in August 1947. Sebald insisted that repatriation was a proper topic for the Allied Council and charged that:

certain propaganda organs of the USSR have attempted to place direct blame for the slow rate of repatriation from Soviet-controlled areas upon the Occupation authorities, specifically, "high officers of the Anglo-American Occupational Headquarters." The editorial in which this statement appears was headlined, "The Displaced Persons Problem Exposed; Why do the United States and Great Britain Obstruct the Repatriation Program?" Another article headlined, "Who is Causing the Repatriation Delay?" states: "All the camps are now overcrowded, and everyone is eagerly awaiting the arrival of his repatriation ship from Japan."[13]

Sebald cited several other Soviet articles and news broadcasts critical of SCAP handling of repatriates, denied the allegations and made an offer to significantly increase the amount of shipping for return of Soviet-held Japanese:

SCAP is prepared to assure you, within forty-eight hours, that there will be enough shipping to return 131,500 repatriates in one month. In thirty days, we can step up this rate of flow to 160,000 per month.[14]

Soviet officials did not accept Sebald's offer. On the contrary, they announced a suspension of all repatriation from December 1947 until April 1948, citing ice and climatic conditions as the basis for their action. When SCAP authorities offered to provide icebreakers to clear frozen ports, the Soviets responded that the proposal was "unacceptable because of difficulties in assembling Japanese at the repatriation ports and the overloaded condition of the Soviet rail transportation system."[15] This delay caused an outcry from the Japanese public. Protest meetings proliferated throughout the nation, and some groups representing POW families attempted, unsuccessfully, to send delegations to meet with General Derevyanko. On one day alone in January 1948, anxious family members sent more than 500 telegrams to the Soviet Mission requesting immediate resumption and return of all Japanese within six months. Welfare Ministry records indicated nearly 700,000 Japanese remained in Soviet hands in April 1948, and the topic was prominent in the news media and in the public consciousness. A giant rally held in Tokyo's Hibiya Park to pressure the Soviets for faster repatriation featured two speakers from the House of Representatives, Miki Takeo and Nakasone Yasuhiro, both destined to serve as prime ministers in later years. In another sign of public reaction, the well-known Mitsukoshi Department Store in Tokyo presented a ten-day exhibit showing the "depressed life and primitive conditions of Japanese illegally held in the Soviet area."[16]

These urgings, however, did nothing to expedite the return of internees held by the USSR. Instead, the Soviets even delayed the resumption of repatriation until May 1948, a month later than previously indicated, due to "unfavorable climatic conditions this year and also taking into consideration transportation and technical facilities." Repatriation priority was announced in *Sobieto Bunka* (Soviet Culture), a Japanese-language publication sponsored by the Soviet Mission:

1. according to rank—civilians, enlisted and officers return in that sequence of priority;
2. according to health—sick and disabled are given priority over healthy;
3. according to conduct—well-behaved prisoners given preference over those with bad records;
4. according to hardship imposed upon the internee's family by his absence, and;
5. according to the type of labor the prisoner is doing, in order that important work will not be interrupted.[17]

About 280,000 Japanese were repatriated from Soviet-held areas between May and December 1948, but Soviet officials paid little attention to priorities announced in *Sobieto Bunka* with the exception that those in poor health were accorded early repatriation. Most of the returned military personnel were older or frail, but young POWs in good physical condition remained in the USSR. SCAP and Japanese Welfare Ministry records indicated that more than 400,000 Japanese still were in Soviet hands at the end of 1948.

BAD NEWS FROM MOSCOW

Soviet officials again suspended repatriation during the early months of 1949 for the same reasons previously cited—unfavorable climatic conditions—and unrest continued to grow in Japan. Repatriation organizations staged frequent protest demonstrations, and the subject received much attention in the press. The situation worsened when Nosaka Sanzō, Secretary-General of the Japan Communist Party, commented in a March 1949 radio broadcast:

> There is no country which does not use war prisoners for intense labor. The USSR knows that if she uses POWs it will cost money. She is not detaining these prisoners because she likes doing so. There are various reasons: for instance, lack of transportation facilities to receive all these men.[18]

Public reaction was swift. One writer, in a letter to the *Mainichi*, a Tokyo daily, expressed outrage at Nosaka's explanation:

> Neither the United States nor the British nations have used POWs for labor in their countries since the war ended. It is well known that the Soviets have done so.
> Nosaka says the USSR is using our men against her will and has not returned the POWs because of the expense involved. Then why did she transport these prisoners thousands of miles into European Russia and the interior of Siberia? If she had returned them immediately after the war, the cost would have been very small.
> Nosaka gives lack of transport facilities as an excuse. If the USSR had facilities to transport a million Japanese from Manchuria to the interior of the USSR in one month after the surrender, what has become of such facilities now? . . . It is quite

evident that the Soviets have ulterior motives in holding these Japanese in bondage four years after a ten-day war.[19]

Repatriation organizations were active in the spring of 1949 with protest demonstrations; petitions to SCAP, the Diet, and the Soviet Mission; pamphlets distributed to the general public; and letters to newspapers; all urging return of the remaining 400,000 Japanese. SCAP's Diplomatic Section dispatched a letter on 25 April 1949 to Soviet Mission officials requesting data concerning death, status, and total number of Japanese POWs retained in the USSR. This request went unanswered, but startling news soon arrived from Moscow. A *Tass* press release of 20 May 1949 announced that "the remaining 95,000 Japanese POWs will be repatriated by November of 1949."[20] The Soviet statement, using the 12 September 1945 *Pravda* statistics as a base, also provided an accounting which made the amazing assertion that there had been no post-war deaths of Japanese in Soviet custody. These data showed:

Total prisoners taken in 1945		594,000
Less:		
Freed on the spot in 1945	70,880	
Repatriated from 1 December 1946 to 1 May 1949	418,166	
To be repatriated in 1949	95,000	
Serving war criminal sentences	9,954	
Total		594,000
Dead, Missing, or Unaccounted for (by deduction)		0

SCAP and Japanese Welfare Ministry claims that 300,000 Japanese remained to be accounted for by the USSR were based on military and colonial government records and reports from returnees. Similar statistics for non-Soviet areas had been proven accurate by matching the number of actual returnees to estimates, but the Soviets would not even discuss the disparity. A SCAP spokesman said the *Tass* press agency release "appears to be a hard-boiled way of breaking the bad news to Japan that Russia through mistreatment or neglect has killed off about 20 percent of the prisoners."[21]

However, there were serious problems with Moscow's accounting for Japanese in Soviet custody. First, the base number of 594,000 was understated. There were approximately 850,000 members of Japan's armed forces in areas conquered by the Soviet Army in August 1945. Furthermore, the *Tass* announcement provided no explanation for the nearly two million Japanese civilians in Northeast Asia at the end of the war, thousands of whom had died in 1945 and 1946. Second, there were no Japanese troops "freed on the spot" at the end of hostilities. It is true that a large number of soldiers escaped, but the Soviet Army replaced many of them with civilians in the contingents carried off to the USSR.

Third, the number shown as repatriated between December 1946 and May 1949 is overstated by 42,759 when compared to SCAP and Japanese government records, and finally, the grim reports carried back to Japan by survivors detailing the thousands of deaths in MVD labor camps lend further evidence to the inaccuracy of the Soviet statement.

In any event, the claim that only 95,000 POWs remained in the USSR resulted in a flood of letters to the Soviet Mission and SCAP seeking an explanation for the missing 300,000 Japanese internees. However, Soviet representatives steadfastly refused to provide any information. In response to queries of a Japanese delegation, V. A. Glinkin, deputy political advisor to General Derevyanko, stated: "We are not responsible for the statistics of SCAP or the Japanese Government."[22] Representatives of Japanese repatriation organizations persisted in their demands for information from Soviet authorities, and a Mission spokesman announced that his government soon would publish the names of Japanese who had died in the USSR. This promise proved to be an empty one—the Soviets provided no list of the dead or missing—and agitation resumed in the fall. The Second Secretary of the Soviet Mission, in response to demands of representatives of the National Federation of Repatriation Organizations in November 1949 said: "I regret that the Japanese do not believe the repatriation figures announced by the Soviet authorities in May."[23] Protest demonstrations at the Soviet Mission accelerated on 22 December 1949 when 400 Japanese staged a sitdown strike in front of closed gates guarded by Soviet soldiers. They left after two days when a Mission representative told them to come back on 28 December. Diet and repatriation organization officials returned on the appointed date, but only received promises that a conclusive statement regarding POWs would be issued by 15 January 1950. It would be "bright information," a Mission official said.

The issue of the missing Soviet-held POWs and civilians was the top story in most Japanese newspapers in December 1949. Emotion was running high, especially among families with relatives still missing. However, there were problems with SCAP and Japanese statistics, too. Although officials insisted that more than 300,000 Japanese were unaccounted for, other sources gave widely varying estimates. The "Society of Waiting Families for the Promotion of Speedy Repatriation" claimed that 500,000 POWs still were in the USSR. *Asahi* commented editorially that deaths may have been far more numerous than estimated—this conjecture turned out to be correct, especially in relation to civilians in Manchuria and North Korea—and speculated that many POWs could be in China instead of the Soviet Union. *Akahata*, the JCP newspaper, published an article designed to discredit the claim that 300,000 POWs remained to be accounted for. The newspaper reported that 8,000 soldiers were killed in August 1945 when their ship was torpedoed by a U.S. Navy ship off the Korea coast. These soldiers, *Akahata* said, were not listed as dead in Repatriation Relief Agency records. Adding to the confusion, recently returned repatriates had their own estimates of the number of Japanese remaining in the Soviet Union. Endō Masao, a former soldier repatriated in the last shipment of 1948, estimated the number of Soviet-held POWs at the end of 1948 to be between 150,000 and 200,000. He based his estimates on statistical data that he and other POWs had developed while still in the USSR, and further explained:

> A large number of people died during the first winter and from my experience I presume that most of them have not been reported. The battalion to which I belonged, for example, shrank from 1,100 to some 400 in the period from November 1945, when it was organized, to the end of February, next year. Due to the absence of regular name lists, the 700 dead became mostly obscure.[24]

A November 1949 repatriate said there were only 20,000 Japanese still in the POW camps but that "there are an additional great number not admitted into internment camps who will never be repatriated."[25]

WALKOUT AT THE ALLIED COUNCIL

Repatriation of the 95,000 POWs was completed in December 1949, and the Soviet government said the only Japanese remaining in the USSR were those serving criminal sentences: 9,945 of them. After this revelation, General MacArthur directed Chairman Sebald to reopen the repatriation issue at the next meeting of the Allied Council for Japan. From the Japanese side, Prime Minister Yoshida called on Sebald to request that strong protests be made to the USSR representative. Yoshida also appealed to "world public opinion in the name of justice and humanity" to resolve the issue, and both chambers of the Diet passed resolutions aimed at "mobilizing world public opinion."[26]

When the 102d meeting of the Allied Council for Japan opened on 21 December 1949, representatives of the four major allied powers were present. An urgent topic—repatriation of Japanese from the USSR—was on the agenda, placed there by the United States representative. However, General Derevyanko denounced the inclusion of this subject and reiterated his previous position that repatriation was not a proper matter for consideration by the council. There were several heated exchanges between council members, and the Soviet member angrily stormed out of the meeting when it became apparent that the issue was going to be discussed in spite of his objections. After Derevyanko's departure, Chairman Sebald presented data for the benefit of other council members and for the record—a detailed transcript later was sent to the Soviet Mission—and cited the unfulfilled agreement to repatriate 50,000 internees per month. Sebald went on to state that no accounting had been given for 316,617 Japanese. The chairman recalled that repeated efforts to obtain information had been unsuccessful; the Soviets had provided no details on the names of deceased prisoners. Sebald cited evidence of the miserable conditions faced by Japanese in Soviet camps. Aides brought in 4 bundles of petitions from Japanese citizens concerning the POWs, and Sebald said there were over 100 more.[27]

Sebald continued the discussion by pointing out that the Soviets had refused to provide any detailed information for more than four years and asserted:

> We can only guess at what may have happened behind the curtain of silence that has shut off these hapless Japanese from their homeland and people for the past four years. We can only surmise the motives of the Soviet Union in refusing to fulfill the pledge given in the Potsdam Declaration. We must resort to pure speculation and conjecture to find any explanation for the Soviet desire to hold the Japanese POWs.
>
> Can it be that Soviet authorities did not know how many of these unfortunate Japanese were in their hands, or where they were located, or what was happening to them? Does the Government of the Soviet Union wish us to believe that it maintained no records in its prison camps, no rosters of internees, no lists, no records of deaths?[28]

Chairman Sebald concluded his remarks with a statement that it was urgently required that Soviet authorities explain what had happened; SCAP, the Japanese government, the Japanese people, and the entire civilized world, he emphasized, wanted to know.

The British Commonwealth member of the Allied Council also had some comments on the repatriation issue. Colonel W. R. Hodgson, an Australian, called the failure to provide information "a callous indifference on the part of the Soviet government to the fate of these POWs." Hodgson pointed out that the Soviet Union, only a few days earlier, had signed the new Geneva Convention concerning treatment of POWs. The agreement required that detaining powers provide specific information on individual POWs, data that the Soviets had neglected to furnish over the last four years. The British Commonwealth member went on to assert that the failure to provide information was also a violation of the Declaration of Human Rights, subscribed to in 1948 by the Soviet government. Hodgson proposed that a third country, such as Switzerland, be designated as a protecting power for repatriation of Japanese from the USSR. Pursuing the matter further, Colonel Hodgson recommended that the council reinforce Sebald's April 1949 letter to the Soviet member (requesting detailed information on POWs) by endorsing its contents and calling for a prompt response.

MacArthur approved Hodgson's proposal and forwarded a request to the U.S. State Department for implementation through diplomatic channels. On the day after Derevyanko's early departure from the Allied Council meeting, General MacArthur issued a statement commenting on the Soviet member's reluctance to "listen to so gruesome and savage a story in all its harrowing barbarity. It could well chill and even sicken a hardened soldier."[29]

BLEAK OUTLOOK

As 1949 drew to a close, the mystery of the missing POWs and civilians was one of the major public issues in Japan. A song of the repatriates, *Ikoku-no-Oka*

(Hills of a Foreign Land), was popularized by a former soldier, Yoshida Tadashi, on the Radio Amateur Hour. Shin Tōhō Studios produced a full-length feature film, narrated by Yoshida, to portray conditions experienced by Japanese prisoners in the USSR. Emperor Hirohito, in his traditional rendering of short poems or *haiku*, at the beginning of 1950, took notice of the plight of missing internees. One poem spoke of the anguish felt by many Japanese:

> With the nation I wait, my heart in pain
> For those for whom we wait in vain!

A companion verse expressed a concern collectively shared throughout the nation:

> Let's welcome home those who have returned
> After suffering so long on alien soil.[30]

Members of the Allied Council for Japan held 62 additional meetings before the end of the Occupation in April 1952. At every one of those meetings, the Soviet representative either walked out, refused to attend, or refused to discuss repatriation. His comment at the first meeting in January 1950 reiterated the Soviet position:

> I want to endorse my statement concerning the problem of Japanese repatriation made at the meeting of the Council on December 21st. I regard the placing of this subject on the agenda of the Allied Council as unlawful and I state that the Soviet Union will not take into consideration any recommendations whatever on this question.[31]

The *curtain of silence* continued, but Secretary of State Dean Acheson, acting on MacArthur's request, sent a letter to Moscow's ambassador to the United States, Alexander S. Panyushkin, urging the Soviet government to agree to the "designation of an international humanitarian body which would be charged with making a complete survey of the situation with a view to obtaining exact information on Japanese POWs." The Australian government also presented a note to the Soviet ambassador to Canberra making the same proposal, but Moscow provided no reply to either request.

In spite of the statement made the preceding month that repatriation had been completed, the Soviets announced in January 1950 that "repatriation of Japanese from the Soviet Union will be continued." Soviet Mission officials in Tokyo, however, refused to comment concerning charges against war criminals, deaths, or names of those still in the USSR. Though not linking the repatriation news to the earlier promise of "bright information," the Soviets said that 2,500 Japanese would be repatriated in January. Coming so soon after the December announcement that repatriation had been completed, a flurry of commentaries in the Japanese press questioned the veracity of Soviet statements. One editorial also pointed out that the USSR had in past years claimed "climatic and icing conditions'' prevented vessel movements in midwinter, but that January 1950 was somehow an exception and that the port of Nakhodka was open.[32] By 1950, however, the Soviets had their numbers straight. Moscow's statement concerning resumption of repatriation was related only to Japanese in the "war criminal" category—2,500 of them were to be released early—and was not a revelation that new hordes of forgotten POWs were about to be released.

Meanwhile, representatives of the Western Allies in Europe also were having repatriation problems with Moscow. There were large numbers of Soviet-held German POWs and civilians for whom no accounting had been given. American authorities charged in early 1950 that 400,000 Germans still were in the USSR, but Kremlin officials insisted that only a few thousand war criminals were held by the Soviet Union. Questioning the reliability of Moscow's statistics, an American official noted that as of the end of 1949 the Soviets had returned 1,131,328 Germans from captivity, "over 200,000 more than Molotov had originally admitted were held as prisoners."[33]

About 4,700 Japanese returned from the USSR in the first two months of 1950. Some of the returnees claimed there were only 4,400 to 5,100 Japanese still held by the Soviets, but others thought there were more. Protest meetings and attempts to see the Soviet Mission chief continued. A Soviet spokesman told a group representing 20 prefectural organizations: "I cannot make any statement about the repatriation problem at this time, but a statement on the problem will be issued in the near future."[34] When a delegation from Yamanashi Prefecture visited the Mission in March to ask for prompt repatriation of the remaining POWs, Soviet officials told them no reply could be given unless a petition was made in writing. Then, more internees came home in April. Approximately 2,800 Japanese citizens, including some generals and high-ranking staff officers, returned. A total of 7,500 former prisoners returned to Japan in the first four months of 1950. Most of them had been serving lengthy prison sentences, but were released early. *Pravda* announced on 22 April 1950 that all Japanese POWs had been returned except for 2,458 still held as war criminals and 9 who were ill. This disclosure elicited more editorial comment and the furor continued.

The Soviets stood by their statistics, but Japanese government officials insisted more than 300,000 civilians and soldiers remained to be accounted for. This number was substantiated by extensive surveys of families who had missing sons or husbands known to have been in areas captured by the Red Army in August 1945. It is an interesting point that Soviet officials never confirmed or denied statistics presented by the Japanese government and SCAP; their only response was to indicate the number of Japanese remaining to be repatriated. It was indeed a *curtain of silence*. Nevertheless, repatriation organizations continued to be highly active in their demands for information on the missing 300,000 and three representatives of the Council on Expedition of Repatriation of Overseas Compatriots were given an unprecedented interview in May 1950 with General MacArthur, who told them:

> The matter giving me the most serious concern since coming to Japan is the repatriation of the POWs. . . . It is regrettable that Communist China and the USSR have been very uncooperative.
>
> I am making efforts for the repatriation as seriously as I would for getting my own men back. I wish you would convey to the families of POWs throughout the country that not only GHQ, but all Americans will continue efforts with deep sympathy for them.[35]

THE UNITED NATIONS INVESTIGATION

More than five years after the conclusion of World War II, the governments of Germany, Italy, Japan, and several other nations alleged that the Soviet Union still held large numbers of their citizens. In October 1950, the United States, Britain, and Australia requested the United Nations General Assembly to appoint an investigative committee to determine the status and number of German, Italian, Japanese, and other POWs held by the Soviet Union. Shortly thereafter, on 14 December 1950, the international body passed a resolution demanding the return of war prisoners held in the USSR. Early in 1951, UN Secretary-General Trygve Lie established an ad hoc Commission on POW Inquiry and appointed representatives of El Salvador, Sweden, and Burma, to investigate the missing POWs. The objectives of the commission, as stated in its charter, were: 1) the repatriation of every prisoner of war who is entitled to repatriation; 2) the accounting for by name, whereabouts, and condition of every prisoner of war who is still detained; and, 3) the utilization of all resources for conducting search for the missing persons in order to establish the fate or whereabouts of those unknown.

The first meeting of the commission was held at the United Nations headquarters in New York in the summer of 1951, and the commission held six additional sessions in Geneva from 1952 to 1957. Eleven nations, those considered most closely concerned with the war prisoner problem, were invited to send representatives to all sessions—Australia, Belgium, France, the Federal Republic of Germany, Italy, Japan, Luxembourg, the Netherlands, the Soviet Union, the United States, and the United Kingdom—but a major impediment to resolution of the problem was the fact that the Soviets never sent a representative to any of the Geneva meetings. Conversely, Japanese Foreign Ministry officials journeyed several times to New York and Geneva to present data on missing POWs. After its third session in September 1952, the commission issued a special report stating that "the lack of cooperation from the Soviet Union, as the principal nation involved in the problem, is paralyzing the work of the Commission which has no means of verifying the information furnished to it by other governments."[36] A year later, the commission reported:

> the Soviet Union has refused invitations to the commission's last three sessions, has rebuffed the group's efforts to obtain the names of prisoners still held in custody or data on war criminals serving jail sentences and has even refused to supply lists of prisoners who died.[37]

After Stalin's death in March 1953, the Soviet government gradually adopted a more conciliatory attitude. In November, representatives of the Alliance of Red Cross and Red Crescent Societies of the Soviet Union advised their Japanese counterparts "that the number of missing and dead Japanese in the Soviet Union is 10,267, and that it is difficult to make name-lists of them."[38] It was the first Soviet acknowledgement of post-war Japanese deaths in USSR-controlled areas.

Although Moscow had provided only scant information on Japanese deaths in the USSR, and no names whatsoever, the Japanese Welfare Ministry by 1954 painstakingly pieced together a list of 253,000 Japanese known to be dead and 16,000 presumed to be dead. These names were obtained through extensive interviews with repatriates and from information provided by families. Japanese Foreign Ministry representatives, led by former Foreign Minister Arita Hachirō, told the UN Commission at its sixth meeting in September 1954 that more than 46,000 Japanese were known to be alive, not only in the USSR but also in other "Communist areas." The data showed 12,000 in the USSR, 2,000 in North Korea, and 32,000 in China, but the reaction of the Soviet government was identical to its position taken in the earlier meetings of the Allied Council for Japan—a *curtain of silence*—and Yakov A. Malik, the Soviet delegate to the UN, declared that the POW Commission was illegal.[39]

Nevertheless, repatriation continued in the 1950s in spite of Moscow's resistance to the UN investigation. From March 1953 to the end of 1955, the Soviet Union returned 1,362 prisoners to Japan. During that same period, the People's Republic of China repatriated 27,904 Japanese civilians and former soldiers, some of whom had been held on war criminal charges.[40] Repatriate organizations continued to press for return of their compatriots. More than 12,000 demonstrated in November 1953 at a huge Tokyo rally; and the Movement to Rescue Japanese Held Overseas, headed by House Speaker Masutani Shuji, held a mass meeting at Hibiya Park in May 1955. By late 1955, the Soviet Union and Japan were attempting to negotiate a peace treaty (the USSR was not a party to the 1951 San Francisco treaty), but the POW issue was a stumbling block. Japan wanted to make an "on-the-spot" investigation of missing war prisoners. The Soviets refused. Talks continued throughout 1956, but agreement on a peace treaty was never reached because of a dispute over the Northern Territories, four islands to the northeast of Hokkaido claimed by Japan.

Since World War II, Moscow steadfastly has maintained that these islands—Shikotan, Kunashiri, Etorofu, and the Habomai group—are part of the Kuriles and that title was transferred to the Soviet Union by terms of the Yalta Agreement. For the Soviets, there is no territorial problem; the matter was resolved in 1945. Tokyo initially based its claim on the theory that the islands, instead of being an integral part of the Kurile chain, where geologically and historically a part of Japan. In 1987, however, officials of the ruling Liberal Democratic Party maintained that:

> although the Japan-Soviet Neutrality Pact was still in effect, the Soviet Union unilaterally declared war on Japan and three days after the termination of the war,

on August 18, 1945, invaded the Northern Territories. On September 3, the Northern Territories came under the military occupation of the Soviet Union.[41]

Abe Shintarō, Liberal Democratic Party (LDP) Secretary-General, asserted: "There cannot be any true friendship between Japan and the Soviet Union as long as the latter continues to take the attitude that the territorial problem is already resolved."[42] The four islands claimed by Japan contain 4,213 square miles of land, about 65 percent of the total area of the Kurile Islands. By comparison, the Ryūkyū Islands (which include Okinawa), occupied by the United States from 1945 to 1972, cover 1,850 square miles.[43]

Notwithstanding their irresolvable differences on the territorial issue, Japan and the USSR reached agreement in December 1956 for the resumption of diplomatic and trade relations. Concurrently, Soviet officials commuted the sentences of all remaining war criminals, and 1,025 former prisoners returned to Japan on 26 December 1956. Moscow said it no longer held any Japanese prisoners, but Tokyo contended that more than 10,000 still were in the USSR.

After six years of work, the UN Commission on POW Inquiry had made some progress, but commission members complained that the Soviet government had not cooperated. The commission, at its seventh and final meeting in September 1957, said it had the names of 9,961 Japanese citizens "believed still to be in the USSR and 35,767 on the mainland of China." A few thousand more Japanese, mostly civilians, returned from the USSR and China during the last three years of the decade. In the late 1950s, a more cooperative Soviet government provided, for the first time, names of Japanese dead. Even so, these lists of 2,776 dead represented only 1 percent of Japanese deaths in areas under Soviet control. At the end of 1959, the Japanese Foreign Ministry claimed that 5,448 POWs still were missing in the USSR.[44] The issue faded away from active concern in the 1960s, but it still is an important part of what is sometimes referred to in Japan as the "grudge" against the Soviet Union.

6
Return to Japan

The long-awaited moment for repatriates came when Soviet political officers and Japanese *aktivs* approved their departure from "intermediate screening camps." Internees boarded trains bound for the repatriation port of Nakhodka, but there was no relief from the ubiquitous indoctrination program. Members of the Anti-Fascist Democratic Committee (AFDC)—Japanese activists—accompanied repatriates to the port and were in charge of trains. Rail cars were decorated with pictures of Stalin, Lenin, and Tokuda Kyūichi, the Japan Communist Party leader, to "help maintain the democratic spirit." Classes and discussions on Soviet-style socialism continued throughout the trip.

As the trains pulled into Nakhodka, a port city 70 miles east of Vladivostok, excitement grew when POWs caught sight of ships in the harbor. They were on their way home, but there were to be more delays before departure for Japan. Repatriates received intensive instruction at Nakhodka, and AFDC members conducted more "screening." Many former soldiers were plucked from their group only a day or two before scheduled departure because of some deficiency in their knowledge of, or lack of enthusiasm for, Marxist-Leninist principles. Repatriates spent at least two weeks in Nakhodka, but many stayed for longer periods—several months for some—and up to a year for internees who refused to parrot the Soviet line. Rumors spread that the United States and Japan were not living up to their commitments, thereby delaying repatriation. When ships left with empty passenger space, Soviet officials said that shortages of food on board "accounted for this depressing situation." SCAP statements that ships were stocked with 10 percent more food than would normally be required were not conveyed to the waiting POWs.[1]

The Soviet indoctrination program at Nakhodka was designed to stir prisoners into fervent enthusiasm for Communism and infuse them with passion that would be carried back to Japan to strengthen the JCP. Soviet political officers led rallies, and Japanese *aktivs* gave strident speeches against "the Americanization of the Japanese race." Repatriates rehearsed pro-Soviet and pro-JCP slogans and songs until they could repeat them without conscious effort. Candidates for return to Japan went through four stages of processing at Nakhodka, as related by Yamamoto Noboru, a physician and former Kwantung Army member, in his account of the "battles of political education" he experienced in October 1949: 1) First stage—Initial processing point (12 days)—for investigation to identify reactionaries and testing to determine knowledge of Communism; 2) Second stage—Intermediate point (short stay)—for instruction on the overall picture of the Soviet way of life and JCP policy concerning each individual soldier's home prefecture; 3) Third stage—Final processing point (2 days)—for rehearsal of slogans and songs and understanding of the plan for revolution in Japan; and, 4) Fourth stage—Remedial section (variable time period)—for repatriates who failed to meet standards imposed at any stage.[2]

Throughout the prerepatriation processing, *aktivs* drilled prospective returnees on behavior they were expected to display upon arrival in Japan. These points were emphasized:

1. Oppose ideological interrogation by U.S. or Japanese authorities.
2. Demand housing and employment.
3. Seek guarantees of freedom for "democratic" groups to receive and greet repatriates in train stations and other public places.
4. Demand freedom of speech and political activity, to include singing and dancing.[3]

After satisfactory completion of all processing steps, POWs were ready for return to Japan. Soviet officials formed repatriates into groups of about 2,000 and assigned Japanese *aktivs* to leadership positions for return voyages. Most POWs, immersed in the indoctrination and passionate fervor for Marxist-Leninist ideals, performed as expected upon arrival in Japan, but some cast aside their pretense at cooperation in short order. Soon after return to Japan, Takebayashi Takeo of Kyoto summed up his experiences:

> I too was driven hard at Nakhodka. I was repeatedly given intensive indoctrination and learned the "Song of the Red Flag." Truly life in Nakhodka is a living hell. The leaders of the democratic movement were most disgusting. If that is communism, to hell with communism.[4]

VOYAGE ACROSS THE SEA OF JAPAN

Japanese ships were a familiar sight in the Soviet Far East port of Nakhodka from 1947 to 1950. Altogether, more than 200 voyages were made across the Sea of Japan to pick up repatriates and transport them to Maizuru, a small port in western Japan about 600 miles to the south of Nakhodka. Ships with names such as Takasago Maru, Shimano Maru, Meiyu Maru, and Eitoku Maru made frequent round trips between the Soviet and Japanese ports whenever the USSR Mission in Tokyo notified SCAP of shipping requirements to transport repatriates on a given date. The usual crossing time was two days. The first POW-repatriates, transported to Japan in 1947, were mostly older or physically incapacitated ex-soldiers who were quiet and politically conservative. By 1948, ships' crews began to notice a marked difference in attitudes of returning Japanese; many were hostile and openly "pro-Communist." The 1949 repatriates showed the effects of thorough indoctrination, and some even attempted to commandeer repatriation vessels. Also, anti-Soviet POWs, after suffering in silence for four years, took vengeance on the *aktivs*, often within less than an hour after departure.

Passengers on many of the 1949 trips were unruly, and the ships' crews frequently faced hazardous situations. Shipowners charged repatriates after one voyage with "intimidation, obstruction of performance of official duties and robbery." Activists on that trip had conducted a People's Court on the high seas and tried ship officers for "undemocratic behavior." Returning POWs on another trip demonstrated against poor treatment and bad food, but subsequent investigation revealed no basis for complaints. Highly indoctrinated repatriates on an August 1949 voyage accused three former Japanese Army officers of being traitors because they refused to participate in political meetings. Activists wanted to hang one of the three as a "first class war criminal" but were stopped by the ship's captain and crew. Although ship regulations prohibited loud singing and chanting of slogans, many did so anyway. This activity led to an unusual problem, as noted in one report:

> Because of heat and dancing of the repatriates on 12 August 1949, a number of repatriates have stomach trouble from drinking too much water. One source said: "Apparently their dancing dislodged dirt and scales in the water tank." The repatriates demand that the ship's captain accept responsibility for their stomach trouble.[5]

Difficulties with repatriates on shipboard often were attributed to the "company commander" and his staff, highly indoctrinated *aktivs* who held a tight grip over most of the others. However, some anti-Communist NCOs and officers took revenge against activists, and a few passengers were lost at sea in the ensuing brawls. A repatriate's account reveals the turmoil on one voyage: "Fights broke out on the ship 20 minutes after departure. Anti-communists took the offensive and their number had suddenly grown larger. Suzuki and the communist contingents were beaten with fists and thrown down a flight of stairs to the deck below."[6] The Repatriation Committee of the Upper House made a special investigation of violence aboard another ship, the Hidehiko Maru. Witnesses claimed that beatings on board had resulted in three deaths and the disappearance of 13 former soldiers.[7]

TURMOIL AT MAIZURU

As each ship neared Maizuru in the summer of 1949, SCAP and Repatriation Relief Agency officials wondered how its passengers would behave: would they show appreciation and joy on their return to Japan after a forced stay in an alien land, or would the repatriates demonstrate wildly, sing praises of the socialist fraternity, and refuse to cooperate? Maizuru officials knew what to expect after the first few groups of former POWs returned: riotous behavior and much turmoil. To be sure, not every repatriate was eager for a public show of pro-Soviet and pro-JCP attitudes, but those who were held the upper hand over their more reluctant compatriots. The vociferous demonstrators caught the attention of the Japanese public and put the small town of Maizuru on the map. Located on Wakasa Bay about 40 miles northwest of Kyoto, Maizuru was known primarily as a wartime port for the Japanese Navy, but because it was the principal port for repatriation from the USSR, its fame surpassed that of the other nine repatriation centers in Japan. About 600,000 repatriates passed through Maizuru.

"We are entering enemy territory!" screamed passengers aboard the Takasago Maru as the ship approached Maizuru in June 1949. Then, lining the ship's deck, the ex-POWs robustly sang the *Internationale* and the *Communist Youth Song*. Chants replete with Marxist slogans filled the air, followed by more singing. One refrain expressed opposition to the Japanese government and called for abolition of the emperor system. These were the voices of young Japanese men, many of whom were only 17 or 18 when captured, who were the product of several years of intensive indoctrination. Although SCAP and Japanese government offiicials, along with the general public, expected some show of pro-Communist demonstrations, the fanaticism of the repatriates shocked the nation. The *Nippon Times* asked editorially: "Are these men or beasts the Soviets are sending back to Japan from their prison camps?"[8] Many repatriates ignored family members who had come to greet them and shouted, "We vowed to join the Communist Party on our return."

Repatriation Relief Agency officials required ex-POWs, before debarking, to fill out cards providing basic information, that is, name, age, former military unit, and place of internment. *Aktiv* leaders, however, ordered repatriates to withhold the requested data. Completion of the forms would be tantamount to "anti-democratic behavior," they said. SCAP officials insisted that cards be filled out prior to debarkation, and a standoff ensued when repatriates steadfastly refused to provide the required data. However, officials soon discovered a solution; they isolated *aktivs*—identified by ship officers—immediately upon arrival and herded them into a quarantined area in the port. Repatriates readily cooperated and filled out cards once their leaders were no longer present. This system worked well for other aspects of processing and became standard procedure for the remainder of 1949. *Aktivs* were permitted to rejoin their comrades only upon departure by train from Maizuru.

Processing at the Repatriation Center required four days and involved several steps: medical, customs, interrogation, demobilization, and orientation. Repatriates were innoculated, deloused, given a medical examination, and, if necessary, quarantined for communicable diseases. A customs search was made for contraband material, followed by an interview conducted by American intelligence officers to obtain information on the Soviet POW system. Demobilization activities entailed preparation of discharge papers, processing of ashes and personal effects of deceased POWs, questioning to determine the fate of missing personnel, and final settlement of pay status. Repatriates attended orientation lectures, and some former POWs were shown films depicting life in postwar Japan. These last two steps were intended to counter Soviet indoctrination.

Although activist repatriates made headlines with their singing and demonstrations, comments from other ex-POWs indicated happiness on return to Japan and promises of revenge against the Soviet Union. A former soldier exclaimed upon arrival at Maizuru: "The first step on the home shore awakens a thousand thoughts, but no love for the Soviet Union. How dare you make us work without letting us eat, you Russian crooks!"[9] An ultra-nationalist even had visions of a Japan on the march in Asia once again:

> There are trials and tribulations ahead of us, but don't worry; we are Japanese! Young men, cooperate toward the reconstruction of Japan with a resolute conviction. Comrades in arms who have died in Siberia, do not grieve. Some day Siberia will be ours. Be patient and wait.[10]

Two groups of Japanese were waiting at Maizuru to greet ex-soldiers returning from the USSR: family members and JCP representatives. *Aktivs* wanted their compatriots' first contact to be with the JCP so that the Communist indoctrination of the past several years would remain uncontested. The activists feared that initial contact with wives, parents, and children would awaken nostalgic thoughts along with the traditional sense of responsibility concerning family obligations. Most family members wanted their husbands, sons, or brothers to return to conventional life within the family and community. These divergent objectives soon led to open conflict between the two groups, and the Japanese government found it necessary to implement an ordinance regulating behavior of greeters at Maizuru and at train stations. In spite of the turmoil at the port, repatriates were amazed at the cordial reception and the number of family members on hand to greet them. *Asahi* reported that ex-POWs were suprised when given *sake*, candy, and tobacco on arrival; their indoctrination had led them to believe Japan was destitute. One repatriate said that the many signs of recovery and availability of numerous commodities made him "realize that Japan still has the power of rehabilitation."[11]

LAST TRAIN HOME

After completion of processing at the reception center; repatriates boarded special trains at Maizuru Station bound for various parts of Japan. Once again, as *aktivs* rejoined other returnees, the tumultous sounds of chanting, shouting, and singing were heard, especially when trains approached larger cities. Repatriates staged loud demonstrations in busy sections of urban areas, causing consternation among police and railway officials. A June 1949 notification from the Secretariat of the JCP Central Committee to regional and local organizations specified immediate steps to welcome the returning soldiers:

1. Welcome returnees at every stop.
2. Wave red flags when train passes.
3. Mobilize labor unions and other associations.
4. Serve tea and other refreshments.
5. Distribute copies of *Akahata*.
6. Approach each repatriate and enlist him into the party if he so desires.
7. Take positive steps to help repatriates find jobs and housing facilities.
8. Arrange for continuing education of repatriates.[12]

Returning soldiers found JCP members waiting to greet them at train stations all along the route home. Party members told repatriates at Tokyo's Shinagawa Station: "You were detained in Siberia for a long time because the Japanese government did nothing to hasten your repatriation. We Communists are the ones who have enabled you to return to your homeland."[13] Party members also distributed handbills charging that the Japanese government was not doing enough for repatriates and that the JCP was struggling to establish a peaceful and democratic Japan. In another instance, about 50 returnees demonstrated in Sapporo Station against the Japanese government and the U.S. Occupation forces. Railway officials told demonstrators to board the train or forfeit their right to free transportation for the rest of the journey. The train left without them, and a dispute ensued for the next 24 hours over tickets to complete their trip on regular trains. Ultimately they were provided free transportation, but other trains bypassed Sapporo to avoid confrontation. Similar events occurred throughout Japan, but one was noteworthy.

Most repatriation trains went from Maizuru to nearby Kyoto before branching off to other parts of Japan. Kyoto, long a center of leftist political activity, was the site of a serious controntation in 1949 between repatriates and police. The demonstration started on a mid-July evening when nearly 100 repatriates left their train and joined leftist union members at a rally in front of Kyoto Station. Police attempted to stop the demonstration, but just then a second train carrying more than 700 repatriates arrived. When this group learned of the rally, they overwhelmed police and poured off the train. Police reinforcements arrived, but before order could be restored a third train with 900 repatriates pulled into Kyoto Station. They soon joined the demonstration, and turmoil followed. Repatriates and unionists engaged in riotous behavior throughout the night with much singing and shouting, along with pledges to overthrow the "imperialist" government. Injuries were numerous, and police arrested several repatriates. It was late the next day before police broke up the demonstration and persuaded the repatriates to resume their journey.[14]

The summer of 1949 saw an outcry of public resentment over the turmoil created by repatriates and the JCP. Newspapers covered the subject extensively, and demonstrators were denounced in editorials and letters to the news media. *Asahi* reported: "Forty-three repatriates alighted from the train amidst a burst of cheers by waiting families and the singing of the *Internationale* by Communists. Some repatriates burst into tears, while others tried to tear themselves away from their families, crying, 'Let me go with my comrades.' "[15] The lead editorial in a Tokyo daily summed up public reaction to the chaos generated by repatriates and the JCP:

> It is no wonder that an anguished mother welcoming her long-absent son should cry out, "What have they done with my son?" Perhaps the repatriates themselves should not be judged too severely for they are the products of Communist training. They are the ones so well indoctrinated that the Soviets allowed them to return. They are Communists.[16]

Public despair over these incidents led the Ministry of Justice to issue an ordinance in August 1949 "binding repatriates to return peacefully to their homes." The directive required repatriates to board designated trains, specified that only family members could accompany repatriates, and regulated welcoming ceremonies at stations. The ordinance cited the Potsdam Declaration requirement that former soldiers be returned to their homes and given a chance to lead peaceful lives. Repatriation was not complete, according to officials, until the ex-soldier was returned to his home. The directive required each repatriate to obey instructions issued by: 1) repatriation ship captains, 2) the chief of the Repatriation Relief Agency at Maizuru, and 3) a locally designated person in charge of the repatriation train. The order also specified that only the Japanese flag could be displayed at train stations.[17] The first arrests came soon when four JCP members at a station in northern Japan were accused of displaying red banners and singing the *Internationale*. Several JCP members were arrested at other train stations for distributing literature and Party application forms.

As repatriates continued to flow back to Japan throughout the remainder of 1949, confusion at Maizuru and the train stations gradually subsided. Enforcement of the cabinet order and intervention of family members were major factors in the decline of radical behavior. Troublesome activity disappeared by the end of 1949, and most repatriates faded into the towns and countryside of Japan.

ADJUSTMENT TO LIFE IN JAPAN

In the late 1940s, Japan was struggling to recover from the devastation of war. Industrial production was below the 1934–1936 average, foreign trade was only 30 percent of the prewar level, and real per capita income was lower than it had been in the 1930s. Rice was rationed, pay was low (the average monthly salary was 6,300 yen, or $17.50), and the standard of living was barely above subsistence level. It was under these unfavorable economic and social conditions that millions of civilian and military repatriates returned to Japan. The Diet approved funds for housing and employment assistance for civilians from Sakhalin and the Kuriles, and loans for other repatriates for business and education purposes, but repatriates had difficulty caring for themselves and their families in spite of this assistance. This was especially true in the case of early civilian returnees.

Some repatriates lived illegally on government lands and earned a livelihood by "lumbering and harvesting in public forests." *Akahata*, the JCP newspaper, reported the eviction of a 21-year-old repatriate from a culvert he had been using for a temporary shelter in Yokohama. He was unable to find housing or a job and said, "Japan should be changed to a country like the Soviet Union where people can work with pleasure."[18] A Radio Moscow broadcast alleged that repatriates were suffering "because the Japanese government and U.S. authorities have done nothing for the returning POWs. In fact, they do not wish to hasten the repatriation of Japanese POWs from the Soviet Union."[19] A Kyoto newspaper reported that 28 percent of the 1949 repatriates were still looking for work in November, but considering conditions at the time, perhaps the remarkable fact was that 72 percent of the returnees had found jobs. Some employers feared repatriates from Soviet areas might "introduce radical agitation," and major newspapers asked for more compassion. The *Yomiuri*, in a 29 July 1949 editorial, urged people to "open their hearts with tenderness and kindness" to the repatriates. *Asahi* asked more fortunate citizens to "transcend their personal hardships and extend a helping hand to repatriates."

Economic conditions improved in Japan after the Korean War began in June 1950, and unemployment decreased. Even before that, however, repatriates were encouraged by government and family efforts to assist them in reentering Japanese society. Ōfune Mikio of Osaka commented: "When I think of the warm treatment I am receiving here, I hate the anti-Japanese education which I received in Russia."[20] Another encouraging sign came from Chiba prefecture where an October 1949 study showed that the majority of repatriates were leading a "settled life." The survey of 808 repatriates revealed that 348 were employed in farming, fishing, or commercial business; 187 had been reinstated in former government and railway jobs; and 27 had found new jobs. Of the remaining 246 repatriates still out of work, 175 were looking for employment and 71 "ha[d] not pushed the search for work."[21] Reports from other areas of Japan indicated favorable employment opportunities for repatriates.

A matter of special interest to SCAP and government officials was the political orientation of the Soviet-held POWs after their return to Japan. The radical behavior of the 1949 repatriates generated fears that a militant Red Army, with the former soldiers as a nucleus, would attempt to overthrow the government and the emperor. These concerns, however, proved to be unfounded. On the other hand, some repatriates joined the JCP and were active members, especially in the first few months after returning. *Akahata* enthusiastically acclaimed new members in the summer and fall of 1949: "six returnees join JCP in Toyama," "ex-lieutenant, son of General Itagaki, joined the JCP," and "two repatriates join Kochi Branch of the JCP and seven join in Oita-ken." However, a survey conducted in late 1949 showed a decrease in repatriate participation in the JCP. *Kyōdō* news agency reported that even though 60 percent of the former POWs had favored Communism upon arrival in Japan, support had decreased to 40 percent by October.[22] Support dropped even more significantly by the end of the year, according to an Osaka newspaper, with only 10 percent of the 1949 repatriates still engaged in Communist activities.

One of the leaders of the Kyoto Station incident broke off completely with the JCP three months after returning home. He said "communism cannot relieve us" and hoped his bitter experiences would open the eyes of other repatriates. Technicians who had been held in Dairen denounced Communism on their return in 1949. "Communism could never be the salvation of Japan," said one of the civilians. A 26 August 1950 *Shūkan Yomiuri* article described ex-POW attitudes on the first anniversary of their return from the USSR and found that most repatriates had become disillusioned with Communism. One ex-soldier blasted the deviousness of the Soviet system: "Communism might be a good doctrine, but even in the Soviet Union you find bribery and blackmarketing. I consider that 80 percent of my four years in the Soviet Union was spent in hypocrisy."

Most repatriates lost their enthusiasm for Marxist-Leninist principles once they had been reintegrated into Japanese society. In the USSR, POWs saw acceptance of Communist indoctrination as beneficial in the MVD camp milieu and as a prerequisite for repatriation. Although most POWs were under the influence of intensive indoctrination when they first returned, repatriates soon found Communist ideology no longer relevant and dismissed it from their environment. However, some did not change.

LINGERING SHADOWS OF STALIN'S CAMPS

Within a year of their return, most repatriates had readjusted to life in Japan without major difficulty, but there were psychological and medical problems for some returnees. Illnesses contracted while in Soviet custody, especially tuberculosis, led to early deaths for some civilians and former soldiers. Others were to be tormented by long-term stress and psychiatric problems for many years after return to Japan.

Kan Sueharu experienced emotional difficulties which led to his suicide. Kan, an *aktiv* leader at a Karaganda POW camp, was summoned to testify at a 1950 Diet committee investigation of charges that JCP Secretary-General Tokuda had played a role in establishing criteria for repatriation of POWs. Tokuda allegedly had written to Soviet authorities requesting that "reactionary" POWs be retained in Siberia and that repatriation be limited to those who had become "truly democratic." This investigation opened old wounds among repatriates called to testify. Tokuda denied the charges, but former POWs testified they had been told of his request by MVD officials. Diet members charged during the hearings that "Communists called on families of repatriates who had testified or intended to testify before the Upper House committee and threatened them with dire consequences for their 'anti-democratic' attitudes."[23] Kan was under intense pressure since he was a key witness. Other repatriates charged that Kan had been instrumental in securing arrests of fellow soldiers on war-criminal charges at the Karaganda camp, and some of these convicted POWs—in early April 1950—were on their way home from Nakhodka even as the committee hearings were proceeding. Succumbing to anxiety, Kan jumped in front of a commuter train on 6 April 1950 at Kichijoji Station in Tokyo's western suburbs. Aramaki Yasuhiko, formerly of the Karaganda *lager*, explained that Kan probably ended his life because of fear of revenge from POWs coming home on the next ship.[24] Diet committee members concluded that charges against Tokuda were true, but the JCP leader disappeared from sight before any legal action could be taken against him.[25]

One of the more bizarre atrocities committed by a POW upon his fellow countrymen, in the *Akatsuki ni Inoru* (Prayer at Dawn) incident, involved a mysterious Corporal Yoshimura. This shrewd, former Kwantung Army NCO ingratiated himself with labor camp officials in Outer Mongolia by establishing work production goals for his unit that were far in excess of what was required. He ruled with an iron hand, severely punishing his men for failure to meet work objectives. Food rations were withheld; worse yet, Yoshimura and his associates tied weak POWs to utility poles, in sub-zero weather, with their hands bound behind them. By morning, the emaciated prisoners would be found frozen to death, heads bowed, as if praying. Yoshimura, repatriated in November 1947, quickly dropped out of sight in fear of retaliation, but public anger over the "Prayer at Dawn" case led to extensive investigation. Newspaper reporters later found Yoshimura on remote Fukae Shima, an island 70 miles west of Nagasaki, and learned that his real name was Ikeda Shigeyoshi.[26] At last, the perpetrator of the "Prayer at Dawn" torture was arrested and brought to trial. The Tokyo District Court found Ikeda guilty in July 1950 and sentenced him to imprisonment for five years, but appeals to higher courts prolonged the case to May 1958 when the Supreme Court of Japan upheld the charges.

By the early 1950s, public concern over the repatriates' leftist ideology began to subside, but rumors persisted that some repatriates had agreed to spy on behalf of the Soviets. Akabane Fumiko, a civilian internee, described MVD attempts to recruit her as a spy. A bemedaled MVD lieutenant colonel interrogated her at a special intelligence camp and asked: "Would you like to be a spy for the Soviet Union?" She refused, explaining that she was in poor health. After additional fruitless attempts to gain Akabane's cooperation, including promises of a good salary, Soviet officers gave up but warned her to keep quiet about the matter. "We'll immediately put you in the Krasnoyarsk prison if you speak about us," the MVD official told her.[27] However, a repatriates' association, linked with the JCP, scoffed at allegations of Soviet attempts to recruit spies:

> These rumors are absolutely false. There are some repatriates who say, "I once was requested to perform a special mission for the Soviets, but I refused. I'm only saying this because I am in Japan now." These repatriates are people with less awareness, false democrats and intentional reactionary elements.[28]

By 1953, however, indications of Soviet spy activity in Japan were detected by government officials. The Maritime Safety Board intercepted a Soviet trawler attempting to rendezvous with a Japanese civilian on a remote Hokkaido beach. National Police officers reported that the Soviet spy ship *Lazezdnov* was attempting to provide Seki Sanjiro, a former Sakhalin resident, with a new set of codes for radio transmissions.[29] The big break in obtaining information on Moscow's intelligence operations in Japan came in January 1954 when Yuri A. Rastvorov, an MVD lieutenant colonel assigned to the Soviet Mission in Tokyo, defected to the United States. Rastvorov, fluent in Japanese, earlier had been an aide to former MVD chief Lavrenti Beria. After Beria's execution in December 1953, the Kremlin issued orders for Rastvorov to return to Moscow. Fearing a fate similar to that of his old chief, Rastvorov quickly sought protection at the American Embassy in Tokyo and asked for asylum in the United States.[30]

Later, in testimony before the U.S. Senate Judiciary Committee, Rastvorov revealed that he had been active in the MVD program for planting former Japanese prisoners as spies in Japan:

> In 1948, I participated, myself, in the recruitment of POWs in the Far East area, especially Khabarovsk. The MVD Intelligence Service recruited approximately 400 Japanese POWs to use as agents after their return to Japan. Some of these agents were used after their return to Japan. Some of them were put on ice temporarily.[31]

Rastvorov provided names to both Japanese and American officials, and Japanese police discovered that some of the repatriate-spies were employed in sensitive positions with government agencies or U.S. Security Forces. Shii Shoji, a former Kwantung Army major repatriated in November 1948, was employed by U.S. military intelligence until February 1954, when Rastvorov identified him as one of the spies. Others worked as news correspondents while some were involved in illegal transactions with U.S. dollars and Military Payment Certificates "in order to disrupt the Japanese economy." Japanese officials indicted some of the agents in government positions, but courts dispensed light sentences—usually suspended—while no legal action was taken against others. Nonetheless, identities were revealed, thereby seriously undermining the Kremlin's espionage program in Japan.

Soviet spy activity continued to vex Tokyo officials in the following decades.

Although there is no evidence that Rastvorov recruited them, in May 1987 two graduates of the former military academy, Date Hiromi and Gotō Sadao, aged 62 and 60 respectively, were arrested on charges of stealing military information from an American Air Force base and selling it to a Soviet intelligence agency and a Chinese source. *Sankei*, a Tokyo daily, commented editorially that the espionage appeared to have been conducted for "love of money" rather than for ideological conviction.[32] Date received more than 100 million yen from the Soviets over a period of several years in return for his information, according to Japanese investigators. Public security sources in Japan indicated a possible connection with Lieutenant General Miyanaga Yukihisa of the Self-Defense Force, who was arrested in a spy case in 1980.[33]

In spite of these lingering shadows of Stalin's camps, however, there appear to have been no major liabilities for Japan as a nation resulting from Soviet detention of Japanese civilians and soldiers. The 1949 fears that large numbers of repatriates would create havoc with their militant radicalism proved to be unwarranted. Most of the former prisoners rejected Communism within six months of their return and quickly passed into the mainstream of Japanese life.

FATE OF THE ELITE

The MVD still held 9,945 Japanese on war criminal charges at the end of 1949, but, perhaps in response to persistent international protests and demands of the Japanese public, the Soviets returned 7,500 former soldiers and civilians to Japan in the first four months of 1950. The remaining internees were destined to spend more time in the Soviet Union, for some an additional six years. For a few, there would be no return. Death was to precede their turn for repatriation. The fate of 7 prisoners of the Soviets is particularly noteworthy.

One of the best-known POWs held by the Soviets was Konoe Fumitaka, son of Prince Konoe Fumimaro, Japan's prime minister in 1937–1938 and 1940–1941. The younger Konoe, educated in the United States at Princeton University, was drafted into the Japanese Army as a private in 1940. He worked his way up through the ranks and was a first lieutenant of artillery at the time of his capture at Mutanchiang (Botankō), Manchuria, in August 1945. Perhaps because of his aristocratic background, the Soviets singled out Konoe for special treatment. MVD officers made repeated attempts to recruit him as an agent for Soviet intelligence in Japan, but Konoe steadfastly refused. Yuri Rastvorov, in testimony before the U.S. Senate Judiciary Committee, explained:

> the Soviet Government refused to free the son of Prince Konoe and decided to keep him in the Soviet Union in order to avoid revelation of all that had happened to him in connection with attempts to recruit him. The Soviets realized what the reaction of the Japanese people and people of the free world would be if the son of Prince Konoe revealed his experiences so he was sentenced as a war criminal

and, I assume, reduced to living conditions which would shorten his life, following the principle that "dead men tell no tales."[34]

Konoe was tried by a military tribunal in 1952 and received a 25-year sentence for "aiding the international bourgeoisie." After imprisonment in Moscow, Taishet, and Ivanovo, he died in the Soviet Union at the age of 41 on 20 October 1956 of a kidney ailment, just two months before he would have been repatriated. A December 1956 repatriate reported that Konoe had been held for several years in solitary confinement in a cramped cell which "may have gradually impaired his health." Konoe's ashes accompanied the last group of repatriates on the Kōan Maru, arriving at Maizuru on 26 December 1956. A former Kwantung Army officer also brought back (hidden in his shoe soles) locks of Konoe's hair and letters to his wife, Masako, which Konoe had written before his death but had not been permitted to mail.[35]

Kwantung Army commander-in-chief, General Yamada Otozō, after conviction at Khabarovsk in December 1949, was detained for six years at Ivanovo, about 180 miles northeast of Moscow. Yamada's detention was frequently publicized by the Tokyo news media along with appeals for the return of other Japanese held by the Soviet Union. However, in late 1953, in traditional Japanese fashion, Yamada's wife asked that her husband not be returned ahead of the others. She explained, "He is the highest ranking Japanese in the USSR and should be in the last group."[36] This request had no influence on Kremlin actions. The Soviets released Yamada from prison in early 1956 and repatriated him six months ahead of the last group. On hearing news of his release, Mrs. Yamada remarked: "I only wish the others could come too." The former Kwantung Army commander arrived at Maizuru on 9 June 1956, more than ten years after Manchuria's fall to the Red Army. In frail condition due to illness suffered during his final year of imprisonment, Yamada was still clear-eyed and "ramrod straight" when he visited the Imperial Palace, Yasukuni Shrine, and the Diet shortly after returning to his home in Tokyo. He expressed amazement at the changes that had occurred during his long absence, but regretted the passing of traditional Japanese ways. Yamada died in Tokyo in July 1965 at the age of 83.[37]

Takebe Rokuzō, director of the General Affairs Bureau of the Manchurian State Council and Japan's top civilian official in Manchukuo from 1940 to 1945, was imprisoned in the USSR from the end of the war until the Soviets transferred him to China in 1950 to stand trial on charges of "crimes against the Chinese people." A People's Court at Shenyang, formerly Mukden, found Takebe guilty on war criminal charges and sentenced him to a lengthy prison term. The People's Republic of China suspended Takebe's sentence in August 1956 due to his poor health and returned him to Japan, but only after the former official expressed "deep repentance and opposition to wars of aggression." Takebe entered a hospital immediately after arrival in Tokyo and died in January 1958 of a cerebral hemorrhage at the age of 65.[38]

Seijima Ryuzō, the former lieutenant colonel flown by the Soviets from Siberia to Japan in September 1946 to testify at the Tokyo war crimes trials, was returned to the USSR in November 1946. He was tried in a Soviet military court on charges of "anti-Soviet aggression" and received a 25-year prison sentence. Seijima was repatriated to Japan in 1956 after Soviet officials suspended his sentence. Subsequent to repatriation, Seijima pursued an active business career with Itō-Chū Shōji (C. Itō Trading Company) and became the firm's board chairman in 1978. In 1987, at the age of 76, he was a consultant to Prime Minister Nakasone and was influential in the affairs of Japan's Liberal Democratic Party.[39]

Uno Sōsuke was 23 when he was captured by the Soviet Army in 1945 and imprisoned in a Siberian labor camp. In 1948, after repatriation, he wrote a book, *Damoi Tokyo* (Going Home to Tokyo), about his experiences in the Soviet Union. Uno graduated with a degree in commerce from Kobe University and embarked on a lengthy career in government and politics. He served ten terms as a Lower House representative from Shiga Prefecture and was appointed to several cabinet posts, including Defense Agency director general and Minister of International Trade and Industry. Uno also held several important positions in the Liberal Democratic Party. He was appointed Foreign Minister in the Takeshita Cabinet in November 1987. Uno announced that one of his objectives was to improve relations with the Soviet Union.[40]

Henry Pu Yi, the puppet emperor of Manchukuo, fell into Soviet hands at the end of World War II and spent the next 14 years under various types of detention in the USSR and China. The Soviets made use of Pu Yi as a witness at the Tokyo trials, and he proved to be a willing accomplice in substantiating Moscow's charges of Japanese anti-Soviet aggression. Pu Yi, flown to Japan in early August 1946, testified for 11 days before the International Military Tribunal for the Far East and "blamed Japan for everything," according to an American journalist. The Soviets flew the last Manchu emperor back to Siberia on 28 August 1946—three weeks before Seijima and two Japanese generals were to make the Tokyo trip—and treated Pu Yi to comfortable accommodations at a health resort for most of the next four years. After a February 1950 agreement between Stalin and Mao, however, Pu Yi was transferred to China to stand trial on charges of "imperialist behavior." The former emperor was imprisoned at Harbin and subjected to intensive indoctrination for the next nine years. Pu Yi, a state witness against Takebe and other Japanese officials at the Shenyang war crimes trials, was released from prison in December 1959. He died at the age of 61 in October 1967 of cancer, according to a Beijing news release.[41]

Hakamada Mutsuo, an *aktiv* leader, was influential in the development of Marxist-Leninist indoctrination programs for Japanese POWs. He was the chief architect of political schools for *aktivs* and was so widely known that POWs sardonically referred to him as *Shiberiya no Tennō*, or Emperor of Siberia. Hakamada refused repatriation in 1949, married a Russian woman, and became a citizen of the USSR. The former *aktiv* joined the staff of Radio Moscow and, at the age of 63, visited Japan in 1976 as a correspondent for the Soviet Radio and Television Commission for the first time since World War II. Former prisoners who had known him in Siberia said Hakamada had refused to return to Japan in 1949 out of fear of retaliation by conservative repatriates.[42]

Japanese charged as war criminals endured harsh and lengthy sentences in the USSR, but Soviet attitudes changed as the years passed. Japanese repatriates in 1955 and 1956 reported there had been no Marxist-Leninist instruction for them. Red Army military bands played for the former prisoners as they prepared to depart, while guards shouted farewell remarks such as, "Take care of yourself!" A festive air prevailed at Nakhodka, especially for the last group—in December 1956—as Soviet authorities said "encouraging words" in farewell speeches. The final group of repatriates from the USSR—some in old military uniforms, others in civilian clothing—showed spontaneity in comments made upon arrival in Japan. By contrast, Japanese returning from China in the 1950s were highly indoctrinated and somberly dressed in high-collar, blue "uniforms" typical of the Mao era. Their remarks were stereotyped, and many expressed regret for their "crimes against the Chinese people."

7
The Final Accounting

Japanese and American records indicated that about 400,000 Japanese remained to be accounted for by the Soviets in May 1949, but a *Tass* press release that month claimed there were only 95,000 POWs plus about 10,000 "war criminals" left in the USSR. SCAP accused Soviet officials of holding large numbers of unrepatriated Japanese, with implications that the Kremlin had sinister motives in its plans for use of the "missing 300,000." In fact, however, most of the missing Japanese were dead. Civilian deaths among Japanese in Manchuria accounted for the largest number of casualties. Furthermore, SCAP and Japanese government estimates of prisoners taken to the USSR in 1945 were overstated. SCAP records had not been revised to show deceased POWs and civilians even though repatriates had told of extensive deaths in Soviet-occupied areas. Soviet officials had provided no accounting of post-war deaths, and American, Chinese, and British Commonwealth members of the Allied Council for Japan wanted an explanation from the Soviet representative. Had SCAP reduced the number of unrepatriated Japanese to reflect estimated deaths, it would have lessened pressure on the Soviets to provide information.

Adjustments were made periodically, however, for other reasons. Some of these changes were arbitrary—the number of Japanese believed to have been in North Korea in August 1945 was increased several times—and SCAP records indicate no reason for the changes. One possible explanation is that the large number of civilians and soldiers moving on foot from Manchuria and North Korea to the South led to confusion in establishing firm estimates. Other changes are more easily explained. The "original number" for Manchuria was reduced from a November 1945 estimate of 1,900,000 to 1,106,000 by October 1946 to account for establishment of separate categories for: 1) Japanese troops and civilians deported to the USSR; and, 2) civilians in the Dairen/Port Arthur area. Decreases to the "original number" for Sakhalin and the Kuriles reflected the escape of an estimated 100,000 civilians to Hokkaido and the transfer of about 80,000 members of the armed forces to Siberia. Conversely, in June 1946, SCAP estimated the total number of Japanese held in the USSR at 700,000, and for the next five years that figure remained unchanged. Later Japanese estimates reduced the number to 575,000.

Any effort to make a precise reconciliation of repatriation from Soviet-controlled areas after World War II is fraught with significant problems. First, the exact number of military troops and civilians in those areas in August 1945 probably never will be known. Second, migration of Japanese from one area to another further complicates resolution of the problem. Third, a few refugees elected to remain where they were at the end of the war, and some were forced to stay. Fourth, several thousand soldiers originally thought to be in the USSR actually were in China. In addition, Soviet authorities transferred about 1,000 Japanese POWs and civilians from Siberia to the People's Republic of China in 1950 to stand trial for "crimes against the Chinese people."[1] Most of these internees later were repatriated by China. Last, but most important, the death rate was appallingly high, especially during the first winter after the war.

By 1949, the hostility of the Cold War had raised the level of rhetoric between the two former wartime allies to such an extent that neither side placed any faith in the explanations of the other. William Sebald, the American representative at the Allied Council for Japan, doggedly insisted that more than 300,000 Japanese remained unaccounted for at the end of 1949. Lieutenant General Kuzma Derevyanko, the Soviet member, refused to discuss the issue, claiming that the *Tass* news release earlier that year fully explained the matter. Soviet statements in 1949 and thereafter concerning the number remaining to be repatriated were generally correct. However, the refusal of Moscow to provide a full accounting of Japanese in areas conquered by Soviet forces in 1945, or even to discuss the issue, far outweighs any merit obtaining from the correctness of Kremlin announcements concerning the number of internees available for repatriation. The Soviet government was accountable for 2,700,000 Japanese, and the 1949 explanation concerning 594,000 POWs—no post-war deaths were acknowledged—amounted to, at best, a feeble reckoning compared to the grim picture later revealed.

Notwithstanding these inadequate explanations and conflicting reports, a final tally based on analysis of SCAP and Japanese government records, news reports, and estimates shows:

Japanese in Soviet hands, August 1945		2,726,000
Less:		
Repatriated	2,379,000	
Deceased (Confirmed)	254,000	
Total accounted for		2,633,000
Missing, Presumed Dead, or Other		93,000

Table 2
Japanese in Soviet-Controlled Areas in August 1945
Analysis of Original Estimate and Adjustments

Area	Original Estimate	Adjusted Estimates for Japanese in Soviet Hands at End of War		
		October 1947	February 1950	Final
Manchuria	1,900,000	1,106,000	1,106,000	1,259,000
Dairen/Port Arthur	-0-[a]	250,000	226,000	228,000
North Korea	232,000	280,000	323,000	359,000
Sakhalin & Kuriles	492,000	492,000	371,000	305,000
USSR	-0-[b]	700,000	700,000	575,000
Total	2,624,000	2,828,000	2,726,000	2,726,000

SOURCE: 1) Daily Intelligence Summaries, 1945-1951, Record Groups 4 and 6, MacArthur Archives; 2) Reports of Japanese Foreign Ministry, 1951-1955; and, 3) Reports of UN Commission on Prisoners of War, 1951-1957.

[a] Japanese in Dairen and Port Arthur originally were included in the Manchuria estimate. A separate category was established in October 1946.

[b] A separate category for Japanese prisoners in the USSR was established in June 1946. The SCAP estimate of 700,000 was overstated. Later estimates placed this number at 575,000, composed of 450,000 military personnel and 125,000 civilians.

This analysis shows that 87.3 percent of Japanese held by the Soviet Union in August 1945 were eventually repatriated. Approximately 9.3 percent died, and the status of 3.4 percent cannot be verified. Table 2 shows an analysis of original estimates and adjustments to the number of Japanese in Soviet-controlled areas in August 1945. Table 3 provides an estimate of the number of Japanese repatriated, dead, and missing, by area.

LASTING IMPRESSIONS

No man knows the harsh realities of a country better than a prisoner in that land. That fact is reflected in the Japanese experience in the land of Lenin and

Table 3
Analysis of Repatriation by Area

Area	Number of Japanese in Area	Repatriated	Confirmed Deaths[a]	Missing, Dead, Other[b]
Manchuria	1,259,000	1,062,000	162,000	35,000
Dairen/Port Arthur	228,000	226,000	1,000	1,000
North Korea	359,000	323,000	34,000	2,000
Sakhalin & Kuriles	305,000	296,000	8,000	1,000
USSR	575,000	472,000	49,000	54,000
Total	2,726,000	2,379,000	254,000	93,000

SOURCE: Repatriation data in Daily Intelligence Summaries, 1945-1951; Japanese Welfare Ministry and Foreign Office Reports, 1951-1960; Reports of the UN Commission on Prisoners of War, 1951-1957; and, news reports in the Japan Times and the New York Times. Above data include escapees from North Korea to South Korea but do not include escapees from Sakhalin and Kurile Islands to Hokkaido.

[a] The Japanese Welfare Ministry confirmed 252,881 deaths in 1954, and the names of a small number of Japanese dead were reported by the Soviet government in the late 1950s.

[b] The Japanese Welfare Ministry declared some internees in this category dead even though there was no actual confirmation. The Ministry announced in May 1954 that 16,254 were presumed to be dead. In the 1950s, the People's Republic of China repatriated about 1,000 prisoners who formerly had been in the USSR.

Stalin. POWs obtained an insider's view of life in the Soviet Union—one totally unavailable to other foreigners and even to most citizens of the USSR—and saw the stark reality of life in Stalin's *Gulag* as contrasted with the image of the workers' paradise portrayed by the Kremlin. Although some accounts revealed acrimonious contempt for their captors, most former POWs look back upon their "Siberian experience" as a time of testing and strengthening. Survival of the hardships of MVD labor camps has made the trials and tribulations of ordinary life facile by comparison. The camaraderie generated among former POWs has prevailed through the years, confirmed by the continued activities of repatriates' associations in Japan. Organizations of former Manchukuo residents also continue to function—the South Manchuria Railways Amity Association is one such group—with reunions and conventions held on a regular basis.

Decades after their return from the USSR, former POWs still had enduring memories of their stay in the Soviet Union. Although most repatriates criticized the Stalin-era Soviet government for its harsh practices, many spoke highly of ordinary citizens as though the government had been staffed with "Soviet" people who were somehow different from ordinary "Russian" people. Repatriates blamed official policies and practices of the Soviet government for their difficulties in the USSR but generally had fond memories of their dealings with ordinary citizens. One former POW spoke in glowing terms of a middle-aged Russian woman who had befriended his work group. When he and two of his colleagues accidentally slipped from a work boat into an icy river, the woman noticed their plight and invited them into her nearby home to dry their clothes. Later she gave them food. The POWs had "completely forgotten sympathy and gentleness" and were overwhelmed by the woman's kindness. Several months later, just before repatriation, one of the POWs visited the woman and

> spoke to her in halting Russian. "Thank you very much for everything you did for us. The time has come for us to return to Japan." She exclaimed, "That's good! That's good!" and ran into her home. Shortly she came back and gave us a basket of boiled potatoes and said, "Return to Japan safely."[2]

POWs gained an insight into the true feelings of Soviet citizens that would not have been possible under other circumstances. On large construction projects, Japanese prisoners frequently worked side-by-side with Soviet laborers who expressed, at times, candid observations about life under Communism, the bureaucracy, and even Stalin. A dialogue, later recalled by a repatriate from a labor camp at Tambov, near Moscow, reveals the attitudes of one Soviet worker:

> Alexander was about 50. He worked with us at Tambov. One day, when there were no MVD guards nearby, Alexander started a conversation with several of the Japanese POWs. "I like Japanese," he said. "The Japanese I associated with at Khabarovsk during my youth was a nice guy." He continued: "Youths of today have no manners. They have the cheek to take the old to task. Things have entirely changed since the revolution. . . . The language used by women has become so vulgar."
>
> Then Alexander, apparently under the influence of vodka, went on to say: "You must know who is to blame." He looked around cautiously, and one of the POWs asked, "Lenin?" Alexander replied: "*Nyet*! Lenin was a great leader, giving freedom to workers and farmers. As long as Lenin was alive, it was all right with the Soviet Union."
>
> One of the POWs then countered: "Who is to blame, then? You enjoy freedom of speech, so you may speak out. Is it not Stalin?" Alexander then looked around, making exaggerated glances over his shoulder. With a sly smile, he put his hand over his mouth and said in a barely audible tone: "*Ya ne snayu* (I don't know)." He would say no more about the matter, but there was no doubt Alexander meant Stalin.[3]

The Soviet detention of Japanese soldiers and civilians, though no longer a current issue, continues to be of interest in Japan. Although Marxist idealism has a strong appeal among college students and intellectuals, relations with the Soviet Union and its tsarist predecessors since the last decade of the nineteenth century have kindled an aura of enmity on the part of many Japanese with respect to their neighbor to the north. Some antagonism has been generated by contemporary issues, such as: 1) the Soviet interception and shooting down of Korean Air Lines flight 007 in September 1983, close to Japanese territory, 2) the dispute concerning the Northern Territories, and 3) Moscow's extensive military presence in the eastern region of the USSR and fleet operations in neighboring waters. Other causes of Japanese animosity toward the Soviet Union are of a historical nature. High among these issues are the 1945 Soviet attack, in violation of the 1941 neutrality pact which—according to the Japanese view—was still in effect, and the lengthy internment of Japanese in forced labor camps after a "ten-day war," as the short August War is sometimes referred to in Japan.

Another side of Japan's "Siberian experience" involves Soviet impressions of their Japanese "guests." Some residents of the USSR have expressed a high regard for the Japanese POWs they encountered in the late 1940s. Aoyama University professor Hakamada Shigeki visited the Central Asian region of the USSR many years after the war. He found a high regard for Japanese work. Buildings constructed by POWs were in good condition—after more than 30 years—and Karaganda citizens spoke highly of the virtues of Japanese workmanship. A townsman who had worked with Japanese POWs praised the quality of their work and was impressed with the high cultural standards of ordinary enlisted soldiers, but he also had some negative opinions: "The Soviet people were shocked at the collapse of the famous Kwantung Army. Japanese acted quite obedient and servile. They were completely different from Europeans. Nobody had much respect for Japanese under such situations."[4]

These observations reflect an interaction between Japanese and people of other lands that is illuminating. Japanese long have been renowned for hard work but also for their obedience to authority. The latter attribute was even more pronounced for the pre-1945 generation than for those that followed. Obedience to the emperor and those in positions of power—parents, teachers, police, and leaders—was stressed in the education and indoctrination of prewar Japanese. With the defeat of Japan, a new succession of authority figures appeared on the scene. In much of Northeast Asia, Soviet officials became the new holders of authority. The former officers and soldiers of the Kwantung Army, dejected and confused after Japan's defeat, obediently followed the directions of their Soviet captors. This submissive behavior contrasted sharply with attitudes of Germans seized by the Soviets who, though compelled by force to obey their captors, did not display the subservient and ingratiating behavior of the Japanese.

Even more surprising than the submissive behavior was the activism of a large number of Japanese in furthering Soviet ideology. Approximately 20 to 25 percent of the former soldiers took an active part in the indoctrination program, and many of the other POWs suffered as a result. To be sure, cooperation with Soviet ideological goals was virtually a prerequisite to repatriation, but there was a significant difference between the passive acceptance displayed by the majority of POWs and the active participation of the minority. Some activists were even more zealous than Soviet political officers in the propagation of Marxist-Leninist goals. In the last year of the "Siberian experience," the collaborators ran the indoctrination program and controlled the fate of other POWs. Where did these *aktivs* come from? Although a few exiled JCP members turned up in POW camps, most members of the Japan Communist Party had been imprisoned since long before the war. The wartime draft probably brought a few "closet" Marxists into the Japanese Army, but their number was small. Instead, almost all activist POWs were young draftees with no previous knowledge of Communism. Their lack of maturity, the vacuum created by Japan's defeat, coupled with immersion in the milieu of the Soviet system and the Japanese predisposition to respect authority, no doubt led to an overly enthusiastic response to the doctrine propagated by their captors.

The intense behavior of the *aktivs* reflects a typical Japanese trait. Whatever interests they pursue, young Japanese apply great enthusiasm and zeal to their efforts. Some former soldiers, only 17 or 18 at the time of the surrender, had had enough exposure to Soviet ideology by 1948 to become not only adherents of Communism, but proponents of its dogma as well. The conversion was probably sincere at the time for most activists, though no doubt there were opportunists who saw cooperation with the Soviets as a means of obtaining power and special privileges. Some older activists probably cooperated with a different objective in mind: revenge against former officers. Whatever their reasons may have been, ex-POWs who had been conspirators soon found it expedient to suppress information about their activities within a short time after their return to Japan. Extensive publicity of the harsh treatment received by many POWs in the USSR put the former *aktivs* in a bad light.

STALIN'S REVENGE

Given the passage of time since the close of World War II, it is possible to analyze Soviet treatment of captured Japanese with less bias or prejudice than was evidenced in the emotionally charged atmosphere of the first postwar decade. Western and Japanese political analysts have pondered the issue, occasionally expressing amazement that the Soviets persisted in holding Japanese for so long in the face of adverse public opinion in Japan. The reaction in Japan to Soviet policies concerning POWs and civilian internees can easily be seen in the declining fortunes of the Japan Communist Party after 1949. The JCP share of the vote for popular election of Diet members decreased from 9.6 percent to 5.2 percent between 1947 and 1950.[5] There were other reasons for this drop in popularity, but Soviet delays and the hostile behavior of the 1949 repatriates no doubt figured prominently in these reverses. An even more dramatic decrease was evident in the number of JCP candidates elected to the House of Representatives. The JCP won 35 seats in January 1949 but failed to win even one seat in the October 1952 election. In fact, it was not until 1969 that the JCP again achieved double-digit status, when 14 or its members were elected to the House of Representatives.[6] Even in the July 1986 election, JCP candidates captured only 27 seats out of a total number of 512 seats, as contrasted to 466 in 1949.[7]

In the late 1940s, however, Joseph Stalin did not appear to be concerned with public opinion in Japan. Instead, his statements show an obsession for revenge. Oddly enough, some of his passion was generated by memories of the 1905 defeat of Imperial Russian forces at the hands of the Japanese. Even though Lenin, at the time, had gloated over the tsarist reverses in Manchuria, predicting an early victory for the revolution in Russia as a result, Stalin spoke in his September 1945 victory speech of vindication for the prerevolutionary loss and railed against "Japanese aggression." Stalin also cited Japanese intervention in Siberia after World War I and border incidents of the 1930s. Revenge was certainly a basic motive in the Soviet attack on Japanese forces in Northeast Asia but was by no means the only factor. Expansion of Soviet territorial limits and access to the Pacific were major considerations. There were several important reasons for the capture and lengthy detention of Kwantung Army troops in the USSR, and there is some difficulty in rating them in order of importance. In fact, priorities appear to have changed in the years after the war. In a chronologically based order of priority, four factors are evident: 1) the need for laborers in the USSR, 2) the use of POWs as hostages to provide Soviet officials with a bargaining lever for modifying Allied occupation policies to further Kremlin goals, 3) Communist indoctrination of POWs to supply the JCP with recruits, and 4) offering the repatriation of the small number of internees still in the USSR in the mid-1950s as an inducement to obtain Japanese agreement to a peace treaty.

From the early 1930s until 1950, the Soviet Union had a crucial need for labor to implement Stalin's modernization and reconstruction programs as set forth in several Five-Year Plans. Soviet citizens were conscripted as laborers to fulfill the industrial goals in the decade prior to Hitler's 1941 attack on the USSR, and hundreds of thousands of German and Japanese POWs were available to supplement indigenous labor in the postwar period. The European regions of the Soviet Union had been devastated by war, and rebuilding of damaged industrial, transportation, mining, and agricultural facilities was one of Stalin's highest priorities. Use of German POWs for forced labor was easily rationalized since Hitler's army was responsible for most of the devastation, but that was not enough. Officials often used trivial justification to place Soviet citizens in forced servitude, and an extension of this reasoning served as a basis for use of captured Japanese soldiers in labor projects. After all, if the Soviets were to sentence thousands of Red Army soldiers to work camps for having allowed themselves to be captured by the Germans during the war, parallel logic would dictate that the same treatment be applied to Japanese soldiers surrendering to the armed forces of the USSR. What is more, Stalin viewed the Japanese as aggressors—not withstanding the fact that it was the Soviets who had denounced the neutrality pact and attacked Japanese forces in 1945—and insisted on their punishment.

The second purpose for detention is perhaps not as precise as the first. Soviet officials were unhappy about many aspects of the Allied occupation of Japan. Stalin initially wanted a partition of Japan in the same manner as Germany, with Red Army forces to occupy Hokkaido, but with only a few months' experience in Germany, the unfavorable results of that quadripartite adventure had been a lesson to the Western Allies, and American officials rejected Stalin's proposal. Second, the USSR (and Australia) insisted upon the indictment of Emperor Hirohito as a war criminal and abolition of the monarchy. This demand was quashed at MacArthur's insistence, even though many top American officials also favored punishment of the emperor. The problem was tempered in early 1946 when Hirohito publicly renounced his divinity, but Soviet officials continued to demand elimination of the emperor system. Third, although SCAP released Japanese Communists from the confinement imposed prior to 1945, Soviet officials pushed for further liberalization and a free hand for the JCP to obtain more power. When MacArthur cautioned against the "growing tendency toward mass violence by disorderly minorities" after the 1946 May Day demonstrations, the Soviet member of the Allied Council charged Americans with encouraging the Japanese government to take an anti-Communist stance. Yet another issue of contention was the charge made by General Derevyanko that SCAP was making plans to resurrect the Japanese General Staff and return Japan to its former imperialist ways. This allegation concerned use of former Japanese officers in the Demobilization Bureau, but SCAP denied any connection. None of these matters were directly related to the repatriation issue, but the Soviets possibly viewed that large number of Japanese in their hands as a pawn to influence SCAP behavior to their advantage. If this supposition is true, the Soviets were generally unsuccessful in their attempts.

Political education of Japanese POWs and detained civilians assumed growing importance with the passage of time. Instruction in Communism and Soviet doctrine reached equal standing with the POW labor contribution in 1948; the goal was to provide new members for the Japan Communist Party once the POWs were repatriated. A strengthened JCP would have furthered Soviet objectives in Japan, and, indeed, thousands of highly indoctrinated former soldiers did return to Japan in the late 1940s. Their fervent show of support for Communist ideology and revolutionary socialism at the Maizuru repatriation port was spectacular and frightful to many Japanese. For a few months in mid–1949, it looked as though the Soviets might have been successful in their political indoctrination goals, but the enthusiasm of the repatriates began to wane after their adjustment to the familiar surroundings of home. Although a considerable number of the former soldiers either joined the JCP or considered themselves sympathetic to party objectives in the first months after their return, most eventually withdrew from any alliance with the leftist organization. Thus, the political indoctrination motive in holding Japanese POWs did not produce the desired results for the Soviets.

Only a little more than a thousand Japanese, mostly alleged war criminals, remained in the USSR in 1955, but the Soviet government saw a use for these POWs in the negotiation of a peace treaty with Japan. Several issues required resolution; the territorial dispute was the most significant matter. The Soviets nevertheless made it clear that early release of the remaining internees, many of whom were serving 25-year sentences, was contingent upon the signing of a treaty. Although a formal peace treaty was not concluded, Japan and the USSR reached agreement in 1956 on a pact normalizing relations between the two countries, and the last POWs were released within a few days.

The use of POWs for labor, then, appears to be the only motive that was fully satisfied. Other goals were not fulfilled, at least not to the degree USSR officials desired.

Inasmuch as Soviet authorities had asked Japanese civilians to become citizens of the USSR and stay on in Sakhalin and the Kurile Islands, it would seem to follow that attempts might have been made to encourage POWs to do the same in labor-short Siberia. Although some Japanese POWs from the 1939 Nomonhan incident chose to stay in the USSR and the Mongolian People's Republic, there is no evidence of any organized effort to persuade soldiers from the August 1945 war to remain in the Soviet Union. Only a handful of POWs refused repatriation. A returning Navy officer said in 1954 that "57 Japanese decided to remain in Siberia."[8]

AFTERMATH

There was a war and Japan lost. That explanation appears to sum up the USSR position concerning the detention of Japanese soldiers and civilians after the Second World War. If there were any virtues in Soviet policies of that era, surely consistency must have been high on the list of attributes. Nationality made no difference; to surrender to an enemy, regardless of circumstances, resulted in a period of forced servitude in the USSR. This fate befell nearly four million German and Japanese POWs and a lesser number of Finnish, Romanian, Italian, Spanish, and other troops. The policy was also applied to Soviet soldiers, hundreds of thousands of whom were captured by the Germans and later sentenced to labor camps upon return to Soviet control.

Treatment accorded Japanese soldiers and civilians held in the USSR was deplorable, but Soviet citizens also experienced miserable conditions in the late 1940s. Japanese and German POWs, in some cases, lived in better conditions than ordinary residents of the USSR. In 1984, Ivan Kovalenko, senior official in charge of relations with Japan for the Central Committee of the Communist

Party of the Soviet Union, visited Tokyo to discuss Soviet-Japan relations. By a twist of irony, Kovalenko had been in charge of administration and welfare of Japanese POWa in the late 1940s. In discussing this matter with Japanese officials, he said: "Japanese prisoners of war . . . in spite of their status as prisoners, enjoyed meals of the same quality as those eaten by our soldiers."[9] Nonetheless, the Germans and Japanese were being detained in an alien land against their will, a major factor in the adverse reaction witnessed in the Western World and Japan. The essence of German and Japanese grievances was not so much a matter of living conditions, but a question of the right of one power to hold captured soldiers of another nation after the cessation of hostilities. None of the other Allied victors of World War II held such large numbers of Japanese prisoners for lenghty periods after 1945. Most Japanese POWs in areas controlled by the United States and Nationalist China were repatriated by the end of 1946. Britain held 82,000 Japanese POWs in Malaya and Burma for two years after the war and a smaller number in Singapore until 1948. The Dutch detained 13,500 Japanese in the Netherlands East Indies until May 1947. These ex-soldiers labored on reconstruction projects.[10] In Europe, however, France held 137,000 German POWs until 1949. The French government claimed that the former Nazi soldiers, especially those whose homes were in the Soviet-occupied zone of Germany, had decided to stay in France as "free laborers," but Soviet officials accused France of using the Germans for forced labor.[11]

Convicted Japanese war criminals were imprisoned for several years in the Philippines, Singapore, Malaya, the Dutch East Indies, and other locations, but all (except for those held in the People's Republic of China) were either pardoned or transferred to Tokyo's Sugamo Prison by 1953. China completed repatriation of Japanese war criminals in 1956. Allied officials authorized release of the last war criminals from Sugamo Prison in May 1958. More than 4,000 war criminals had been held at Sugamo between 1945 and 1958.

Kremlin leaders viewed their detention of nearly 600,000 Japanese as correct behavior, but the rest of the world disagreed. The 1929 Geneva Convention on war prisoners required prompt repatriation of soldiers held by former enemy powers after the cessation of hostilities, but the Soviet Union was not a signatory to the 1929 convention and cannot be held accountable to its provisions. In its declaration of war on Japan, however, the Kremlin announced its adherence to "the statement of the Allied powers of July 26, 1945." That statement was none other than the Potsdam Declaration which specified "the Japanese military forces, after being completely disarmed, shall be permitted to return to their homes." However, this obligation was not honored by Moscow. The Soviets, seeking an improved international standing, agreed to the terms of the Third Geneva Convention of August 1949, which also called for the unconditional repatriation of POWs after the discontinuance of fighting. Kremlin representatives signed the new convention in December 1949 concurrent with Moscow's announcement that general repatriation of Japanese POWs had been completed.

Next in importance after the issue of the lengthy detention of POWs is the matter of providing an accounting for the former soldiers and civilians under Soviet control. The Kremlin has never provided a complete reconciliation of the total number of Japanese military personnel and civilians in areas occupied by the Red Army in August 1945. Although more than 250,000 Japanese died while in their custody, Soviet officials furnished only scant information concerning those deaths. The sparse data provided by the Soviets in the 1950s was basically correct as far as it went but was only a small fraction of what should have been forthcoming.

Not only is the information concerning deaths inadequate, but Moscow has never allowed organized visits to the graves of deceased POWs. Family members were allowed to visit cemeteries in the northern territories in the 1970s and again in 1986 and 1987, but there are no POWs buried there. Only the remains of pre–1945 Japanese dead are interred on those islands. A few Japanese have visited POW cemeteries in Khabarovsk, but their number is small in comparison to the total number of dead. The Japanese Welfare Ministry announced plans in 1958 to send a team of relatives and government officials to the Soviet Union to hold memorial services at more than 300 graveyards and bring home remains, but the Kremlin has never given approval. Japanese have conducted visits of this nature to all the other areas where members of their armed forces died in World War II. During the 1984 Kovalenko visit to Japan, Hiraizumi Wataru, a Liberal Democratic Party official, attempted to discuss this issue. He told the Soviet representative: "Many prisoners died of starvation and cold. Therefore, I would appreciate your permission for the survivors to worship at their colleagues' or relatives' graves." The next entry in the transcript of talks between the two officials indicates: "Kovalenko: (no response)."[12] Thus the dark shadows of the *curtain of silence* continued into the fourth decade following Japan's "Siberian experience." This intransigent attitude did not endear the Soviet official to Tokyo. A senior Japanese official, commenting on the 1987 expulsion of two Japanese from Moscow for allegedly spying against the USSR, said of Kovalenko: "He still treats the Japanese as war prisoners."[13]

It could be argued that the Soviet detention and treatment of Japanese, German, and other POWs is but one further example of the unprecedented horrors witnessed during World War II. Certainly none of the major participants can claim to have been totally virtuous. To begin with, Japan's own armed forces were notorious for their brutal treatment of enemy citizens. The 1937 "Rape of Nanking," as just one example, was an orgy of terror that left more than 300,000 people dead, according to Chinese estimates. The Nazi bombing of British cities in 1940–1941 took a heavy toll on civilians, and American warplanes dropped incendiary bombs in the spring of 1945 igniting entire German and Japanese cities. Hundreds of thousands of civilians burned to death in fiery infernos. On one night alone, 9 March 1945, fires started by napalm bombs killed 72,000 Tokyo civilians and made more than one million people homeless. In another holocaust, on the opposite side of the Euro-Asian landmass, Hitler's systematic execution of six million civilians surely must rank as the all-time atrocity of recorded history. The two atom bombs dropped from American B–29s in August 1945 caused about 120,000 deaths in Hiroshima and 70,000 in Nagasaki. This appalling destruction resulted from the awful heat experienced at the climax of the most dreadful war ever known to man.

On a scale of less epic proportions, the forced relocation of people of Japanese ancestry in the United States, beginning in February 1942, bears analysis and comparison to the Soviet detainment of Japanese prisoners of war. About 110,000 ethnic Japanese, two-thirds of whom were American-born and the rest resident aliens, were forced to move from the West Coast to relocation centers in remote areas of western states. Not even one of these uprooted residents had been charged with a crime. No one was allowed to obtain legal counsel, nor was anyone permitted a chance to establish his loyalty to the United States. The official reason advanced for the forced relocation was "military necessity to protect the West Coast against sabotage and espionage," but the real reasons, easily seen from the perspective of a later era, more likely were rooted in panic and racism. In 1941, few Americans were sufficiently knowledgeable to separate the actions of Japan, its armed forces, and its citizens, on the one hand, from people with the same kinds of names, cultural background, and racial identity living in California, Oregon, and Washington. The Pearl Harbor attack, previously thought to be beyond Japan's capability, pushed both official and private American opinion over the brink of reasonableness into the chasm of emotional reaction.

When logic and reason returned to the collective American conscience after the war, it became apparent that: 1) the Pearl Harbor attack was solely the responsibility of the Japanese Navy and high officials in Tokyo; 2) there was no planned attack against the West Coast; and, 3) Japanese Americans were just as stunned and surprised by the events of 7 December 1941 as were other Americans. Although the panic and emotional reaction following Pearl Harbor may explain the forced relocation of Japanese Americans, these circumstances did not provide a justification that would stand up in the light of postwar scrutiny. Shortly after the war, Congress saw a need for financial compensation for property damage and loss as a "reasonable and natural consequence of the evacuation or exclusion" from the West Coast. Under the Evacuation Claims Act of 1948, approximately $37 million was paid out to 25,000 claimants. In 1976, President Gerald Ford issued a proclamation acknowledging: "We now know what we should have known then—not only was that wrong, but Japanese Americans were and are loyal Americans." Ford closed his proclamation with the resolve "that this kind of action shall never again be repeated."[14]

More than four decades after the war, American officials were looking for much broader remedies. A majority in Congress supported legislation that would make a formal national apology and provide compensation for violation of constitutional rights and unlawful detention. In addition, litigation was proceeding through federal courts to provide restitution and redress. Final resolution of this problem may take years, but the fact that legislative and judicial channels were fully available to pursue remedies for earlier injustices reflects a society that is willing to make amends for errors of the past.

The one uniting thread in all of these atrocities and misguided actions is that they were perpetrated in the heat and intensity of a world at war, an all-out effort bringing to bear the total resources of the major combatants, even at the risk of inviting Armageddon. Conversely, how must the Soviet detention and ill treatment of several hundred thousand Japanese after the war be viewed? Did the Soviet Army whisk away nearly 600,000 Japanese soldiers and civilians to the USSR out of some perceived need for military security to prevent espionage and sabotage? Was the forced labor of so many POWs necessary to meet the urgency of a wartime crisis? Did Japanese in Manchuria and other Northeast Asian locations pose a threat to the survival of the Soviet Union? Was an aggressive and imperialist Japan on the verge of overrunning the land of Lenin and Stalin? There was no "heat of war" for Japan after August 1945. When the fires of war had subsided, there were no resources available for waging war, no fighting spirit left, and not even enough life-sustaining necessities to maintain existence without outside help.

The "heat of war," then, had no connection with the deportation and long confinement of Japanese in the Soviet Union. Instead, the real reason is clearly revealed in the need for workers to aid in the industrialization of Siberia and the reconstruction of the European regions of the USSR. The effort was a success, thanks in large part to the labor of millions of war prisoners.

Decades have passed since Japan's "Siberian experience," but peering behind the *curtain of silence* raises questions about the future. What course will the Soviet Union take should large numbers of enemy soldiers again fall into its hands? Will the Kremlin honor its commitment to the Geneva Convention of 1949? Of special interest is Article 109, as quoted in the 1974 edition of the *Great Soviet Encyclopedia*: "After cessation of military operations, the belligerent countries are obligated to repatriate unconditionally prisoners of war."[15] The Soviet government approved a new constitution in 1977; protection of human rights was promised, as it had been in two earlier constitutions dating back to 1924. Since these guarantees existed even during the Stalin years, on paper at least, something more concrete is needed. General Secretary Mikhail Gorbachev held out promises of an improved climate for human rights through his *glasnost* (openness) policies of the late 1980s. These hopeful starts need to be substantiated by guarantees for the protection of all political and civil rights, and legal assurances for the proper and humane treatment of detainees. Specifically, the 1949 Geneva Convention requirement for prompt repatriation of war prisoners after cessation of hostilities must be understood by the Kremlin to be a mandatory obligation.

Lastly, what of amends to those who suffered at the hands of Stalin and his *Gulag* henchmen? Is it too much to ask for compensation for wrongful detention and violation of human rights? Certainly an expression of regret is long overdue. Even an acknowledgement of the fact that millions of citizens of other nations were held for forced labor in the USSR in the years after World War II would, if nothing else, permit the Soviet Union to face up to its past. Unfortunately, none of these steps—not even in Gorbachev's 1987 denunciation of the "enormous and unforgivable" crimes of Stalin—have materialized. Without some act of atonement, the *curtain of silence* will shroud history into the twenty-first century.

Notes

1. THE AUGUST WAR

1. Japan's field army in Manchuria was known as the Kwantung Army, after the Kwantung Leased Territory (on the Liaotung Peninsula) transferred to Japan after the Russo-Japanese War of 1904–1905.

2. Alvin D. Coox, *Nomonhan, Japan Against Russia, 1939* (Stanford: Stanford University Press, 1985), 1:84.

3. For a complete account of this incident see Alvin D. Coox, *The Anatomy of a Small War: The Soviet-Japanese Struggle for Changkufeng/Khasan, 1938* (Westport, Conn.: Greenwood Press, 1977).

4. For the definitive work on this major border conflict see Coox, *Nomonhan.*

5. George Alexander Lensen, *The Strange Neutrality: Soviet-Japanese Relations During the Second World War, 1941–1945* (Tallahassee, Fla.: The Diplomatic Press, 1972), pp. 3–17.

6. U.S. Department of State, *Foreign Relations of the United States, The Conferences at Malta and Yalta, 1945* (Washington, D.C.: U.S. Government Printing Office, 1955), p. 984.

7. Kase Toshikazu, *Journey to the Missouri* (New Haven: Yale University Press, 1950), pp. 154–55.

8. U.S. Department of State, *Foreign Relations of the United States, Conference of Berlin (Potsdam), 1945* (Washington, D.C.: U.S. Government Printing Office, 1960), 2:1474–76.

9. Ibid., 2:1293.

10. London *Daily Telegraph*, 15 March 1983, p. 4.

11. Pacific War Research Society, *Japan's Longest Day* (Tokyo: Kodansha International Ltd., 1973), p. 75.

12. Headquarters, U.S. Army Forces Far East/Eighth Army, Military History Section, Camp Zama, Japan, "Japanese Studies on Manchuria," March 1955, 1:77, Record Group 338, Washington National Records Center, National Archives and Records Administration, Suitland, Md.

13. Ibid., 1:111–12.

14. Hayashi Saburō, *Kōgun, The Japanese Army in the Pacific War* (Quantico, Va.: Marine Corps Association, 1959), p. 173.

15. U.S. Army Forces Far East/Eighth Army, "Japanese Studies on Manchuria," 10:58–59.
16. S. M. Shtemnko, *The Soviet General Staff at War, 1941–1945* (Moscow: Progress Publications, 1970), p. 341.
17. Satō Naotake, *Futatsu no Roshiya* (Two Russias), (Tokyo: Sekai no Nihonsha, 1948), p. 207.
18. U.S. Department of State, *Conference of Berlin (Potsdam)*, 2:1474.
19. Yamamoto Tomomi, *Four Years in Hell* (Tokyo: An Asian Publication, 1952), pp. 7–8.
20. Shtemnko, *The Soviet General Staff at War*, p. 331.
21. Raymond L. Garthoff, "The Soviet Manchuria Campaign, August 1945," *Military Affairs* 33 (October 1969): 318–26.
22. U.S. Army Forces Far East/Eighth Army; "Japanese Studies on Manchuria," 9:54–55.
23. *New York Times*, 15 August 1945, p. 3.
24. Louis Allen, *The End of the War in Asia* (London: Hart-Davis, MacGibbon, 1976), p. 197.
25. Shtemnko, *The Soviet General Staff at War*, p. 346.
26. Garthoff, "The Soviet Manchuria Campaign," pp. 326–28.
27. *Pravda*, 3 September 1945, p. 1.
28. Japan, Foreign Ministry, "Letter to President of UN General Assembly on Repatriation Problems," 25 July 1951, p. 13.
29. U.S. Department of State, *Foreign Relations of the United States, The Conferences at Cairo and Teheran, 1943* (Washington, D.C.: U.S. Government Printing Office, 1961), p. 448.
30. Ibid., p. 566.
31. General Staff, General Headquarters (GHQ), Supreme Commander for the Allied Powers (SCAP), *Reports of General MacArthur, MacArthur in Japan: The Occupation, Military Phase* (Washington, D.C.: U.S. Government Printing Office, 1966), 1:149–51.
32. Military Intelligence Section (MIS), GHQ SCAP, Daily Intelligence Summary, 8 April 1947, p. 1, Record Group 6, General Douglas MacArthur Memorial Archives, Norfolk, Va.

2. JAPANESE SETTLERS AND THE RED ARMY

1. MIS, Daily Intelligence Summary, 8 May 1946, p. 1.
2. MIS, Daily Intelligence Summary, 9 February 1946, p. 5.
3. MIS, Daily Intelligence Summary, 23 January 1946, p. 5.
4. MIS, Daily Intelligence Summary, 21 December 1945, p. 3.
5. MIS, Daily Intelligence Summary, 26 September 1946, p. 10.
6. Ibid.
7. *Nippon Times* (Tokyo), 23 March 1954, p. 3.
8. Allied Council for Japan, Minutes of 20 December 1950 meeting, annex 7, Record Group 5, MacArthur Archives.
9. MIS, Daily Intelligence Summary, 9 January 1948, pp. 4–5.
10. *Japan Times* (Tokyo), 15 January 1958, p. 3.
11. *Japan Times*, 29 July 1957, p. 3.
12. Japan Times, 15 January 1976, p. 2.

NOTES

13. Aikō Hiroyuki, Hitoyoshi City, Kumamoto Prefecture, response to author's questionnaire, 20 February 1987.
14. MIS, Daily Intelligence Summary, 16 September 1946, p. 2.
15. Iijima Shiro, "Hoku-Man Kaitaku Dan no Saigo" (End of the North Manchuria Pioneer Settlers Corps), in Inada Masazumi, Itō Masatoku, and Tomioka Sadatoshi, eds., *Jitsuroku Taiheiyo Sensō* (A Firsthand Record of the Pacific War), (Tokyo: Chūō Kōron Sha, 1960), 7:183–95.
16. *Washington Post*, 4 March 1987, p. A–26.
17. MIS, Daily Intelligence Summary, 30 January 1946, p. 3.
18. Yamamoto, *Four Years in Hell*, p. 21.
19. Aikō, response to author's questionnaire.
20. MIS, Daily Intelligence Summary, 16 September 1946, p. 2.
21. Hashimoto Katsuyuki, Hiroshima City, response to author's questionnaire, 1 June 1987.
22. Aikō, response to author's questionnaire.
23. MIS, Daily Intelligence Summary, 24 July 1946, p. 3.
24. Hashimoto, response to author's questionnaire, 1 June 1987.
25. Kuriyama Aiko, interview with author, Tokyo, about October 1954.
26. Jack Belden, *China Shakes the World* (New York: Monthly Review Press, 1949), pp. 377–78.
27. Reiko Schwab, interview with author, Norfolk, Virginia, 12 February 1985.
28. *Asahi* (Tokyo), 15 March 1946, p. 1.
29. Lionel Max Chassin, *The Communist Conquest of China* (Cambridge, Mass.: Harvard University Press, 1965), pp. 66–85.
30. Tang Tsou, *America's Failure in China, 1941–50* (Chicago: University of Chicago Press, 1963), pp. 327–37.
31. U.S. ambassador in China to Secretary of State, Radio Message No. 1017, 23 September 1947, quoted in U.S. State Department, *Foreign Relations of the United States, 1947* (Washington: U.S. Government Printing Office, 1972), 7:996–98.
32. *Nippon Times*, 1 November 1947, p. 1.
33. Donald G. Gillin and Charles Etter, "Staying On: Japanese Soldiers and Civilians in China, 1945–1949," *Journal of Asian Studies* 42 (May 1983): 510.
34. *Japan Times*, 24 April 1958, p. 3.
35. *Liberal Star* (Tokyo: Liberal Democratic Party of Japan), 10 August 1987, p. 5.
36. Barbara Jelavich, *St. Petersburg and Moscow* (Bloomington: Indiana University Press, 1974, pp. 237–47.
37. Paul Paddock, *China Diary: Crisis Diplomacy in Dairen* (Ames: Iowa State University Press, 1977), pp. xii–xv.
38. MIS, Daily Intelligence Summary, 26 November 1949, p. 6.
39. MIS, Daily Intelligence Summary, 2 November 1949, p. 8.
40. U.S. Department of State, *Conferences at Malta and Yalta*, p. 770.
41. Leonard E. Barsdell, "Memorandum Based on Observation of Russian-occupied Korea with an American POW Recovery Unit," 22 September 1945, Record Group 4, MacArthur Archives.
42. *Asahi*, 15 October 1945, p. 3.
43. Military Government Section, U.S. Army Forces in Korea, "Summation of Military Government Activities in Korea," May 1946, p. 76, Record Group 4, MacArthur Archives.

44. Civil Intelligence Section, GHQ, U.S. Army Forces Pacific, "Trends, Japan-Korea and Philippines," 16 July 1946, p. 30, Record Group 4, MacArthur Archives.

45. *Minchoo Chosun*, official newspaper of the North Korean Government, quoted in MIS, Daily Intelligence Summary, 30 November 1946, p. 5.

46. MIS, Daily Intelligence Summary, 30 November 1946, p. 5.

47. *Japan Times*, 16 September 1957, p. 3.

48. Military Intelligence Section (MIS), GHQ SCAP, Periodic Intelligence Summary, 1 March 1947, p. 69, Record Group 6, MacArthur Archives.

3. JAPANESE IN STALIN'S LABOR CAMPS

1. Sakoda Yoshihiko, "Kokkyō Kanshi Shō Zenmetsu" (The Annihilation of the Frontier Observation Unit), in Inada Masazumi, Itō Masatoku, and Tomioka Sadatoshi, eds., *Jitsuroku Taiheiyo Sensō* (A Firsthand Record of the Pacific War), (Tokyo: Chūō Kōron Sha, 1960), 7:99–105.

2. Aikō, response to author's questionnaire.

3. Gotō Shukaku, *Shiberiya Yūshū Ki* (Specter of a Siberian Prisoner), (Tokyo: Nihon Gaku Kyōkai, 1977), pp. 35–36.

4. Hashimoto, response to author's questionnaire.

5. Chaen Yoshio, *Sugamo Purizun/Shiberiya Nihon Shinbun* (Sugamo Prison/Siberia Japan Newspaper), (Tokyo: Fuji Shuppan, 1986), pp. 208–9.

6. Edward Norbeck, "Edokko, A Narrative of Japanese Prisoners of War in Russia," *Rice University Studies* 57, no. 1 (Winter 1971): 20.

7. MIS, Periodic Intelligence Summary, 1 January 1947, p. 26 (SECRET, declassified 20 August 1975), Record Group 6, MacArthur Archives.

8. James F. Byrnes, *Speaking Frankly* (New York: Harper & Brothers Publishers, 1947), p. 213.

9. Gerhard Escenhagen, "The Prisoners of War, the Civilian Prisoners and the Returnees," in Delmut Arntz, ed., *Germany Reports* (Bonn: The Press and Information Office of the Federal Government, 1966), p. 36.

10. For the definitive work on forced labor in the Soviet Union see Aleksandr I. Solzhenitsyn, *The Gulag Archipelago, 1918–1956* (New York: Harper & Row, 1976), 3 volumes.

11. Itō Haruki, "Kita Chishima Jitsuroku" (A Firsthand Account of the North Kuriles), in Inada Masazumi, Itō Masatoku, and Tomioka Sadatoshi, eds., *Jitsuroku Taiheiyo Sensō*, 7:84–98.

12. MIS, Daily Intelligence Summary, 12 November 1946, p. 2.

13. Allied Translator and Interpreter Service (ATIS), GHQ SCAP, Bulletin No. 1, "Interrogation of Repatriates," 15 January 1947, Record Group 6, MacArthur Archives.

14. Allied Council for Japan, Minutes of 21 December 1949 meeting, p. 11, Record Group 5, MacArthur Archives.

15. Chaen, *Sugamo Purizun/Shiberiya Nihon Shinbun*, p. 208.

16. MIS, "Interrogation of Japanese Returning from the USSR," 18 June 1947, p. 3, Record Group 6, MacArthur Archives.

17. Yamamoto Tomomi, *Four Years in Hell*, pp. 135–36.

18. Gotō, *Shiberiya Yūshū Ki*, p. 65.

19. Ishii Takashi, "Japanese Prisoner of War Labor in Soviet Russia" (Master's Thesis, University of Illinois at Urbana-Champaign, Urbana, Ill., 1953), pp. 81–82.

20. G–2 Report, "Communist Indoctrination of Japanese Repatriates from Soviet Territory," 2 February 1949, Tab 15, Record Group 6, MacArthur Archives.
21. Letter appended to G–2 Report, "Communist Indoctrination of Japanese Repatriates of Soviet Territory."
22. Yabe Akira, "Kamen no Dōshi" (Companion in Disguise), *Bungei Shunjū* (Tokyo) 60 (September 1982):210.
23. MIS, Periodic Intelligence Summary, 15 August 1947, p. 31.
24. Coox, *Nomonhan*, 2:949–50.
25. Joseph Stalin, *Problems of Leninism* (Moscow: Foreign Language Publishing House, 1947), p. 356.
26. Anatole G. Mazour, *Soviet Economic Development, Operation Outstrip, 1921–1965* (Princeton: D. Van Nostrand, 1967), p. 62.
27. Ishii, "Japanese Prisoner of War Labor," p. 87.
28. Yamamoto, *Four Years in Hell*, pp. 225–29.
29. Ishii, "Japanese Prisoner of War Labor," pp. 98–102.
30. Yamamoto, *Four Years In Hell*, p. 167.
31. Allied Council for Japan, Minutes of 21 December 1949 meeting, p. 14.
32. *Sobieto Bunka* (Soviet Culture), June 1948, quoted in "Communist Indoctrination of Japanese Repatriates," Tab 10.
33. MIS, Periodic Intelligence Summary, 15 September 1947, p. 30.
34. Joseph Scholmer, *Vorkuta* (New York: Henry Holt & Co., 1954), p. 64.
35. *New York Times*, 30 September 1984, p. I–16.
36. Higuchi Kinichi, *Uraru-o Koete* (Beyond the Urals), (Tokyo: Kangen sha, 1949), p. 124.
37. Based on average number of Japanese in the USSR for each year from 1945 to 1949, multiplied by 3,650 work hours per year; times 50 yen per hour, the average wage in Japan in 1949, at an exchange rate of 360 yen to the dollar. Values for 1987 are based on an average hourly rate of 1,600 yen for production workers, at an exchange rate of 125 yen to the dollar.
38. Hozaka Masayasu, "Seijima Ryuzō no Kenkyū" (A Study of Seijima Ryuzō), *Bungei Shunjū*, (Tokyo) 65 (May 1987):272–97.
39. Seijima's experiences parallel those of the protagonist in Yamasaki Toyoko's novel, *Fumō Chitai*, the story of a Japanese Army officer held in Siberia and flown by the Soviets to Japan for the Tokyo war crimes trials. Yamasaki, however, denies that her main character was modeled on Seijima's experiences. *Fumō Chitai*, translated into English by James T. Araki as *The Barren Zone* (Honolulu: University of Hawaii Press, 1985), was written as fiction, but portrays conditions that closely resemble those reported in documentary records.
40. Philip R. Piccigallo, *The Japanese on Trial: Allied War Crimes Operations in the East, 1945–1951* (Austin: University of Texas Press, 1979), p. 152.
41. Akiyama Hiroshi, "Saikin Senwa Junbi Sarete Ita!" (Germ Warfare Preparations!), *Bungei Shunjū*, 33 (August 1955): 250–60.
42. *Washington Post*, 19 November 1976, p. 1.
43. Shimamura Kyō, *Sanzennin no Seitai Jikken* (Vivisection of 3,000 People), (Tokyo: Hara Shobo, 1967); Morimura Seiichi, *Akuma no Hōshoku* (Gluttony of the Devil), (Tokyo: Kōbunsha, 1981); and Yamada Seizaburō,, *Saikinsen Gunji Saiban* (Military Court of Biological Warfare), (Tokyo: Shinkō Shuppansha, 1982).

44. John W. Powell, "Japan's Biological Weapons: 1930–45," *Bulletin of the Atomic Scientists*, 37 (October 1981): 44–52.
45. Yamamoto, *Four Years in Hell*, pp. 162–63.
46. "Speech of Nikita Khrushchev Before a Closed Session of the Twentieth Congress of the Communist Party of the Soviet Union on February 25, 1956," Committee Print, Judiciary Committee of the U.S. Senate, 85th Congress, Washington, D.C., 1957.
47. David J. Dallin, *Forced Labor in Soviet Russia* (New Haven: Yale University Press, 1947), pp. 37–38.
48. Allied Council for Japan, Minutes of 20 December 1950 meeting, Annex 1, Record Group 5, MacArthur Archives.
49. *New York Times*, 9 June 1956, p. 4.
50. *New York Times*, 27 December 1956, p. 10.

4. MARXIST-LENINIST INDOCTRINATION

1. Saigen Sōsuke, "Saigen Sōsuke no Nikki" (Diary of Saigen Sōsuke), Ishiki Masao, ed., *Maizuru Chihō Hikiage Engo-kyoku Shi* (History of Maizuru Area Repatriates Support Office), (Kyoto: Kōseisho Hikiage Engo-Kyoku, 1961), p. 97.
2. Military Intelligence Section (MIS), G–2 Section, GHQ SCAP, Spot Intelligence Report, 17 August 1948, Record Group 6, MacArthur Archives.
3. MIS, Periodic Intelligence Summary, 15 March 1948, p. 5.
4. Imadate Tetsuo, *Nippon Shinbun* (Japan Newspaper) (Tokyo: Kagami-ura Shobo, 1957), p. 36.
5. Ibid., pp. 36–37.
6. MIS, "Communist Indoctrination of Japanese Repatriates from Soviet Territory," 2 February 1949 (SECRET, declassified 20 August 1975), p. 9, Record Group 6, MacArthur Archives.
7. Ibid., pp. 10–11.
8. Imadate, *Nippon Shinbun*, p. 39.
9. MIS, Daily Intelligence Summary, 30 September 1949, p. 7.
10. Imai Genji, *Shiberiya no Uta* (Song of Siberia), (Tokyo: San-ichi Shobo Ltd., 1980), p. 223.
11. MIS, "Communist Indoctrination," p. 11.
12. Chaen, *Sugamo Purizun/Shiberiya Nippon Shinbun*, pp. 152–53.
13. Government Section, GHQ SCAP, "Review of Government and Politics in Japan," April 1950, p. 180, Record Group 5, MacArthur Archives.
14. MIS, "Communist Indoctrination," pp. 37–39.
15. Ibid.
16. Ibid., p. 43.
17. Ibid., p. 17.
18. Imai, *Shiberiya no Uta*, pp. 279–80.
19. Gotō, *Shiberiya Yūshū-ki*, pp. 66–68.
20. MIS, "Communist Indoctrination," p. 20.
21. Imadate, *Nippon Shinbun*, p. 65.
22. MIS, Daily Intelligence Summary, 19 May 1947, p. 7.
23. MIS, "Communist Indoctrination," p. 29.
24. Imadate, *Nippon Shinbun*, p. 66.

NOTES 137

25. Yabe Akira, "Kamen no Dōshi," (Companion in Disguise), *Bungei Shunjū* (Tokyo) 60 (September 1982):211.
26. MIS, "Communist Indoctrination," p. 31.
27. Imadate Tetsuo, *Rageri no Naka no Nihonjintachi* (Japanese Inside the *Lager*), (Tokyo: Niju Isseiki Shobo, Ltd., 1974), pp. 211–12.
28. Ibid., p. 211.
29. MIS, "Communist Indoctrination," p. 28.
30. MIS, Daily Intelligence Summary, 28 June 1949, p. 6.
31. Chaen, *Sugamo Purizun/Nippon Shinbun*, p. 210.
32. MIS, "Communist Indoctrination," p. 31.
33. Ibid., Tab 2.
34. MIS, Daily Intelligence Summary, 19 March 1950, Press Summary.

5. ATTEMPTS TO EXPEDITE REPATRIATION

1. General Staff, *Reports of General MacArthur*, 1:71.
2. Ibid., 1:179.
3. Allied Council for Japan, Minutes of 26 June 1946 meeting, p. 18, Record Group 5, MacArthur Archives.
4. Allied Council for Japan, Minutes of 2 October 1946 meeting, p. 6.
5. Lt. Gen. K. Derevyanko, USSR Member of the Allied Council for Japan, letter to the Supreme Commander for the Allied Powers, General of the Army D. MacArthur, 12 March 1946, Record Group 5, MacArthur Archives.
6. GHQ SCAP, letter to Lt. Gen. K. Derevyanko, subject: "Return from Japan of families of residents of Southern Sakhalin," 20 March 1946, MacArthur Archives.
7. Lt. Gen. Derevyanko, letter to the Chief of Staff, U.S. Armed Forces, Pacific, 1 July 1946, MacArthur Archives.
8. George Atcheson, Jr., Diplomatic Section, GHQ, letter to Lt. Gen. K. Derevyanko, 23 July 1946, MacArthur Archives.
9. Lt. Gen. Derevyanko, letter to the Chief of Staff, USAF, Pacific, 20 August 1946, MacArthur Archives.
10. George Atcheson, Jr., letter to Lt. Gen. Derevyanko, 26 August 1946, MacArthur Archives.
11. General Staff, *Reports of General MacArthur*, p. 181.
12. Allied Council for Japan, Minutes of 29 October 1947 meeting, p. 5.
13. Ibid.
14. William J. Sebald, *With MacArthur in Japan* (New York: W. W. Norton & Company, 1965), p. 138.
15. General Staff, *Reports of General MacArthur*, p. 184.
16. MIS, Spot Intelligence Report, 29 September 1948.
17. MIS, Daily Intelligence Summary, 19 June 1948, p. 8.
18. Tokyo News Service, 28 March 1949, quoted in MIS, Daily Intelligence Summary, 18 April 1949, p. 5.
19. Ibid.
20. *Pravda*, 20 May 1949, p. 2.
21. MIS, Daily Intelligence Summary, 3 June 1949, p. 7.
22. *Nippon Times*, 22 May 1949, p. 1.
23. *Nippon Times*, 10 November 1949, p. 3.

24. Letter to *Jiji Shimpo*, quoted in *Nippon Times*, 4 June 1949, p. 4.
25. MIS, Daily Intelligence Summary, 2 December 1949, Press Summary.
26. Sebald, *With MacArthur in Japan*, pp. 140–42.
27. Allied Council for Japan, Minutes of 21 December 1949 meeting, pp. 6–17.
28. Ibid., p. 18.
29. Sebald, *With MacArthur in Japan*, p. 145.
30. Richard L. G. Deverall, *Japan's Soviet Held Prisoners of War* (Bombay: The National Information and Publications, Ltd., 1951), p. 5.
31. Allied Council for Japan, Minutes of 4 January 1950 meeting, p. 2.
32. *Nippon Times*, 11 January 1950, p. 4.
33. *Nippon Times*, 19 January 1950, p. 1.
34. MIS, Spot Intelligence Report, 30 January 1950.
35. *Asahi* (Tokyo), 2 May 1950, p. 1.
36. *United Nations Review*, 4 (December 1957): 13–15.
37. *New York Times*, 23 September 1953, p. 3.
38. *United Nations Review*, 1 (November 1954): 41.
39. Ibid., p. 44.
40. *Nippon Times*, 3 January 1956, p. 3.
41. *Liberal Star*, 10 October 1987, p. 12.
42. Ibid.
43. Leon E. Seltzer, ed., *Columbia Lippincott Gazetteer of the World* (New York: Columbia University Press, 1962).
44. *New York Times*, 15 November 1959, p. 4.

6. RETURN TO JAPAN

1. MIS, "Communist Indoctrination," Tab 2.
2. Welfare Ministry of Japan, Repatriation Support Office, *Maizuru Chihō Hikiage Engo-kyoku Shi* (History of Maizuru Area Repatriation Support Office), (Kyoto: Kōseisho Hikiage Engo Kyoku, 1961), 1:98.
3. MIS, Spot Intelligence Report, 9 August 1949.
4. MIS, "Communist Indoctrination," Tab 15.
5. MIS, Spot Intelligence Report, 13 August 1949.
6. Edward Norbeck, "Edokko, A Narrative of Japanese Prisoners of War in Russia," *Rice University Studies* 57, No. 1 (Winter 1971): 65.
7. *Nippon Times*, 27 March 1949, p. 3.
8. *Nippon Times*, 5 August 1949, p. 4.
9. MIS, Daily Intelligence Summary, 9 September 1947, p. 3.
10. Ibid.
11. *Asahi* (Osaka), 14 October 1949, p. 1.
12. Government Section, "Review of Government and Politics in Japan," March 1950, p. 153, Record Group 5, MacArthur Archives.
13. MIS, Spot Intelligence Report, 15 May 1948.
14. MIS, Daily Intelligence Summary, 16 July 1949, p. 1.
15. *Asahi* (Tokyo), 6 July 1949, p. 4.
16. *Nippon Times*, 5 August 1949, p. 4.
17. Government Section, "Review of Government and Politics in Japan," August 1949, p. 131.

NOTES

18. *Akahata* (Tokyo), quoted in MIS, Daily Intelligence Summary, 19 November 1949, press summary.
19. MIS, Daily Intelligence Summary, 18 April 1949, p. 2.
20. MIS, "Communist Indoctrination of Japanese Repatriates," Tab 15.
21. *Chiba Shimbun* (Chiba), 12 October 1949, quoted in MIS, Daily Intelligence Summary, 15 October 1949, press summary.
22. MIS, Daily Intelligence Summary, 26 October 1949, press summary.
23. Government Section, "Review of Government and Politics in Japan," March 1950, pp. 127–38.
24. *Mainichi* (Tokyo), 10 April 1950, p. 1.
25. SCAP issued an edict purging 24 JCP central committee members on 6 June 1950. Most of the purged communists escaped to China and remained there until 1955. Tokuda died in Beijing in November 1953.
26. "Yoshimura Tai wo Sabake" (Judgment of the Yoshimura Unit), *Shūkan Asahi*, 13 March 1949, pp. 3–9.
27. Akabane Fumiko, *Dasbedania* (Tokyo: Free Asia Press, 1955), pp. 147–51.
28. Kurihara Yasuyo, *Shinjitsu wo Uttaeru* (Speaking the Truth), (Tokyo: Hachigatsu Shobo, 1949), p. 71.
29. *Nippon Times*, 13 August 1953, p. 3.
30. *Nippon Times*, 6 February 1954, p. 1.
31. Report of the Internal Security Subcommittee to the Committee on Judiciary, U.S. Senate, 84th Congress, 31 December 1956 (Washington, D.C.: U.S. Government Printing Office, 1957), pp. 141–44.
32. *Sankei* (Tokyo), 21 May 1987, p. 10.
33. Kyōdō news agency (Tokyo), 23 May 1987.
34. Internal Security Subcommittee hearings, Judiciary Committee, U.S. Senate, 18 and 19 December 1956, Part 47 (Washington, D.C.: U.S. Government Printing Office, 1957), p. 3170.
35. *Japan Times*, 27 December 1956, p. 1.
36. *Nippon Times*, 24 November 1953, p. 1.
37. *New York Times*, 19 July 1965, p. 27.
38. *Japan Times*, 21 January 1958, p. 3.
39. Hozaka Masayasu, "Seijima Ryuzō no Kenkyū" (A Study of Seijima Ryuzō) *Bungei Shunjū* 65 (May 1987): 272–97.
40. *New York Times*, 7 November 1987, p. 3.
41. Arnold C. Brackman, *The Last Emperor* (New York: Charles Scribner's Sons, 1975), pp. 266–338.
42. *New York Times*, 16 January 1976, p. 34.

7. THE FINAL ACCOUNTING

1. Allied Council for Japan, Minutes of 2 August 1950 meeting, p. 5.
2. Higuchi Chikara, "Bareisho to Roshiya Fujin" (Potatoes and the Russian Lady) *Bungei Shunjū* 60 (September 1982): 206.
3. Higuchi Kinichi, *Uraru-o Koete* (Beyond the Urals), (Tokyo: Kangen sha, 1949), pp. 61–62.
4. Hakamada Shigeki, Omuro Mikio, Tanaka Katsuhiko, and Uchimura Kosuke,

"Sutarin Shuyōjo Rettō no Nihonjin" (Japanese at Stalin's Prison Camp Archipelago) *Bungei Shunjū* 60 (September 1982):193.

5. Hugh Borton, Preface, in Evelyn S. Colbert, *The Left Wing in Japanese Politics*, (New York: Institute of Public Relations, 1952), p. viii.

6. Theodore McNelly, *Politics and Government in Japan* (Boston: Houghton Mifflin, 1972), pp. 122–23.

7. *Liberal Star*, 10 August 1986, p. 11.

8. *New York Times*, 21 March 1954, p. 38.

9. *Liberal Star*, 10 February 1984, p. 5.

10. General Staff, *Reports of General MacArthur*, 1:178–79.

11. *New York Times*, 1 January 1949, p. 6.

12. *Liberal Star*, 10 February 1984, p. 5.

13. *New York Times*, 21 August 1987, p. 1.

14. Gerald R. Ford, President of the United States, Executive Proclamation No. 4417, 19 February 1976, in *Federal Register* (Washington, D.C., National Archives and Records Service, 20 February 1976), 41:7741.

15. A. M. Prokhorov, et al., eds., and Maxine Lesser Bronstein, et al., trans., *Great Soviet Encyclopedia, A Translation of the 3d Edition, 1974* (New York: MacMillan, Inc., 1977), 22:126.

Selected Bibliography

Beloff, Max. *Soviet Policy in the Far East, 1944–1951*. London: Oxford University Press, 1971.
Bohlen, Charles E. *Witness to History, 1929–1969*. New York: Norton, 1973.
Byrnes, James F. *All in One Lifetime*. New York: Harper, 1958.
Clubb, O. Edmund. "Manchuria in the Balance, 1945–1946." *Pacific Historical Review* 26 (4): 377–89 (November 1957).
Dallin, David J. *Soviet Russia and the Far East*. New Haven: Yale University Press, 1948.
Endō Masao. *Hokusen, Shiberia Senyū Roku* (A Record of Comrades in Arms in North Korea and Siberia). Tokyo: Oshi sha, 1986.
Feis, Herbert. *Contest Over Japan*. New York: Norton, 1968.
Fujikawa Kosei. *Hen na Heitai* (A Peculiar Soldier). Tokyo: Kindai Shuppan sha, 1970.
Fujikawa Masahide. *Hateshinaki Sanga ni* (To Endless Mountains and Rivers). Tokyo: Fujiwara, 1977.
Fukase Nobuchiyo. *Orochon no Banka* (An Elegy in Orotukan). Tokyo: Fukase Nobuchiyo, 1974.
Furuta Kōzo. *Koya no Seishun* (Youth in the Fields). Hiroshima: Furuta Mitsuko, 1979.
Fuse Isao. *Shiberiya Tōbō no Kiroku* (Record of an Escape from Siberia). Tokyo: Kokutetsu Rōkumin Zenkoku Shitetsu Kyōgi Kai, 1969.
Garthoff, Robert L. *Soviet Military Policy*. New York: Praeger, 1966.
Graves, William Sidney. *America's Siberian Adventure*. New York: P. Smith, 1941.
Grew, Joseph C. *Turbulent Era: A Diplomatic Record of Forty Years, 1904–1945*. Boston: Houghton Mifflin, 1952.
Harada Haruo. *Akatsuki ni Inorumaji* (Let's Not Pray at Dawn). Tokyo: Uzushio Shuppan sha, 1972.
Hasegawa Yuichi. *Shiberiya ni Torawarete* (As We Were Captured in Siberia). Sendai: Sōhoku sha, 1975.
Hashimoto Sawazo. *Byakuya ni Inoru* (Prayer in the White Nights). Tokyo: Chūō sha, 1948.
Hata Hikosaburō. *Kunan ni Taete* (Endure Hardships). Tokyo: Nikkan Rōdo Tsushi sha, 1958.
Hirabaru Takeji. *Uran Batoru e no Michi* (The Road to Ulan Bator). Shimonoseki: Sekimakan Shobo, 1975.

Hirasaka Kenji. *Horyo no Iseki* (Remembrances of a War Prisoner). Okayama: Hirasaka, 1979.
Hiyama Kunisuke. *Shiberiya Ryoshūki* (Siberia Diary). Tokyo: Nihon Jitsugyō Shuppan sha, 1975.
Honda Tadashi. *Higashi Manshu Shi no Dai Kōshin* (The Great Death March of East Manchuria). Tokyo: Honda Tadashi, 1974.
Hori Kiyoshi. *Furyo: Sobieto Yori Kaeru* (Prisoners: Returning From the Soviet Union). Tokyo: Shoin Shoin, 1948.
Iguchi Asao. *Kōryū ki* (Journal of Captivity). Tokyo: Aoki sha, 1968.
Imai Genji. *Tsuki ni Inoru* (Praying to the Moon). Osaka: Osaka-ya Hatsu bai, 1977.
Ishida Saburō. *Muteikō no Teikō* (Resisting by Not Resisting). Kawasaki: Ishida, 1976.
Ishiguro Tatsunosuke. *Sanga Ariki* (Mountains and Rivers). Tokyo: Bunka Kensetsu sha, 1949.
Kagawa Shigenobu. *Ningen Haigyō Juichi-nen* (Suspension of Humanity for Eleven Years). Tokyo: Nikkan Rōdo Tsushin sha, 1958.
———. *Watakushi no Mita Shūyōjo* (The POW Camp I Saw). Tokyo: Hakuo sha, 1975.
Kan Sueharu. *Katararezaru Shinjitsu* (The Untold Truth). Tokyo: Chikuma Shobo, 1950.
Kawaguchi Hiroshi. *Soren Furyo Kenbunki* (Seeing More of the Life of Prisoners in the Soviet Union). Tokyo: Hasugatani Yoshiharu, 1975.
Kinoshita Hideaki. *Kōryū Seikatsu Juichi-nen* (Eleven Years of My Life in Captivity). Tokyo: Nikkan Kōgyō Shinbun sha, 1957.
Kitagawa Masao. *Kantō-gun Kaimetsu* (Annihilation of the Kwantung Army). Tokyo: Ogetsu Shobo, 1949.
———. *So-Man Kōryūki* (A Journal of Detention in the Soviet Union and Manchuria). Kyoto: Daiga Dō, 1948.
Kobayashi Shigejiro. *Kiseki no Shiberiya Shūyōjo* (Miracle of the Siberian POW Camps). Osaka: Osaka Sosaku Shuppan Kai, 1984.
Komatsu Shigero. *Shiberiya Saigo no Kikanhei* (The Last Repatriate from Siberia). Tokyo: Kojin sha, 1986.
Levine, Steven I. *Anvil of Victory: The Communist Revolution in Manchuria, 1945–1948.* New York: Columbia University Press, 1987.
Maeno Shigeru. *Ikeru Shikabane* (A Living Corpse). Tokyo: Shunsun sha, 1961.
McWilliams, Wayne C. *Homeward Bound: Repatriation of Japanese from Korea After World War II.* Hong Kong: Asian Research Service, 1987.
Matsumura Tomokatsu. *Kantō-gun Sanbō Fukuchō no Shuki* (Journal of the Assistant Chief of Staff of the Kwantung Army). Tokyo: Fuyō Shobo, 1977.
Mizutani Eiji. *Akai Tōdo* (The Red Frozen Earth). Tokyo: Hara Shobo, 1969.
Morley, James William. *The Japanese Thrust into Siberia, 1918.* New York: Columbia University Press, 1957.
Nakamura Ryūichi. *Nagareboshi* (Shooting Stars). Odaira: Nakamura Ryūichi, 1972.
Nakamura Taisuke. *Shiberia wo Sayonara* (Farewell to Siberia). Tokyo: Daini Shobo, 1966.
Nakamura Yuriko. *Akai Kabe no Ana* (A Hole in the Red Wall). Tokyo: Musashi Shobo, 1956.
Nihon Kōan Chōsa chō. *Gai Mo Kikansha no Shuki* (Memoirs of Repatriates from Outer Mongolia). Tokyo: Kōan Chōsa chō, 1957.
Nishi Kazuhiro. *Akai Hoshi, Shiroi Oka, Kuroi Ie* (Red Star, White Hills, Black Houses). Tokyo: Sorin sha, 1948.

Ogata Mitsuo. *Tennō no Fumie* (A Trampled Image of the Emperor). Tokyo: Sankei Shinbun sha, 1969.
Ogata Nakaba. *Kurai Rōka* (Dark Corridor). Tokyo: Tachibana Shoten, 1957.
Pegov, N. M. "Stalin on War with Japan." *Soviet Studies in History* 24 (3): 26–38 (Winter 1985–1986).
Rzheshevskii, O. A. "Bourgeois Assessments of the Soviet Victory Over Japan." *Soviet Studies in History* 24 (3): 69–79 (Winter 1985–1986).
Sakama Fumiko. *Setsugen ni Hitori Torawarete* (Captured Alone in a Snowfield). Tokyo: Kōdan sha, 1975.
Scalapino, Robert A. *The Japanese Communist Movement, 1920–1966*. Berkeley: University of California Press, 1967.
Shimizu Takehisa. *Soren no tai-Nichi Sensō to Yaruta Kyōtei* (The Soviet War against Japan and the Yalta Agreement). Tokyo: Kasumigaseki, 1976.
Stephan, John J. *The Kuril Islands: Russo-Japanese Frontier in the Pacific*. Oxford: The Clarendon Press, 1974.
——. *Sakhalin: A History*. Oxford: The Clarendon Press, 1971.
——. "The USSR and the Defeat of Imperial Japan, 1945." *Soviet Studies in History* 24 (3): 3–25 (Winter 1985–1986).
Suzuki Seigoro. *Damoi Yaponsuki* (Japanese Going Home). Tokyo: Sōzo, 1976.
Suzuki Yoshihiro. *Yukidoke* (Melting Snow). Otaru: Otaru Asahi, 1975.
Swearingen, Rodger. *Communist Strategy in Japan, 1945–1960*. Santa Monica: Rand Corp., 1965.
——. *Red Flag in Japan: International Communism in Action, 1919–1951*. Cambridge, Mass.: Harvard University Press, 1952.
——. *The Soviet Union and Postwar Japan*. Stanford: Hoover Institution Press, 1978.
Tagusari Genichi. *Uragirareta Heitai* (A Betrayed Soldier). Tokyo: Chishiki sha, 1948.
Takeuchi Kinshi. *Nihon no Furyo wa Soren de Donna Sekatsu no Shitaka* (How Japanese Prisoners Lived in the Soviet Union). Tokyo: Kōbun sha, 1950.
Tsumura Kenji. *Nahotoka no Jinmin Saiban* (The People's Court of Nakhodka). Tokyo: Bunka Hyōron sha, 1949.
Uno Sōsuke. *Damoi, Tokyo* (Going Home to Tokyo). Tokyo: Katsu Shiro Shobo, 1948.
Viktorov, Ya. "Sebald's Deliberate Lies." *Soviet Press Translations* 5: 523–26 (1 October 1950).
Vishwanathan, Savitri. *Normalization of Japanese-Soviet Relations, 1945–1970*. Tallahassee: The Diplomatic Press, 1973.
Walm, Nora. "Japanese Prisoners Home From Russia." *Atlantic Monthly* 184: 28–30 (November 1949).
Warner, W. F. "Repatriate Organizations in Japan." *Pacific Affairs* 22: 272–76 (September 1949).
Yamada Seizaburo. *Sobieto Yokuryū Kikō* (A Journal of Captivity in the Soviet Union). Tokyo: Tōhō Shuppan sha, 1973.
Yamazaki Katsuji. *Haisen to Ningen* (Lost Battle and People). Yokohama: Marui Sangyō Shuppan-bu, 1975.
Yomiuri Shinbun, Osaka Shakai-bu. *Aa, Shiberiya* (Ah, Siberia). Tokyo: Yomiuri Shinbun sha, 1979.

Index

Abe Shintarō, 97
Acheson, Dean, 93
Afghanistan, 43
Agriculture Ministry, Japanese, 23
Aikawa Haruki (a.k.a. Yanami Hisao), 68
Aikō Hiroyuki, 22, 24–26
Akabane Fumiko, 108
Akahata (JCP newspaper), 68, 90, 106–7
Akatsuki ni Inoru (Prayer at Dawn), 108
Akiyama Hiroshi, 60–61
Alliance of Red Cross and Red Crescent Societies of the Soviet Union, 95
Allied Council for Japan, 83–85, 91, 93, 115–16
Allied Intervention, Siberia, 6
Allied Occupation of Japan, 5, 15, 71, 74, 104; behavior of troops, 36–37, 69
Alma Ata, 43, 47
Amur River, 9–10, 40
Anti-Fascist Democratic Committee (AFDC), 76–78, 80, 99
Aramaki Yasuhiko, 108
Arita Hachirō, 96
Army Unit 731, 60–61
Asahara Masaki, 69
Asano Fukuichirō, 51
Atcheson, George, 83, 85–86
Australia, 83, 93, 95, 123

Baikal-Amur-Mainline (BAM), 58
Barsdell, Leonard, 32–33
Beria, Lavrenti, 109

Biological warfare, Japanese preparations for, 60–61
Blagoveshchensk, 41
British Commonwealth, 83, 92, 115
Byrnes, James F., 44

Cairo Conference, 15
Caspian Sea, 43
Central Asia, 43, 48, 66, 120
Changchun (Shinkyō), 8–9, 12, 14, 24, 30
Changkufeng, 2
Chiang Kai-shek, 3–4, 15
China Expeditionary Army, 5
China, Nationalist, 2, 4, 26, 83
China, People's Republic of, 26, 31, 96, 111–13, 116, 125
Chita, 42, 50
Churchill, Winston S., 3, 15

Dairen, 29–32; Japanese in, 30–31, 117; repatriation from, 31, 86, 118; reversion to Chinese control, 31–32, reversion to USSR control, 17, 30
Dan Tokusaburō, 66
Date Hiromi, 110
Declaration of Human Rights, 92
Demobilization Bureau, Japanese, 84, 123
Derevyanko, Kuzma N., 83–86, 91–92, 116, 123
Dutch East Indies, 125

Eighth Route Army, 40
The Emperor of Japan, 10–11, 39, 59, 69, 73, 77, 93, 120, 123
Endō Masao, 90

Five-Year Plan, Soviet, 53–54
Ford, Gerald, 127
Foreign Ministry, Japanese, 4, 63–64, 95, 97, 112
France, 125
Friendship Society (*Tomo no kai*), 68, 73–76

Geneva Convention on War Prisoners, 92, 125, 128
German-Soviet Non-aggression Pact, 1939, 3
Germany, 3–4, 7, 13, 124–25
Glinkin, Vladimir A., 90
Gorbachev, Mikhail, 128–29
Gotō Sadao, 110
Greater East Asia Co-Prosperity Sphere, 1, 8, 39
Gulag, 62–63, 118, 128

Hakamada Mutsuo, 112–13
Hakamada Shigeki, 120
Halahei, 23
Harbin, 1, 8, 10, 12, 14, 21, 24, 112
Hashimoto Katsuyuki, 26, 41
Hata Hikosaburō, 12
Health and Welfare Ministry, Japanese, 15, 88–89, 96
Heilungkiang (Black Dragon River). See Amur River
Hiraizumi Wataru, 126
Hiroshima, 7, 127
Hodgson, William R., 92
Hulutao, 14, 28

Ikeda Shigeyoshi, 108
Imadate Tetsuo, 78
Imai Genji, 74
Imperial General Headquarters, 2, 5–6, 11
India, 83
Intelligence Operations, 6–9; postwar Soviet operations in Japan, 108–10

Intermediate Screening Camp, 80, 99
International Military Tribunal for the Far East, 59–60, 112
Iran, 43
Iryumin (residents' association), 27

Japan Communist Party (JCP), 16, 66, 70, 72, 76, 80–81, 88, 99, 100, 104–5, 107, 109, 121–23
Japanese Americans, Internment during World War II, 127–28
Japanese Army, 2, 5, 8–9; deaths in North Korea, 45; defensive operations against Soviet attack, 9–13; deportation to USSR, 40–48; deserters in Manchuria, 39–40; intelligence operations, 6–9; surrender, 12–13; treatment of Allied POWs and civilians, 36; troops in post-surrender Manchuria, 39–40
Japanese Association of Mukden, 27
Japanese in Soviet areas, 2, 13–19, 21, 30, 32, 116–18, 126
Japan-USSR, normalization of relations, 96–97, 122, 124

Kan Sueharu, 107–8
Karaganda, 43, 48, 58, 63–64, 66, 107–8, 120
KGB, 46
Khabarovsk, 8, 10, 14, 41–42, 47, 58, 60, 64, 67–68, 72, 76–77, 109, 111, 119, 126
Khalkin Gol, 2, 52, 124
Khobarenkopf, Vladimir (a.k.a. Ōba Sanpei), 67
Khrushchev, Nikita S., 62
Kirin, 10, 22
Kislenko, Aleksandr, 85–88
Kokuryūkō (Black Dragon River). See Amur River
Konoe Fumimaro, 110
Konoe Fumitaka, 110–11
Korea, 1, 10, 12
Korean Airlines, Flight 007, 120
Korean War, 35, 40, 106
Kovalenko, Ivan, 124–26
Kurile Islands, 1, 12, 17–18, 45, 106;

INDEX

Japanese civilians in, 17–21, 124; repatriation from, 47–49, 115–18
Kusaba Tatsumi, 59
Kwantung Army, 2–3, 5–6, 8–9, 11–12, 27, 67, 111, 120, 122; battle plans, 5, 10; biological warfare preparations, 60–61; intelligence operations, 6–9; Nomonhan (Khalkin Gol), 2; Soviet Red Army attack on, 9–13; surrender, 12
Kwantung Leased Territory, 17, 22
Kyoto Station, leftist demonstration, 104–5

Lake Baikal, 5, 14, 57–58
Lake Khasan, 2
Lenin, Vladimir I., 99, 117, 119, 128
Liaotung Peninsula, 29, 31
Liberal Democratic Party of Japan (LDP), 97, 112, 126
Lie, Trygve, 95
Li Gui-qin, 23–24

MacArthur, Douglas, 15; and Allied Council for Japan, 84, 91; attempts to obtain Soviet entry in war against Japan, 3; and Derevyanko, 92; and leftist demonstrators, 123; *Nippon Shinbun* article on, 70; and repatriation from USSR, 95
Magadan, 47, 58
Maizuru, 71, 100–103, 123
Malaya, 125
Malik, Yakov A., 9
Manchuria, 1, 5, 8, 11–12, 15, 17, 21–29, 39–41, 61, 67, 111, 128; arrest and deportation to USSR of civilians from, 39, 61–62; deaths of civilians in, 25, 28, 90, 115; Koreans in, 1, 21; orphans in, 23–24, 28–29; repatriation of civilians from, 27–29, 115–18; Soviet Army treatment of civilians, 22–29; withdrawal of Soviet Army, 27
Mantetsu. See South Manchurian Railway
Maritime Province District, USSR, 8, 58
Maritime Safety Board, Japanese, 109
Marshall Plan, 70, 72
Marxist-Leninist indoctrination of prisoners, 65–81, 120–21, 123; *aktivs*, 66, 69, 71, 73, 77–80, 99, 100–103, 107, 112, 121; Anti-Fascist Democratic Committee, 76–78, 80, 99; Friendship Society, 68, 73–76; intermediate screening camp, 80, 99; Nakhodka processing, 80, 99–100; *Nippon Shinbun*, 67–71, 74–77, 80; political schools, 71–73, 112; wall newspapers (*kabe shinbun*), 79–80
Masutani Shuji, 96
Matsumura Tomokatsu, 59–60
May Day celebrations, 70, 79
Miki Takeo, 87
Ministry of Justice, Japanese, 105
Miyanaga Yukihisa, 110
Molotov, Vyacheslav, 4, 7, 44
Morimura Seiichi, 60
Movement to Rescue Japanese Held Overseas, 96
Mukden (Shenyang), 9, 12, 14, 21, 24, 30, 40, 111–12
Mukden Incident, 22
Mutanchiang (Botankō), 10, 26, 110
MVD (Ministry of Internal Affairs), 46, 48–49, 52, 58–64, 67, 72, 78, 81, 90, 107–10, 118–19

Nagao Yoichi, 63
Nagasaki, 127
Nakhodka, 14, 80, 93–94, 99–100, 113
Nanking, 126
National Federation of Repatriation Organizations, 90
New Zealand, 83
Nippon Shinbun, 67–71, 74–77, 80
Nishihara Yasuhiro, 63
NKVD, 46, 61–63
Nomonhan, 2, 52, 124
Northern Territories (*Hoppō Ryōdo*), 13, 96–97, 120, 126
North Korea, 28, 32–35, 96; closing of 38th parallel, 32; deaths in, 45, 90, 118; Japanese civilians in, 17, 32–35, 117; Japanese military personnel, escape from, 45; repatriation from, 33–35, 115–18; Soviet attack on, 10, 12

North Pacific Flotilla, 12
Nosaka Sanzō, 70, 75, 88

Ōfune Mikio, 106
Ōnishi Takijiro, 5
Orphans, search for, 28–29
Outer Mongolia (People's Republic of Mongolia), 8, 13, 41, 108, 124

Panyushkin, Alexander S., 93
Pearl Harbor, 3, 127
Philippines, 3, 125
Political Schools, 71–73, 112
Port Arthur (Ryōjun), 6, 29–32, 86
Potsdam Conference, 4, 27, 39, 72, 92, 125
Powell, John W., 60
Pravda, 13, 89, 94
Prisoners in the USSR, German, 44–45, 48, 53, 58, 73, 94, 120, 122, 124–25
Prisoners in the USSR, Japanese, 39–64, 124–25; civilians, 17, 39, 43, 61–62; conditions in work camps, 46–53; construction and work projects, 53–59, 119–20, 128; criminal sentences, 59–64; deaths, 43, 89, 96, 115–18; deportation to USSR, 40–45; escape attempts, 50; female prisoners, 44, 108–9; food, 51–52; Maizuru Repatriation Center, 100–103, 123; Marxist-Leninist indoctrination, 65–81; medical treatment, 52; Nakhodka, 99–100; number in USSR, 89–91, 94, 115–18, 126; physical examination, 49–50; repatriation, 51, 99–113, 116, 118; sea voyage from Nakhodka, 100–101; train travel to hometown, 103–5
Prisoners in the USSR, Soviet, 45, 53, 58, 122, 124
Provost Marshal, Eighth U.S. Army, 37
Pu Yi, Henry, 22, 112
Pyongyang (Heijo), 33–34

Racial prejudice, absence of in USSR, 44, 52, 76
Rastvorov, Yuri A., 109–11
Red Army (Soviet), atrocities against civilians in Manchuria, 22–29; border incidents, 2; casualties, 35; intelligence operations, 6; Transbaikal Front, 9; treatment of civilians in North Korea, 32–34; troop movements, 6–7; war on Japanese forces, 9–13; withdrawal from Manchuria, 27
Reparations, 24–25, 44
Repatriation, 15–16, 99–113; adjustment to life in Japan, 105–7; after effects, 107–10; attempts to expedite, 83–97; Dairen and Port Arthur, civilian, 31; Korea, civilian, 33–35; Maizuru Repatriation Center, 101–3; Manchuria, civilian, 22–29; reverse repatriation, 84–86; Sakhalin and Kurile Islands, civilian, 17–21; sea voyages, 100–101; statistics on, 116–18, 126; train to hometown, 103–5; war prisoners, 99–113
Repatriation Relief Agency, 90, 101–2, 105
Ribbentrop, Joachim von, 3
Roosevelt, Franklin D., 3–4, 15, 32
Russo-Japanese War, 1, 5, 16–18, 22, 122

Sakhalin, 1, 12, 17–18, 106; Japanese civilians in, 17–21, 124; Koreans in, 19, 21; repatriation from, 17–21, 115–18; reverse repatriation, 84–86
Satō Naotake, 4–5, 7
Schwab, Reiko, 26
Sebald, William J., 86–87, 91–92, 116
Seijima Ryuzō, 59–60, 112
Seki Sanjiro, 109
Shelakhov, Georgi A., 12
Shii Shoji, 109
Siberia, 17–18, 52, 58–60, 103–4, 108, 111–12, 116, 124
Singapore, 125
Society of Waiting Families for the Promotion of Speedy Repatriation, 90
Sorge, Richard, 6
South Manchurian Railway (*Mantetsu*), 6, 25–26, 30, 41, 118
Soviet-Japanese Neutrality Pact of 1941, 2–4, 6, 16, 97, 120
Soviet Mission in Japan, 66, 81, 85–86,

91, 109; demonstrations at, 87, 89–90; announcements on repatriation, 90, 93–94
Special Military Mission, Harbin, 8
Stalin, Joseph, 3, 5, 15, 53, 72, 79, 100, 112, 118–19, 123, 128; agreement on trusteeship for Korea, 32; death of, 96; denunciation by Gorbachev, 129; denunciation by Khrushchev, 62–63; endorsement of Potsdam Proclamation, 89; memories of Russo-Japanese War, 13, 122; victory speech, 13, 122
Sugamo Prison, 125
Supreme Commander for the Allied Powers (SCAP), 15, 37, 66, 81, 83–84, 87–90, 99, 101–2, 106, 115–16, 123
Suzuki Kantarō, 4

Takebayashi Takeo, 100
Takebe Rokuzō, 22, 111–12
Takeda Tsuneyoshi, 12
Tass, 67, 89, 115–16
Teheran Conference, 3, 15
Tōgō Shigenori, 7
Tokuda Kyūichi, 70, 80–81, 99, 107–8
Trans-Siberian Railroad, 5, 41, 46, 58
Truman, Harry S., 4, 70, 72

United Kingdom, 4, 87, 95, 125; Allied Intervention in Siberia, 6
United Nations, Commission on POW Inquiry, 81, 95–97
United States, 3–4, 87, 95, 99, 115, 125; Allied Intervention in Siberia, 6; Cold War tension, 16; incendiary bombing of Germany and Japan, 126
Uno Sōsuke, 112
USSR and Japan, 2–3, 7, 124–26; accounting for war prisoners, 13, 88–91, 94, 96–97, 116; peace treaty negotiations, 124; Soviet declaration of war, 7–8; territorial dispute, 96–97

Vasilevsky, Aleksandr M., 9, 12
Vladivostok, 14, 30, 40–42, 72, 99
Vorkuta, 58

Wallace, Henry A., 72
War criminals, Japanese, 125
War Prisoners and Civilians Administration, Mukden, 28
White Russians, 1, 21, 48

Yabe Akira, 51, 77
Yalta Conference, 3–4, 5, 7, 17, 32; territorial agreements, Far East, 3–4, 96
Yamada Otozō, 11–12, 60, 111
Yamamoto Noboru, 100
Yanami Hisao (a.k.a. Aikawa Haruki), 68
Yoshida Kohei, 70
Yoshida Shigeru, 91
Yoshida Tadashi, 93
Yoshinaga Haruko, 60

Zhukov, Georgi K., 2

About the Author

WILLIAM F. NIMMO is a researcher and historian specializing in foreign relations and military affairs. He held civilian positions with the Department of the Army in Washington and Japan.